MEHM

101 QU
YOU
ABOU

101 QUESTIONS YOU ASKED ABOUT ISLAM

WRITTEN BY

MEHMET OZALP

BRANDL & SCHLESINGER

BOOK PUBLISHERS

First published by Brandl & Schlesinger Pty Ltd in 2004

PO Box 127 Blackheath NSW 2785 Australia
www.brandl.com.au

Copyright © Mehmet Ozalp, 2004

All rights reserved. No part of this publication may be reproduced in any form or by any means, electronic or mechanical, including photocopying, recording, or by any information storage and retrieval system, without the prior written permission in writing from the publisher.

Cover & book designed by András Berkes

Set in 10½ pt Bembo Book

National Library of Australia Cataloguing-in-Publication entry:

Ozalp, Mehmet 1968-.
101 questions you asked about Islam.

ISBN 1 876040 63 7

1. Islam. 2. Muslims. 3. Democracy – Religious aspects – Islam. 4. Women in Islam. 5. Terrorism – Religious aspects – Islam. I. Title.

297.2

Printed in Australia by Griffin Press

CONTENTS

Preface   11

Introduction   15

PART I ■ FAITH ESSENTIALS OF ISLAM

God and Religion

Q1   What is the key message of Islam?   23
Q2   What is the concept of God in Islam?   27
Q3   Do Muslims believe in an active God?   30
Q4   Is God considered part of the universe?   32
Q5   Do Muslims believe in man being created in the image of God?   34
Q6   Is it sufficient to believe in God but not belong to a religion?   35
Q7   How does Islam relate to science?   38
Q8   Does Islam accept Jesus as the "Son of God"?   40
Q9   What are the major differences between Islam and Christianity?   42
Q10   Does Islam believe in God incarnating as Jesus or as anything else?   44
Q11   How is Islam different to other religions?   49
Q12   How does Islam view other religions?   55
Q13   Do you believe that God has an overriding Will?   58

Chain of Prophethood and Revelation

Q14   Does one need to believe in all prophets?   63
Q15   What are the roles of prophets in Islam's ethical system?   66
Q16   Why do Muslims believe that Muhammad was a genuine prophet?   69

CONTENTS

Q17 What was the personality and character of Muhammad? 74
Q18 Can you explain the background of the Qur'an? 79
Q19 How do we know that the Qur'an did not lose its authenticity? 81
Q20 What is the content of the Qur'an? 84

Judgment Day and Life After Death

Q21 Will there be a physical resurrection after death? 89
Q22 What will be the basis of judgment in the Hereafter? 92
Q23 Does being a Muslim guarantee the Paradise? 95
Q24 Is there punishment after death if injunctions are not followed? 98
Q25 According to Islam can a non-Muslim go to Paradise? 100
Q26 If a child dies, where does she end up – Heaven or Hell? 103
Q27 Can good atheists be saved on the Day of Judgment? 105
Q28 Is the final place of destination eternal? 107
Q29 What is the description of Hell? 109
Q30 Could you describe Paradise from an Islamic perspective? 111

PART II ■ LIVING ISLAM

Personal Practice and Spirituality

Q31 How does faith affect a Muslim's spiritual life? 117
Q32 What is the daily life and practice of a Muslim? 119
Q33 Could you describe public and private worship? 121
Q34 How important are the five pillars in Islam's ethical system? 123
Q35 How and when do Muslims worship? 126
Q36 Why do Muslims pray five times a day? 129
Q37 What is the purpose behind the movements in Muslim prayer? 131
Q38 What are the benefits of daily prayers? 133
Q39 How important are daily prayers to a Muslim? 137

CONTENTS

Q40 At what age does religious responsibility start for a Muslim? 139
Q41 What preparations take place before worship and why? 141
Q42 What are the main charities in Islam? 143
Q43 Why do you fast for a whole month in Ramadan? 146
Q44 Why do Muslims go on pilgrimage to Mecca? 149
Q45 What is it like to experience Pilgrimage? 152
Q46 What are the responsibilities of men and women in Islam? 155
Q47 Why do Muslims see Muhammad and God as role models? 158
Q48 What are the fundamentals of Islamic ethics? 160
Q49 How important are Islamic traditions in a Muslim's life? 162
Q50 Why do Muslims have strong connections to their religious heritage? 164
Q51 How does committing sins affect one's morality? 166
Q52 Why do some Muslims have beards and some not? 170

Spirituality in a Mosque

Q53 What are the sacred places of Islam? 175
Q54 What is the *Ka'bah*? Why do Muslims face the *Ka'bah* when praying? 178
Q55 What are the main features of a Mosque? 181
Q56 Why aren't there any pictures or idols inside a mosque? 184
Q57 What significance does the mosque have for Muslims? 186
Q58 What really happens in a mosque? 188
Q59 What is the role of *imam*? Can a woman be an *imam*? 191
Q60 Can an *imam* get married? How does one become an *imam*? 194
Q61 What is the significance of *azan* (call to prayer)? 196
Q62 Why is Friday the Muslim holy day? 199

Communal Experience of Islam

Q63 Islam seems different from one country to the next. Why? 203
Q64 Where does culture begin and religion stop in Islam? 206

CONTENTS

Q65 What is Sufism? Is it Islamic or just another religion?   209
Q66 What are the differences between Sunni and Shiite Islam?   212
Q67 Can you explain Qur'anic or Sharia law?   216
Q68 Can laws of Islam change and to what degree?   219
Q69 Did Muslim 'clergy' make fundamental changes in Islam?   226
Q70 Why does Islamic law appear so restrictive?   229
Q71 Why are punishments for adultery and theft so severe?   232
Q72 What does *halal* mean? What makes food *halal*?   235
Q73 What is the Muslim community's involvement in charities?   238

PART III ■ ISLAM IN THE MODERN WORLD

Saved by the Veil – Women in Islam

Q74 Why do I only see men praying in a mosque?   245
Q75 Why does Islam restrict the rights of women? Is this true?   248
Q76 What is the role of women in Islam and in Muslim society?   251
Q77 Why do women have to cover their bodies and hair?   255
Q78 Why are women treated badly in Muslim countries?   259
Q79 Why does Islam allow men to marry up to four women?   261
Q80 How does marriage and divorce happen in Islam?   264
Q81 Are arranged marriages part of Islam?   269
Q82 Can a Muslim marry a non-Muslim?   271

Muslims' Perspectives on Life

Q83 What are the fundamental Muslim values?   277
Q84 Is Islam a way of life?   281
Q85 What is the significance of ceremonies of birth and death?   283
Q86 What is the place of Qur'an in the life of a Muslim?   286
Q87 How do Muslim teenagers react to Islam in a Western country?   288

Q88	What is it like to live as a Muslim in a secular culture?	291
Q89	How does Islam view sex before marriage and homosexuality?	295

Contemporary Issues Facing Islam and Muslims

Q90	What is *jihad*?	303
Q91	Does Islam encourage terrorism?	307
Q92	Why are Muslims so opposed to non-Muslims?	310
Q93	Muhammad fought wars – is violence in the nature of Islam?	315
Q94	What is Islam's view of euthanasia and abortion?	319
Q95	What are the main Islamic symbols and their significance?	323
Q96	Is there a spiritual leader of all Muslims in the world?	325
Q97	How does Islam view the environment?	327
Q98	Is Islam compatible with democracy?	333
Q99	Why can't Muslims separate politics and religion and be secular?	336
Q100	Why is there misunderstanding between Muslims and the West?	341
Q101	What is the future of Islam?	348

PREFACE

Islam is, without doubt, the most misunderstood of all religions. While people will readily admit they know nothing of Zoroastrianism and little about Taoism, they believe they do know about Islam. Unfortunately, what they think they know is invariably wrong, often horribly wrong, a creation of an ethnocentric media fuelled by a very unrepresentative group of alleged Muslims. One of the things people think they know about Islam is that it is violent by its very nature. Our media spares no opportunity to make this connection. In one national daily soon after "9/11", I counted the phrase "Islamic terrorism" or "Islamic terrorists" 26 times in the first 4 pages, with the word "terrorism" on its own appearing not once.

In fact, there is no religion less appropriately used to justify violence than Islam. There is no religion that has such strong and explicit tenets towards tolerance in its sacred text, and no religion with such a strong track record of tolerating other religions and other beliefs within its jurisdictions. In the early Middle Ages, when there was not much tolerance to be found anywhere, Islam built model civilisations based on multi-cultures and multi-beliefs. By and large, a Jew, Christian or Hindu was far better off living in most Islamic princedoms than anywhere else, including, in many cases, their own princedoms, especially if the prince happened to belong to a different persuasion of the same religion.

This tolerance was not accidental nor was it part and parcel of ancient Arabic culture; that culture had been as faction-ridden as any other in pre-Islamic times. The tolerance was practised because of the Muslim's strong belief that Islam truly was the fulfilment of God's ancient promise (to Abraham initially) that He would establish a model community in the midst of the nations. This would be a community that would reflect God's deep desire that humankind should live in peace and practise all forms of personal integrity and social justice. This would be the community that would show the rest of the world how to live well and under God. This community was the Ummah of Allah, the People of God.

For Muhammad, it was Islam that finally took up the challenge to be the People of God. Inspired by Moses and Jesus, the founders of Judaism and Christianity, Muhammad went on to establish the religion that he believed was what both of them were striving for all along. In his own mind, he seemed quite clear that Moses, Jesus and himself were at one in their vision and adherence to the promise. They are all prophets of God and he declared himself to be "the last and greatest" because he finally established the model community in the form of Islam. For Muhammad, Moses and Jesus were Muslims (submitters to God) in the true sense, as was Abraham, the ancient prophets, John the Baptist and Mary, all of whom strove to do God's will. So too, any Jew who lives by the Ten Commandments or any Christian who follows Jesus' Great Commandment (to love God and neighbour), was a submitter to God, and so to be respected and accommodated. By inference, the authentic followers of any religion could also be accommodated as being "anonymous" submitters to God.

Importantly, Muhammad seemed bent on giving the benefit of the doubt to those who followed other religions, especially Jews and Christians. As "People of the Book" (fellow believers in the true God), they should be assumed to be genuine in their beliefs and so be respected. For the time, this was a remarkable gesture of multicultural largesse. Within the great Islamic Civilization that went on to capture the hearts and minds of most of the Middle East and much of Europe, Africa and India, the concept of the *dhimmi* (important minority group) communities was unique. The *dhimmi* communities were those minority groups that lived within an Islamic society that followed another religion yet were tolerated, respected and often regarded as an indispensable contributor to the richness of the Islamic society. For hundreds of years, generations of Jewish and Christian communities lived and prospered within Islamic worlds as *dhimmi* communities.

It cannot be over-emphasised how ground-breaking the social attitude and practice of *dhimmi* was, and the important thing to note is that it came directly from the Muslims' understanding of the will of Muhammad about these things. As such, the injunction towards tolerance came directly from God and was clearly part of the model community that was established in God's name. It was part of being the "People of God" that difference should be respected in this way. To be Muslim was to be fair, just and tolerant in the way enjoined by God.

This is why I make the assertion that no religion is more inappropriately used as an instrument of intolerance and least of all violent intolerance than Islam. It is sad that a religion with such a strong ethic for tolerance should descend to being the bogeyman of intolerance that has become the popular image of Islam in recent times. Happily, there are important Muslims who are striving to resurrect the original and authentic image of Islam and to create a better image and enhanced understanding of this most misunderstood but profoundly beautiful religion. Among other things, for the Jew or the Christian, there is no true understanding of their own traditions without understanding Islam, a religion that was influenced by both but has gone on to influence the later development of both in ways that are all too rarely appreciated.

PREFACE

Mehmet Ozalp's book should be seen as one of the noble efforts to create better understanding and improve our education about Islam. This book offers painstakingly precise and well-sourced details about a myriad of aspects of Islamic belief and practice. It is a work of art, having been crafted in loving detail yet with the commitment of one who clearly knows the challenge, and is committed to meeting it, of offering education to a world that too often prefers stereotype and the culture of blame. I commend Mehmet Ozalp's book to anyone who prefers to live in a more informed and civilised way than this. I commend it also for its potential to spread the word about the wisdom and the beauty of Islam.

Professor Terence Lovat
Pro Vice-Chancellor (Education and Arts)
The University of Newcastle, Australia
November, 2003

INTRODUCTION

Islam is the religion of one in five people on earth. Since its inception in the 7th century, it became a world religion almost immediately within the lifetime of the Prophet Muhammad. Regrettably, people in the Western World have only heard of Islam in association with violence and politics on top of a negative historical background fuelled by the unhelpful propaganda of the Crusades. Although Islam has always been in the world centre-stage, a rising awareness of Islam is observed in modern times. At the beginning of a new millennium, world events have triggered a desire in people to get to know Muslims and Islam at a personal level.

The new Studies in Religion subject in high schools of Australia has also led some schools to teach Islam to their students as a world religion in addition to Christianity. This has led schools to organise excursions to local mosques. Auburn Gallipoli Mosque of Sydney, Australia, which was built based on classical Ottoman architecture, attracts a fair share of such excursions. Overwhelmed by the demand, the president of Auburn Gallipoli Mosque asked me to assist him in meeting the needs of the growing number of visitors in the year 2000. Seeing a good opportunity to make a contribution to peace and understanding, I have accepted the invitation and helped establish a team of men and women tour guides.

In addition to the mosque tours, I have received numerous speaking invitations, along with my associates, to schools, churches and various organisations to inform them about Islam and Muslims.

INTRODUCTION

The experience has made us realise that there was a pattern to the questions asked by people who came to listen to us. We started to collect the questions asked in order to train our tour guides with answers. After organising three mosque open-day events, about 200 mosque tours and 50 speaking arrangements in the last three years, the number of questions on our list grew to more than 150 questions. Initially we decided to write short answers to these questions. In the course of time, some of the visitors and students asked for written answers to their questions as well. It soon became obvious to me that there was a need to have a book answering these questions and to make it available to a wider audience.

There are a number of books available that aim to inform people about Islam. I believe this book is unique in number of ways. Firstly, the questions are asked by people who are not Muslim and come from a Western cultural background. The questions are not what I think should be asked of Muslims and answer them accordingly, but they are real questions asked by ordinary Australians. On the whole, I have preserved the originality of these questions. Secondly, there are 101 questions in the book and the list is quite comprehensive. In most cases, I have combined a number of questions of similar nature as one question. Thirdly, although I have answered each question with an objective mind, there is an element of bias in the book since I am a Muslim myself. I believe this aspect adds more value to the book and readers will appreciate it more as they really want to know how a Muslim understands and lives Islam. In my answers I have tried to be as objective as possible and give support to my explanations from the core sources of Islam, which are the Qur'an and the collection of Prophet Muhammad's sayings and actions. I have also tried to reflect the rationale of Muslim thinking and the wisdom behind the teachings of Islam rather than just passing on information.

INTRODUCTION

I believe this book will give non-Muslim readers an insight into Islam from a Muslim who grew up amongst them and lives and works with them. It will also benefit Muslim readers who are also confronted with these questions on a daily basis and need to relate Islam to a life in a Western country.

I want to thank thousands of curious people for asking these questions and contributing to the formation of this book. I acknowledge the Auburn Gallipoli Mosque visitor services team for helping me in collecting the questions. I also extend my thanks to Stephanie Boyle, Zuleyha Keskin, Husam Deeb and Mehmet Saral with their assistance in drafting answers to some of the questions. I am especially grateful to Phillip Claxton who spent long hours in editing the book amongst his busy schedule. I am also grateful to my wife Yasemin for being patient with me and for tolerating me in taking some of her time in completing this book.

Mehmet Ozalp
Sydney, July 2004

PART I

FAITH ESSENTIALS OF ISLAM

Chapter 1

God and Religion

Misconceptions and misunderstandings about Islam and its teachings are most strikingly seen in people's assumptions concerning Islam's perception of God. Some people think that Islam is a pagan or even a polytheistic religion, and some also assume that "Allah" is a strange deity or an idol. In fact, Allah means no more than "The God", the one and only true deity who created the universe, and therefore the God of all creation and humanity. In this chapter, you will find out about the uncompromising monotheism of Islam that is simple in its concept and yet profound in its implications.

It is also a common human response to compare a new concept with what one already knows. Questions are often asked that compare the religious concepts of Islam with those of a familiar religion such as Christianity. In this chapter you will also get an opportunity to see how Islam is similar or different to other major world religions.

Q1

Could you please give us an idea of the concept of Islam and its main aspects?

A man came to the Holy Prophet Muhammad (pbuh[1]) and said, *"Give me information about Islam such that would suffice me and I should not have to ask anyone else"*. The Prophet concisely replied, *"Say, 'I believe in one God', and then be straight"*. [ALSO SEE THE QUR'AN, 41:30.] This statement summarises the two halves of Islam, right belief and right action. *"I believe in one God"* asserts the monotheism of Islam, that is, the oneness and uniqueness of God; and *"be straight"* (*istaqeem*) refers to being balanced, following the middle ground and having integrity in one's self and one's actions. At another level, the message of Islam rests on four forms of oneness:

- Oneness of God
- Oneness of the message of God
- Oneness of the order of Prophets
- Oneness of humanity

Oneness of God refers to the unity of God, in that God is the one and only God; there is none comparable to Him; He does not share his Lordship and Divinity with any other being and He alone has the attributes of perfection. [REFER TO QUESTIONS 2–5 FOR MORE ABOUT GOD IN ISLAM.]

Oneness of the message of God. "Message" means that Islam is not a new religion, *"We sent Noah to his people. He said: 'O my*

---

[1] Out of reverence for his role as the Messenger of God, Muslims are required to say "peace be upon him" whenever the name of the Prophet Muhammad or, in fact, the name of any other prophet is mentioned. In books this is usually abbreviated to "pbuh" after the name. This is only a recent practice. Since Muslims already know about this and non-Muslim readers are not required to say the phrase, I have not included the abbreviation "pbuh" after the name of the Prophet Muhammad in this book.

people! **Worship God, have no other god but Him...**'" [QUR'AN, 7:59] The same theme, "believing and worshipping one God", appears in many places in the Qur'an with reference to all the previous prophets. Muslims believe that Islam is the final reminder of the eternal message of God, one that seems to have been compromised by people in previous centuries. Islam is this primordial religion of God. The Qur'an (the holy book of Muslims) declares, *"And this was the legacy that Abraham left to his sons, and so did Jacob; 'Oh my sons! God has chosen the faith for you; then die not except in the faith of Islam."* [2:132] Over time, as humanity progressed and new needs emerged, the same core message was packaged differently until the religion as revealed to the Prophet Muhammad was complete and perfected with a special guarantee that it will stay authentic until the Last Day. The Prophet Muhammad was to be the last prophet and Islam was to be the final, complete and perfected form of God's core religion, *"...this day have I perfected your religion for you and completed My favour unto you, and have chosen for you as religion, Islam..."* [QUR'AN, 5:3]

Oneness of the order of Prophets means that the prophets do not compete with one another, but rather that they came to confirm one another and guide people in a particular time and location. *"We have sent revelations to you as We sent them to Noah and the Prophets after him: We also sent revelations to Abraham, Ishma'il, Isaac, Jacob and his descendants, to Jesus, Job, Jonah, Aaron, and Solomon. We have revealed Psalms to David.* **Of some prophets We have already told you their story; of others We have not**; *and to Moses God spoke directly..."* [QUR'AN, 4:163–165]. Thus, Islam accepts all true prophets appointed by God whether their names appear in the Qur'an or not. This universal approach leads Muslims to investigate other religions and treat their followers with tolerance rather than prejudice.

Oneness of humanity refers to the absolute equality of every human. One's race, colour, social status, wealth, etc., are not to be used as criteria for human superiority. *"O mankind! We created you from a single (pair) of a male and a female, and made you into nations and tribes, so that you may know each other (not that you may despise each other). Verily the most honoured of you in the sight of God is the most righteous of you. And God has full knowledge and is well acquainted (with all things)"* declared the Qur'an in 49:13, fourteen centuries ago.

Furthermore, Islam is both a religion and a way of life covering four essential and complementary aspects of human existence for one in every five people on earth.

1. Islam explains existence and relates human life to God and the universe in a manner that satisfies the mind and the heart alike.

2. It teaches that the prime function of human existence is the recognition and worship of God.

3. It shows how naturally belief in angels, prophets, holy books, the hereafter and the Divine Will emanate from faith in the One true God.

4. Islam establishes universal and timeless principles of human conduct to ensure continuous human development resulting in individual and communal happiness in this life and the next.

Collectively, these four aspects of Islam provide Muslims with a very profound self-realisation and meaning, a firm conviction and a strong commitment to its practice.

Literally, the word "Islam" means "submission" and the word "Muslim" means "the one who has submitted". "Islam" comes from the root word *"seleme"*, meaning "peace" in Arabic. Therefore, in a religious context, a Muslim is defined as a person who has surrendered himself or herself to God in deep faith and as a result has found peace within himself or herself and with his or her social and natural environment. The Qur'an says, *"Do (some people) seek a deen other than the deen of God? Is this what they do even though everything within Space and Earth surrenders willingly or unwillingly to Him? Certainly*

QUESTION 1

they will return to God?" [QUR'AN, 3:85] In this verse, the word *"deen"* refers to "religion" or a "way of life". The message of this verse and others like it invite humans to the belief and worship of one God using their reason and free will. Although God has created all creatures and people as servants to God without asking them first, He is inviting humanity to accept willingly the honourable role of servanthood. In doing so, the Qur'an points our attention to how the rest of the universe has surrendered in obedience to God. Consider how every entity in the universe follows certain laws. The earth always follows the same route set for it by God: bees always make honey and spiders always craft their webs. Hence, in their submission to God's design (will), the whole creation is Muslim. Anybody who has submitted himself or herself to God can be considered a Muslim. Islam, therefore, asks human beings to synchronise themselves with the natural world in their recognition of, and submission to, God.

Islam is a divine system comprising a set of clear, self-evident, timeless and universal truths that consider the human being as an integrated whole, basing its propositions on the natural human disposition and the universe.

Q2

What sort of God do you believe in? Who is the God of Muslims? Do Muslims have lots of gods? Why do you worship a person? Who do you pray to?

The concept of God in Islam is described concisely in one of the short chapters of the Qur'an: *"Say: He is God, the One (and only); God, the Eternal, Absolute; He begets not, nor is He begotten; And there is none like unto Him."* [QUR'AN, 112:1-4] In this verse the Qur'an gives a very clear idea of God. At the same time it tells us what God is and what He is not.

The central concept in Islam is the absolute unity of God. No other entity, human or non-human, has any share in God's Lordship, Attributes or Divinity. He alone has created and governs the universe, to Him belongs all attributes of perfection, and to Him should all devotion and worship be offered.

God in Islam is both transcendent and personal. He is transcendent because in His essence He is not like anything in his creation. We cannot know God's essence as he is beyond human comprehension. In this respect the Prophet Muhammad gave us a rule of thumb, saying that *"whatever mental picture you have for God, God isn't that"*. God has no gender. He is neither male nor female. The pronoun "He" is sometimes used because the word "it" does not exist in Arabic.

Even though transcendent, God in Islam is not distant or unconcerned with human life. He is nearer to us than our own jugular vein [QUR'AN, 50:16]. He is also a personal God because we can get to know His attributes by reflecting on His works in the universe. In Islam, God has many names, including a list of 99 names. This list includes such names as All-Merciful, Most Compassionate, The Mighty, All-Knowing, The Loving, The Caring, The Living, The Bringer of Peace, The Avenger of Evil, The

Generous, and so on. Through these names we get a feel for God and see His presence in everyday life, in nature and the universe. Therefore, we no longer need to concern ourselves with what God may look like as we can relate to Him by His observable actions and therefore appreciate His qualities. For example, by reflecting on the balance and equilibrium in the universe and life on earth and how this is maintained without human control, we can conclude that God exists and that He is The-Just. Since God has given us freedom of choice, He asks us to establish justice in the human domain. Since from time to time humans transgress justice, after death they will be called to give account in a Supreme Tribunal where justice will be fulfilled.

Islam came to end idol worship and the association of partners with the one true God. In Islam it is a major sin to worship a person, statue or any other thing except the Creator, God Almighty. The only divinity worshipped in Islam is God, who is not a person and does not have limitations as do human images. No matter how holy a person is, he or she cannot be prayed to or worshipped because these acts of devotion should only be offered to God and without the need of any intermediaries.

The assumptions in the question may come from the use of the word "Allah". If people do not know the meaning of this word they may think that Muslims believe in a person called Allah. The word for "God" in Arabic is "Allah". Since the Qur'an was originally revealed in Arabic, the name "Allah" was used to mean "the God". Christian Arabs, as well as Muslims, call God "Allah" in their Scriptures. On the other hand, the word "Allah" is special in that it does not have plural forms (like "gods" in English) or female or male connotations (e.g., "goddess") or miniature connotations (eg., "demigod"). In this respect, Muslims consider the word "Allah" as the most appropriate name for God.

Moreover, Muslims do not worship Muhammad in any way. He is not considered to be divine. He is a human being just like us, but with the important role of being a revelation-bearing Prophet to guide Muslims and humanity.

Do you believe in an active God?

Muslims believe in an active God. Since all the attributes of God are eternal, their manifestations in the universe are continuous. For example, He is the Creator and He is continuously active in the act of creation. We clearly observe that the universe is constantly changing with new creation. Since these activities are not governed by humans or by other created beings, they require a constantly active God. For instance, all particles and celestial objects are in constant motion. Stars and galaxies are being born and destroyed all the time. Every moment, something or someone dies or is born. The earth is like a beautifully ornamented palace with its landscape constantly changing. All these require constant governing of affairs so that order is maintained.

We know that the sun is internally active and as a result constantly radiates its light in every direction. It becomes present in the light, heat and other attributes of every object. In a similar way, **God is constantly active and present at every place with His Knowledge and Power**. In this way, His names and attributes manifest in the whole Universe. It is important to note that the whole creation, including human beings, cannot physically get beyond space and time. On the other hand, space and time do not bind God, as He is the one Who created them in the first place. In this respect, **as space and time do not bind God, we say that God is nowhere and transcendent**.

God acts consistently through what is termed "natural laws", which are constantly at work. Therefore, God is always active. The following verse from the Qur'an alludes to this: "*God! None has the right to be worshiped but He, the Ever-Living, the One Who sustains and protects all that exists. **Neither slumber nor sleep overtakes Him**. To Him belongs whatever is in the heavens and whatever is on earth. Who is he that* *can intercede with Him except with His Permission? He knows what happens to them (His creatures) in this world, and what will happen to them in the Hereafter. And they will never compass anything of His Knowledge except that which He wills.* **His Throne** *[in a figurative sense representing God's command and control in the universe]* **extends over the heavens and earth, and he feels no fatigue in guarding and preserving them. And He is Most High, the Most Great"** [QUR'AN, 2:255].

You say that you believe in one God who created the universe. Is God considered part of the universe?

In Islam, God is neither part of the universe nor is the universe considered to be a part of God. God is completely different to His creation. The Qur'an says, *"And there is none like unto Him."* [QUR'AN, 112:4] The Prophet Muhammad said that whatever one imagines God to be, that is not God, meaning that God's Self and Essence are beyond our imagination and comprehension.

We can further clarify the point that "God is not part of the universe" by giving an analogy. Let us assume there is a book and every word in this book is intelligent, just like a person. A word can only see letters, other words, sentences, paragraphs and pages, because only these entities exist in the realm of a book. A particular word stops and thinks. He looks at himself, and realises he is composed of letters that are put together in a particular order to give a meaning. He then looks at sentences, paragraphs and pages realising that even greater order and meaning can be observed. Hence, he concludes this book that he is in must have an author. He then extrapolates, saying, "I wonder what my author looks like?" At this point, the word will start to make mistaken conjectures, because he will try to liken the author to pages, paragraphs and other features of the book, as these are the only things he knows in his own world of existence. In reality though, the author is completely different to the book.

In a similar manner, the universe is like a book. The earth is like a page and we are like the words of the book. Just as a book has an author, the universe must have a Creator. And, just as an author of a book is completely different to the book itself, God is completely different to His creation. If a person starts to imagine the essence of God or tries to give certain images to God, he will always be in error, since we are all limited by our knowledge of this universe and God is completely unlike anything in His creation or in the universe. The existence of human-like and animal-like gods in some religions is a result of this great mistake.

When we talk about God's names and attributes manifesting in the universe, we mean that those qualities reflect themselves in the works of God. For example, God has the name *Al-Jameel* (The Beautiful). The beauty of a flower or of spectacular scenery is a reflection of this name. God has the name *Al-Adl* (The Just). The balance and equilibrium that we see in nature and the universe is a reflection of this name. Another name is *Ar-Rahman* (The Most Compassionate). The caring a monstrous crocodile gives its young is a manifestation of this name. Thus, each name of God given in the Qur'an informs us of an innate "skill" or "quality" of God.

Q5

Do you believe that man is created in the image of God?

Muslims do not believe man is created in the image of God's essence. God does not physically look like human beings or have the inherent limitations of humanity. He does not have arms and legs as we do, nor is He of flesh and blood. The Qur'an reveals that God is not like any of His creatures in essence. [QUR'AN, 112:1–4]

On the other hand, God has created human beings with attributes similar to those of His own, but in a very limited fashion. This is highlighted in the verse, "*…I have made him (Adam) complete and breathed into him of My spirit…*" [QUR'AN, 15:29] Notwithstanding the fact that Islam clearly rules out any assertion that may suggest the divinity of any human being, it also allows that the human being possesses the perfect and infinite attributes of God in a limited and finite fashion, so we can get to know God.

As human beings we only know and comprehend things in terms of opposites, such as hot-cold, positive-negative, and so on. But God does not have any opposites. For us to comprehend God he has embedded in us attributes similar to His own. We use our attributes as a unit of measure to understand the absolute, eternal and perfect attributes of God. For example, we only see the seven colours of the spectrum at a certain distance. When we reflect on the fact that the universe ticks in perfect order in spite of its size, we can truly understand that God is All-Seeing in order that He can govern everything in the universe. Through our limited artistic and creative skills, we can comprehend the matchless Artistry and Creativity of God.

Knowledge of God is essential as it leads to love of God. We cannot love someone we do not know. Lack of knowledge of God will result in a very superficial and pretentious claim to love God. God has endowed us with the right tools to reach to the higher stations of knowing and loving Him.

Q6

Is it enough to accept and believe in a universal consciousness or power? Can a person be saved from punishment by just accepting God? Is it OK if I believe in a Supreme Being but not follow a religion?

When we closely examine the creation, we realise that state-of-the-art technology is deployed and there is much complexity within a fine display of art. The form that each creation takes is selected from many different possible forms. The variety and abundance of life forms seem to be never-ending on this tiny planet, which is among hundreds of billions of stars that make up our Milky Way galaxy, one among billions of galaxies in the universe. All these observations lead to the necessity of having infinite *knowledge*, *will* and *power* to make it all happen. If these attributes are not given to one Creator, then gods to the number of particles in the universe have to be implicitly accepted. This is because without a God every particle in the universe has to have infinite knowledge, will and power so that the harmony and perfect operation of the universe can be maintained. To explain this further, we can draw the analogy of the sun's image appearing in every object on earth. If the idea of a single sun in the sky is rejected then the existence of innumerable suns equalling the number of transparent objects must be accepted if we are to explain the images seen in those transparent objects. Similarly, if the purposeful acts that particles, plants and animals seem to perform without consciousness are not attributed to one God, then divine attributes must be attributed to every entity in the universe.

Having established the fact that there has to be a God and His Supremacy cannot be challenged, we can also claim that it is not acceptable for someone to only believe in a Creator but not a religion, because belief in God requires other things, such as belief

QUESTION 6

in prophets, books and resurrection. For instance, consider the following rational argument:

- God created and ordered the Universe in perfect harmony with His infinite Knowledge and Power. The mind-boggling detail, the delicate inter-working of all the parts of creation and the grand scale of total existence shows that the One who created all this has infinite knowledge.

- It is natural that anyone who has knowledge speaks when issues in the areas of their expertise and concern are raised. Since God Almighty is concerned with the whole creation and has infinite knowledge, He will surely speak.

- When God speaks, He will surely speak to conscious beings that are also able to speak. God will speak to mankind, as having the most complete and balanced composition, capacity and faculties among conscious creatures.

- Within mankind He will surely speak to the one most worthy of the Divine conversation and the one who has the most perfect composition and capacity to represent the Divine message. He will surely select the golden generations of Prophets and the Prophet Muhammad, since both friend and foe acknowledge his perfect character.

It is undeniable that balance characterises the whole universe. Consider the way stars and galaxies are held in balance, the fact that annual rainfall throughout the earth equals the amount of water that vaporises from the waters and how each species is balanced within its ecological system. All these show that balance is universal and a manifestation of the justice of the All-Just God in nature. However, absolute justice is not apparent in the human domain. Hitler died without receiving his due punishment and many good people have passed away without being rewarded. God's absolute justice requires that there must be another realm where absolute justice will be fulfilled.

Therefore, according to Islam and in accordance with reason, when one accepts God one must also accept Revelation, the Prophets and the notion of life after death.

It is also inconceivable that a compassionate God would ignore humanity and not provide them with principles and guidelines to lead them to happy lives in this world and the hereafter. As manifested throughout the universe, Divine Compassion meets the smallest needs of the most insignificant of God's creatures. Is it at all possible for God not to meet the needs of humanity, the best of His creation?

At birth, a human being is born with many faculties in potential form waiting to be developed. Unlike other creatures, he or she enters the world like a seed waiting to blossom. A baby knows nothing but to suckle its mother's breasts. Compared to animals, which are born with whatever knowledge and skills they need to survive in this world, a baby needs a long period to physically develop. Thus human beings need to learn everything. In fact, the most distinguishing aspect of humanity is its ability to learn [QUR'AN, 2:31–33]. Learning requires teaching, which in turn requires instructions or manuals from its Maker, God. Hence religion becomes an essential necessity for human existence.

We also have spiritual needs that nothing materialistic can satisfy. The increasing number of people who suffer depression in the developed countries is testimony to the need for spirituality. In Islam, religion in the form of revelation (Qur'an) and its model in the life of the Prophet Muhammad is a way of life and a set of principles and guidelines to meet the physical, mental, spiritual and social needs of individuals as well as communities.

How does Islam relate to science?

Not only does Islam and its revealed holy book the Qur'an not contradict established scientific facts but they also encourage humanity to observe and reflect upon the universe and the laws governing its operation. Almost 15% of the Qur'an, over 700 verses, is composed of messages such as, *"Behold! In the creation of the heavens and the earth, and the alternation of night and day, there are indeed Signs for men of understanding. Men who celebrate the praises of God, standing, sitting, and lying down on their sides, and contemplate the (wonders of) creation in the heavens and the earth, (and say): 'Our Lord! You did not create this in vain...'"* [QUR'AN, 3:190–191]

Not only does the Qur'an encourage humanity to investigate and reflect upon the universe, it actually contains scientific truths which were only discovered in the 20th century. Since the Qur'an was revealed 14 centuries ago and the Qur'an that exists today is the same as the original, Muslims see this phenomenon as undeniable evidence that the Qur'an is the word of God.

For example, verses that say *"Do not those who disbelieve see that the heavens and the earth were **together**, but We have split them **apart**, and We made **every living thing out of water**, will they not then believe?"* [QUR'AN, 21:30] and *"And the heaven, We raised it high with power, and most surely, We are expanding it."* [QUR'AN, 51:47] clearly talk about the Big Bang, the expanding universe and living bodies being made up largely of water, are all concepts unheard of in the 7th century. The verse, *"Glory be to Him Who created **pairs of all things**, of what the earth grows, and of their kind and what they do not know"* [QUR'AN, 36:36] explicitly describes the Law of Parity that is prevalent throughout the universe. The roundness of the earth, the earth going around the sun, the precise description of embryonic development, the germination of plants and many more scientific facts are openly mentioned in the Qur'an. Many scholars who saw these verses centuries ago were bewildered as they contradicted the accepted, however false, scientific notions of the times. Having full trust in the Qur'an, they concluded that the earth was round about five centuries before Galileo.

Since the early advent of Islam, being conscious of Qur'anic teachings, learned Muslim men and women studied material and religious sciences with deep spiritual practice at the same time. This has resulted in Muslims preserving the scientific heritage of the time, adding invaluable contributions and more importantly developing modern scientific methodology before passing it on to Europe to fuel the development of contemporary civilisation.

Islam does not subdue science or reason. On the contrary, it encourages their use and development. Science is a reflection of the universe, which is God's created entity. Reason is also an essential created aspect of human disposition that differentiates humanity from the rest of creation. No revealed religion that has remained authentic should be antithetical to facts we can observe about the universe and the use of reason. Islam in this sense is comfortably compatible with both science and reason.

Q8

Does Islam accept Jesus? What is Islam's view of Jesus? Do you accept Jesus as the son of God?

Jesus' name is mentioned 25 times in the Holy Qur'an whereas the name Muhammad is only mentioned five times. It is in the creed of Islam to accept Jesus as an honoured prophet of God, one of the highest in rank. Therefore, no Muslim would even dare to reject Jesus outright.

The Qur'an tells us that Jesus is held in high honour and will be one of those closest to God in the Hereafter; *"Behold! The angel said: 'O Mary! God gave you glad tidings of a Word from Him. His name will be Christ Jesus, the son of Mary, held in honour in this world and the Hereafter and of (the company of) those nearest to God'"* [QUR'AN, 3:45].

Jesus was strengthened with the Holy Spirit[2] while he performed miracles such as speaking in his infancy, giving life to a dead bird, raising the dead, giving sight to the blind and curing lepers with the permission and power of God [QUR'AN, 5:110]. Muslims also accept that Jesus was raised into Heaven, *"(And remember) when God said: O Jesus! Lo! I am gathering you and causing you to ascend unto Me"* [QUR'AN, 3:55].

The Qur'an speaks highly of Mary, mother of Jesus. *"Behold! The angels said: 'O Mary! God has chosen you and purified you; chosen you above the women of all nations'"* [QUR'AN, 3:42]. Not only is she one of few people in the Qur'an mentioned by name, but also her name appears thirty-one times in the Qur'an. The statement *'God has... chosen you above the women of all nations'* is rather interesting considering the fact that the first audience of the Qur'an was a highly tribal and nationalistic society in Arabia.

---

2 As referred to in other Qur'anic verses, the Holy Spirit in Islam is believed to be the Archangel Gabriel, who is a created being and cannot create anything and has no divinity.

According to Islam, Jesus was born miraculously without a human father and his mother Mary was a pure virgin, *"She said: 'O my Lord! How shall I have a son when no man had touched me?' He said: 'Even so: God creates what He wills. When He had decreed a plan, He but said to it, 'Be' and it is!'"* [QUR'AN, 3:47] The command "be" is believed to be the "Word" that brought Jesus into existence in his mother's womb.

Muslims love and genuinely revere Jesus. However, Islam does not agree with the Christian doctrine that "Jesus is the son of God" or is "God". The Qur'an consistently emphasises that Jesus was a human being and the "son of Mary" [QUR'AN, 2:253]. The main reasons for this are:

■ According to Islam, accepting someone as the literal "Son of God" infers that Divinity of God is shared or passed on to the "son". This in turn violates the tenets of monotheism and belief in one true God. The Qur'an states *"...He begets not, nor is He begotten; And there is none like unto Him."* [QUR'AN, 112:3–4]

■ The circumstances in which Adam came to be without any father and mother show that being without a father does not imply divinity [QUR'AN, 2:59]. If it were so, we would also have to accept Adam as the "Son of God".

■ Performing miracles does not imply divinity since all the prophets preceding Jesus also displayed a wide variety of miracles.

Islam and Christianity seem similar in many ways. What are the fundamental differences?

Islam and Christianity are similar in their codes of morality. They both accept God, revelation, the prophets, angels and resurrection. As discussed in the answer to QUESTION 8, Muslims also revere and accept Jesus. As far as Muslims are concerned, these similarities are quite natural and, in fact, necessary because Muslims believe that the God who sent Jesus to guide humanity before also sent the Prophet Muhammad for a similar mission at a later time.

Nevertheless, there are also important differences between Islam and Christianity. Muslims believe that one of the reason why Muhammad was sent as a prophet was to correct and clarify some aspects of Christian faith concerning which Christian scholars and clergy were not in full agreement and because the true teachings of Jesus had become somewhat distorted over time. The fundamental differences between Islam and Christianity are as follows:

1. The concept of God. The notion of God having a son is directly opposed to the Islamic faith. According to Islam God does not *"beget nor He is begotten"*.

2. The Trinity is not accepted in Islam. According to Islam, only God has divinity. Both Jesus and the Holy Spirit are created beings without divinity.

3. The Divinity of Jesus. Islam does not admit divinity to anyone other than God. Jesus is proclaimed in the Qur'an as *"the word of God and a spirit from Him"*. However, the birth of Jesus was miraculous, as was the creation of Adam.

4. Original sin. Islam teaches that Adam and Eve have sincerely repented for their joint mistake and they were eventually forgiven by God in their lifetime. According to Islam no-one bears the sin of another. Everyone is born sinless but with the capacity to sin. Therefore, there is no reason for the "atonement" of the sins of humanity. God is All-Forgiving. If He wills He can forgive the sins done towards Him. Sins done to other beings will be settled by God between the parties involved on the Day of Judgment. Here, Islam introduced the idea of "human rights" and "animal rights" centuries before the West.

5. Confession. There is no need to have an intermediary between God for forgiveness. God has promised in the Qur'an that He will forgive sins if sincere repentance is expressed directly to God, for He is All-Hearing.

6. Salvation. According to Islam, salvation is achieved through a person's faith and good deeds, acting with the guidance and grace of God. *"Most surely man is in loss. Except those who believe and do good, and enjoin on each other truth, and enjoin on each other patience."* [QUR'AN, 103:2–3] Salvation is the outcome of a virtuous life, not just a moment of conversion.

7. Clergy. There are neither clergy nor church establishment in Islam. Islam also does not prohibit men or women who want to lead religious lives or take spiritual leadership in the Muslim community. There is also no practice of monasteries or convents. Religion should be a part of one's natural and communal life.

In Christianity it is believed that "God has reincarnated in Jesus". Is this acceptable in Islam? Are there similar reincarnations of God in a human or other form in Islamic beliefs?

The notion of God incarnating in any physical or spiritual form is unacceptable to Islam and its teachings. It is neither necessary, useful nor possible for God to incarnate in a human being or any other physical entity.

How does Islam arrive at this conclusion? If one does not accept a religion, its prophet and revelations, then there has to be an objective source of information that is accessible to everyone equally, no matter what cultural and geographic background one might come from. In proving its set of propositions, the methodology of the Qur'an (Islam) uses the universe and the natural world as the objective source of information to which everyone has access. Since eternal salvation depends on the set of propositions one is expected to believe, any proposition of faith must pass the following two criteria:

■ It must be clear and beyond the realm of interpretation. It must be verifiable by reason.

■ There must be a very important purpose for the proposition in the universe or in human life.

For example, let us apply these two criteria to belief in resurrection. A Muslim has to believe in life after death, where we will give an account of our earthly life. The Qur'an clearly reiterates this in many of its verses. In order to prove the notion of life after death, the Qur'an says, "*So consider the signs of God's mercy; how He gives life to the earth after its death. Indeed, it is He Who gives life to the dead, for He is powerful over all things.*" [QUR'AN, 30:50] This verse illustrates the fact that there is life after death by using information from nature and argues that just as life seemingly flourishes out of nothing after a good rainfall in an arid landscape, it is also possible for life to be created out of substances that appear dead in the grave. Since God is capable of giving life to dead earth in an observable fashion, so too He is powerful enough to give life to dead humans. Thus, the first criterion is fulfilled.

The second criterion is also fulfilled in the case of resurrection, as it has very important repercussions in social life and the idea of justice. Belief in life after death allows the policing of every individual through their conscience resulting in the death of evil inclinations, even before they are born in the mind. The idea that this worldly life is the only one is one of the greatest dangers to human happiness and safety. This philosophy is an open invitation to people to commit crimes if they think they can get away with it. The soaring crime rate in countries where belief in a hereafter is weak, irrespective of material comfort, education and laws, is proof of this fact.

There are many similar lines of argument in the Qur'an that give rational arguments on all matters of belief. These verses usually end with the phrases, "there are signs in this for people who think", and for "people who reflect", "people of understanding" and so on. There are also many verses in the Qur'an that are critical of people who blindly follow the religion of their fathers. The faith that Islam wants is a certain, educated, verified and rational conviction.

If we apply the two Islamic criteria to the idea of God reincarnating in a human being, we see that Islam cannot agree with this notion. Muslims feel that the belief that God reincarnated in Jesus or the Hindu proposition that God reincarnates in every object are interpretations without firm evidence. When there is lack of demonstrable evidence, assumptions step in. Assumptions lead to conjectures, which in turn lead to differing interpretations. Great debates and disagreements follow suit as happened in Christian and Hindu circles in relation to the nature of the Divine. From an Islamic perspective, the fact that we witness extraordinary events taking place in nature does not mean natural matter has divinity in it, but rather means that there is a God who has the attributes of Knowledge, Will and Power to bring those events into reality. Similarly, the fact that Jesus performed miracles does not mean he was divine, but means that he was supported by God just as the Bible says, *"After the people saw the miraculous sign that Jesus did, they began to say, 'Surely this is the Prophet who is to come into the world.'"* [JOHN 6:14]

It is often said in support of Christianity that one of the reasons why "God incarnated in Jesus" at the moment of the crucifixion was to feel the pain of suffering that human beings undergo in life. Moreover, in human form "God in Jesus" reduced Himself to the human level so that he could relate to humanity better. Also, in this way, we are able to relate to a God in human form personally as God is otherwise distant and unreachable. God granted humanity a favour by assuming a human form.

Islam's view is that it is not necessary for God to enter into a physical body to know pain and suffering. He is the one who created the nervous system and the brain sensations that give the feeling of pain and suffering. Therefore, He does not have to experience it in order to know what we go through in life. Since God maintains the balance in an atom as He does in galaxies, His knowledge and power know no boundaries. God is not distant and is even closer to us than our jugular vein and knows what we think and go through [QUR'AN, 50:16]. Therefore there is no reason why God should enter into a human body.

Suffering and pain is a result of our natural disposition, designed to channel our emotions and awareness towards God. We are intrinsically weak and powerless. An unseen virus can kill us. We have innumerable enemies and ailments. Our ability to get what we want is finite yet our wants and desires are limitless. We are rather lazy and short in power and influence, yet life's requirements are many. Events in nature and the universe unavoidably touch us as we are connected with the whole universe. Our mind directs us towards lofty goals, yet we are limited in capacity, short in patience and have a brief earthly life. No knowledge and no technological advance will adequately address this inherent human disposition. All of these paradoxical situations in which we find ourselves were designed by the Creator so that we might seek the Eternal, long for the Perfect and reach out to find God. Islam's position is that only through a certain faith in God, a strong spirituality, transcending the self and desires, and submission in God will adequately close the gap and place a person on the right wavelength and groove in life. Therefore, suffering and pain are not there to punish humans, but to lead them to find purpose in life and as a result of this, to find God.

Islam has a unique way of meeting the human needs to personally relate to God without anthropomorphising God (that is, giving Him human attributes). In Islam, God has many names including All-Merciful, Most Compassionate, The Mighty, All-Knowing, The Loving, The Caring, The Living, The Bringer of Peace, The Avenger of Evil, The Generous, and so on. Through these names we get a feel for God and see His presence in everyday life, in nature and the universe. Therefore, we no longer need to concern ourselves with what God may look like as we can relate to Him by His observable actions, thereby appreciating His qualities.

Islam's position is also that the acceptance of God's incarnation in human form is neither possible nor purposeful. It is against God's majesty to reduce Himself to the level of His creation. The idea of God's incarnation brings with it theological and rational problems.

QUESTION 10

It entails an acceptance of the notion of the Trinity, which Muslims find irrational and impossible to accept. Muslims ask endless questions, such as, "Who was governing the universe when God was fully human in Jesus while he was eating, sleeping and being limited by space and time?" "Who was creating new stars in other galaxies during this time?" "What happened to God when Jesus died?" "Who caused his death?" "Was the incarnation physical or spiritual? If the incarnation was physical, is God composed of matter or did part of God became matter?" "If incarnation was a spiritual one, what happened to Jesus' spirit?" and "Did Jesus have a human spirit at all?"

How is Islam different to other religions?

Although Islam has significant similarities with all religions, it differs from other religions in belief, worship and certain aspects of social and moral principles.

The Qur'an claims that Islam is a religion of balance and represents the middle ground between the Jewish and Christian traditions. For example, in relation to justice, while Judaism asserts an attitude of *"an eye for an eye"* and Christianity teaches that one is to *"turn the other cheek"*, Islam, on the other hand, gives the right to seek justice while encouraging the affected parties and victims to forgive and reconcile [QUR'AN, 5:45].

God in Islam is both transcendent and personal, unlike Buddhism, which does not talk about God at all due to the transcendent reality of God, and unlike Christianity, which only accepts a personal God in the incarnation of Jesus. Islam does not ascribe absolute and perfect attributes of divinity to any image or person other than God, unlike Hinduism, where every divine attribute is ascribed to a separate God.

Islam does not give divinity to any human or created being other than God, unlike the concept of the Trinity in Christianity. In Islam, unlike Hinduism, God is not a distant entity but closer to us than our jugular vein [QUR'AN, 50:16]. Muslims worship and pray directly to God without any intermediaries.

Islam claims that no-one nation or race or religion can claim ownership of the earth. The dominion of God belongs only to God and He may endow it to whomever He wills out of His righteous servants. The Qur'an points to this fact: *"And Moses said unto his people: Seek help in God and endure. Lo! The earth is God's. He gives it for an inheritance to whom He wills. And lo! The sequel is for those who keep their duty (unto Him)."* [QUR'AN, 7:128]

QUESTION 11

In Islam, unlike Judaism, God also speaks to all humanity through revelation and the prophets without favouring one over the other, *"And for every nation there is a messenger. And when their messenger comes (on the Day of Judgment) it will be judged between them fairly, and they will not be wronged."* [QUR'AN, 10:47]

Since I have already covered the differences between Islam and Christianity in QUESTION 9, I will focus on the differences between Islam and Judaism, Hinduism and Buddhism.

Judaism

Islam has a lot in common with Judaism in its concept of God, resurrection, reward and punishment. Islam agrees with at least ten out of the thirteen articles of Jewish faith listed by Moses Maimonides. However, there are some differences:

- Judaism asserts that the Torah will not be changed and there will never be any other Law. Islam would say that the Torah was changed and rewritten several times in history. Just as Jesus came with a changed Law, so has Islam brought a new Law appropriate to a developed society. The Qur'an also says that the Jewish law is overly harsh due to human revisions and it needed to be changed [QUR'AN, 16:118].

- Judaism says that Abraham and his immediate sons were Jewish. Islam on the other hand starts the Jewish nation with Jacob and his sons [QUR'AN, 2:140].

- While Jews still await the coming of the Messiah and do not recognise Jesus as a prophet, the Qur'an says that Jesus was appointed by God as the Messiah.

- In Judaism, God has made an all-time covenant with the Jews and appointed them as a chosen people who were granted land by God forever. Islam says that the covenant with Jews was conditional and, in time, they broke the covenant [QUR'AN, 2:83]. The world also only belongs to the righteous not just a particular race of people [QUR'AN, 21:105].

Buddhism

Islam, especially the spiritual aspect of Islam known as Sufism, has important similarities with the philosophy of Buddhism. Just as in Buddhism, Islam also asserts that the motivation and intention of one's actions have important bearings in one's life on earth and beyond death. The main differences are as follows:

- The feeling of "unsatisfactoriness" is not a problem in Islam. It is this feeling that gives us the impetus and motivation to develop spiritually as a human being. It only becomes a problem if it is channelled to the self and worldly pleasures.

- Buddhism asserts that there is no immortal soul. In Islam, the human soul exists and continues to exist after death. The human spirit is a decree of God. Its essence does not change but it unfolds just like the petals of a rose in its development. Death is not destruction, but is a transition and a separation of the soul from the physical matter of the body and for the soul to continue on its journey towards its permanent realm.

- In Buddhism, God does not exist and humans have created God. In Islam God is necessarily existent. Since everything has a beginning and an end there must be a being that begins everything. Islam asserts that we cannot be blind to the fact that the universe exists. The art, complexity, imminence, scale and purposeful design in the universe requires an Artist with the Will, Knowledge and Power to make it all happen. The existence of God has an important bearing on our own existence.

- Although Islam also recognises that human desires are the cause of human spiritual suffering, it does not aim to blunt the desires but to channel them for the purpose for which they were created. The desires are given to us to survive on this planet, just like animals. The difference between animals and humans is that our desires have no end so we can continuously endeavour in our spiritual development. In a balanced state, the harmful effects of desires are neutralised. Suffering will always persist if a person does not find God.

■ Buddhism is not a public religion. The ideal Buddhist is a monk who is detached from the world. It is based on the cultivation of spiritual understanding. Although Islam also fosters spiritual understanding, it does this through a rational approach that has strong communal ties and practices. Islam does not encourage the lifestyle of a monk, but leads a person to achieve a restful spiritual state within a community so that spiritual understanding can be shared with other people in everyday life.

■ Buddhism says that a person will go through continuous rebirth if enlightenment is not achieved. The state of a person at reincarnation depends on his or her state of being which is a culmination of negative and positive energy generated by one's actions. Although Islam says that one's actions will influence the way one is eventually resurrected, resurrection will only occur once. Everyone will give an account of their lives and accordingly will end up in a final place of reward or reprimand. This life is enough to reach a positive, restful and enlightened state. Countless individuals who have rid themselves of desires and found high levels of spirituality from the empirical state of a baby shows that one lifetime is enough to attain an enlightened state. Those who did not achieve such a state have simply wasted their capacity to do so.

Hinduism
Islam also shares some similarities with Hinduism. As with Hinduism, Islam also teaches that there is a divine law and order in the

universe and that we must be in harmony with it. While the ultimate reality in Hinduism is Brahman, one of the 99 names for God in Islam is Rahman (Most Gracious) – strikingly similar words used to name God. In Islam, as in Hinduism, the motivation and intention of one's actions have an important bearing on one's life on earth and beyond death. The main differences are as follows:

- Hinduism teaches that there is neither an absolute beginning or end to human life nor to the life of the cosmos. A person is caught in cycles of creation and destruction unless he or she seeks liberation through religious practice. Islam, on the other hand, teaches that everything in the universe has a beginning and an end, except for God. This inevitably shows the permanence of God, just like the appearance and disappearance of the image of the sun on water bubbles in a stream shows the relative permanence of the sun.

- In Hinduism, Brahman is the ultimate reality behind all appearances. The whole world is the body of the Divine, hence sacred. Animals, rocks, rivers, human beings etc. are all expressions of the Divine. Islam says that God transcends space and time and God is neither part of, nor like, any of His creations in the universe. Yet Islam also acknowledges every creation has a divine purpose and hence is sacred in its own right.

- Hinduism teaches that there are millions of gods and goddesses with the assumption that all of them are one. Brahman cannot be worshipped directly. One can only worship Brahman through lesser personal gods. Islam teaches that there is one and only one God, and no-one else shares God's divinity. There is nothing to prevent humans worshipping God directly as God is closer to us than we think.

- In Hinduism, a way of achieving harmony with the world is ordering human groups into classes, each having certain obligations and privileges. According to this caste system, one's class is

QUESTION 11

determined at birth. Islam, on the other hand, teaches that all human beings have equal status and all humanity is one. No-one has a born advantage or disadvantage over the other. Being rich or poor, ruler or servant only serves as a test for us in this life. The only differentiator of people is their level of righteousness, which can only be judged by God.

Muslims recognise that there is an element of truth in every religion, for either a religion is explicitly cited in the Qur'an as having a divine origin or there is a strong chance that it has. However, Muslims believe that Islam is the only religion that achieves balance in all aspects of religion. Whatever is the highlight of a particular religion, Islam has it. Islam has the monotheism and legal aspects of Judaism, the love and compassion of Christianity, the richness of Hindu philosophy and the spirituality of Buddhism all in a unique blend.

Islam wants its followers to have a faith based on intellect and reason, a deep spirituality that brings a person into direct relationship with the one and only God and a healthy social activism to influence the society in goodness and progress. It does not want its followers to go to extremes in belief, worship or social conduct[3].

This is not to say that Islam was composed by putting together pieces from all the religions. It means that Islam has found the perfect combination of faith and practice of religion as a way of life covering all aspects of humanity. It has preserved the ideals of the oneness of God and the oneness of humanity. God, according to the Qur'an, says, *"This day have I perfected your religion for you and completed My favour unto you, and have chosen Islam for you as **deen** (religion and way of life)"* [QUR'AN, 5:3].

---

3 See the answer to QUESTION 100 for an explanation of current status of Muslims that may seem to contradict this assertion.

Q12

How does Islam view other religions? Is it open to other religions? What is the Muslim attitude to members of other faiths that believe in one God (e.g. Christians & Jews)? Is there a different approach to non-monotheistic faiths (e.g. Buddhist, Hindu)? Are there any interfaith relationships, especially with Christianity?

The Qur'an's definition of a believer (*Mu'min*) is somewhat broader than the common expectation that "a believer is one who believes in Islam". In fact, one can *accept* Islam as a way of life and practice it, which is the definition of a Muslim, but he or she does not necessarily *believe* in Islam. A *mu'min* (believer) is defined broadly as one who believes in the One and Only God, angels, revelation, the prophets and resurrection. The Qur'an says, *"Not all of them are alike: of the People of the Book (Christians and Jews) are a portion that stand (for the right): They rehearse the Signs of God all night long, and they prostrate themselves in adoration. They believe in God and the Last Day; they enjoin what is right, and forbid what is wrong; and they hasten (in emulation) in (all) good works: They are in the ranks of the righteous. Of the good that they do, nothing will be rejected of them; for God knows well those that do right."* [QUR'AN, 3:113–115]

Thus, true believers as described above can be found anywhere irrespective of what religious title the person might have. As long as they fulfil the Qur'an's criteria, they are believers. Muslims believe that Islam is not a new or unique message, but is the most complete update of the same timeless and universal message that God sent to previous prophets and people [QUR'AN, 2:132]. That is, the message that God reminded humanity as a whole for one last time.

Muslims call Christians and Jews the "People of the Book", that is, people to whom God's revelation was sent through Jesus and Moses respectively. Although the Qur'an does not specifically mention Hinduism, Buddhism or Zoroastrianism as divine religions, it does not reject them or their founders either. Islam's position is that, since God has sent prophets to all nations throughout history, it is likely that the founders of these religions may well have been true prophets. Since we have no way of knowing, Muslims neither clearly accept these religions nor do they reject them outright. Instead, Islam focuses on the criteria that deem a person an acceptable believer. In Islam, it is a transgression to worship more than one God or any presumed deity other than the one God [SEE QUESTION 25 ON ISLAM'S VIEW OF NON-MUSLIM'S POSITION IN THE HEREAFTER].

Because of the above position, Muslims have always had good relations with people of other religions. Islam essentially calls for its followers to establish good relationships with people of other faiths and nations: *"God does not forbid you to be kind and equitable to those who have neither made war on your religion nor driven you from your homes."* [QUR'AN, 60:8] Let alone encouraging hatred or acts of violence, Islam forbids Muslims even to offend people of other faiths through insulting remarks, *"And insult not those whom they worship besides God..."* [QUR'AN, 6:108]

Throughout Muslim history, Muslim rulers never suppressed religious freedom. They went even further to build and fix churches and synagogues for Christian and Jewish subjects. Abbasid caliph Harun al-Rashid even held dialogues and theological meetings with representatives of other religions.

Today there are many interfaith dialogue initiatives taking place all around the world, especially with Christians, since half the world's population is Muslim or Christian. These relationships stretch to Buddhism, Hinduism and Judaism as well. Influential Muslim spiritual leaders such as M. Fethullah Gulen are encouraging their students and followers to enter into dialogue with people of other faiths. Locally in Australia, great strides have been taken to foster dialogue and understanding since the year 2000. Muslim organisations such as the Australian Federation of Islamic Council (AFIC), Muslim Women Network, Affinity Intercultural Foundation (Sydney) and Australian Intercultural Society (Melbourne) are examples of organisations that focus on interfaith relations and dialogue. They have engaged in reciprocal church and mosque visits by members of the respective congregations, workshops and interfaith panels in churches and schools and the staging of international interfaith dialogue conferences, to name some of the joint projects.

In a short time, strong relationships have developed to ensure the continuation and growth of such initiatives into the future to result in tangible projects and bear the fruits of mutual understanding and acceptance.

Do you believe that God has an overriding Will?

We need to consider this question with respect to nature and the universe as well as to human life. In the case of the universe, we observe that there is a definite measure and selection of particular options from amongst many possibilities taking place in creation. The fact that the total amount of rainfall on earth is exactly the same every year and the dimensions of the human face and its symmetry show such a measure. Islam's perspective is that it is God who determines everything that exists. Everything in the universe occurs within God's knowledge: *"With Him are the keys of the unseen, the treasures that none knows but He. He knows whatever there is on the earth and in the sea. Not a leaf does fall but with His knowledge. There is not a grain in the darkness (or depths) of the earth, nor anything fresh or dry (green or withered), but is (inscribed) in a Clear Record."* [QUR'AN, 6:59]

There are many examples of how the composite parts of the universe have been divinely determined that we can glean from nature and the universe:

- There is a grand plan and sequence of events to be observed in the Universe that are beyond our control. The Big-Bang, the creation of the Milky Way and the earth, the geological periods and the creation of living beings including humans can be given as examples.
- As proven by science, natural laws point to a restriction and a measuring, hence directing matter into a chosen course. No creation can escape the forces of divine laws. For example, the law of gravitation applies to every object in the universe.
- There is a delicate balance of life (ecology) on earth that indicates a plan and determination.

As far as humanity is concerned, on the other hand, there is freedom of choice. The Will of God is not forced upon humanity, but is disclosed in the form of revelation. Just as the universe is governed perfectly by submitting to the Will of God, humanity is expected to willingly submit to the Will of God to find peace, harmony and happiness in the human domain. This ultimate submission to God is what it means to be a Muslim.

In Islam, Divine Determination is a title for God's knowledge, which transcends time and space. God's knowing and recording of future events does not force a person to act in an ill manner. Meteorologists through their science and knowledge can predict and record that it will rain two days later. If it actually rains in two days time, it did not come to pass because of the prediction. It was going to rain anyway. Similarly, through his infinite knowledge, God knows what we will do in our lives and records it. However, this does not force us to perform the acts that He has thus recorded.

Humanity has freedom of choice and an independent will to exercise this freedom. We choose to respond to events in a particular way. God Almighty creates the act and the resultant consequences. For example, when we move our arms, we have no conscious control over the physiological processes that produce the desired movement. There are also quadriplegic people who want to move their limbs, but cannot.

All good is from God and the evil associated with us is from our own soul. Evil is produced by the lack of fulfilment of an essential ingredient or condition for good to be created. Humans through the misuse of their will cause this and the consequence is evil.

The creation of evil or allowing evil to happen is not evil, but choosing evil is. God does not choose evil, we do. He allows it because He has granted us freedom of choice. For example, a child might ask his father to carry him on his shoulders and take him into the rain. Although his father warns him that he will get wet and sick, the child insists. If his father takes him into the rain and the child starts complaining, he would deserve to be rebuked for not heeding his father. Similarly, we choose a great portion of what we do in life and consequences flow from those choices.

Since no other being other than God can have creative powers, it follows that God creates both good and evil. However, evil is created as a consequence of man's misuse of his independent will. If God did not create evil as a consequence of man's misuse of his independent will, we could not talk about freedom of choice and being a human being. **Responsibility and accountability come with the freedom of choice.**

Chapter 2

The Chain of Prophethood and Revelation

One of the most fundamental tenets of Islam is the notion that giving revelation to appointed prophets is a continuous act of God. Islam is a religion that recognises that God did not miss or neglect any group of humanity and sent an innumerable number of prophets as guides to all people. The illustrious list of prophets includes Abraham, Moses, David, Jesus and of course Muhammad – peace be upon them all. You will be pleasantly surprised that, just as Islam does not distinguish between any two human beings in race, colour, looks, etc. it also does not hold any one prophet as superior to any other.

In this chapter, I will examine the concept of prophethood and revelation in Islam. In particular, I will answer questions about the mission and character of the Prophet Muhammad as well as the nature, content and history of the Qur'an.

Is it acceptable if a person accepts some of the prophets of God and does not accept some others?

The existence of the prophets is a necessity. God created and ordered the universe in perfect harmony with His Infinite Knowledge and Power. The intricate detail, the delicate inter-working of all parts of creation and the grand scale of existence in its totality show that the one who created all this has infinite knowledge. It is natural that someone who has specialist knowledge speaks when issues in that area of expertise are raised. Since God Almighty is concerned with the whole creation and He has infinite knowledge He will surely speak. When God speaks, He will surely speak to conscious beings that are also able to speak. God will speak to mankind, since man among creatures with consciousness has the most complete and balanced composition, capacity and faculties. Within mankind He will surely speak to the one most worthy of the divine conversation and the one who has the most perfect composition and capacity to represent the divine message. He will surely select the golden generations of Prophets.[4]

Each religion has a differing perspective as to whom they recognise as prophets and the place of prophethood within God's plan for humanity. While Judaism acknowledges many prophets such as Noah, Abraham, Joseph, Moses, David, Solomon and so on, and only excepting Jesus and Muhammad, Christianity recognises all the prophets except the Holy Prophet Muhammad. Judaism limits prophethood to the Jewish nation, even as Jesus and his claimed divine nature eclipse all other figures of religion in Christianity.

---

4 Nursi, Said, *Letters*, Truestar, Turkey (1994), pp. 99–100.

QUESTION 14

It appears that there is a tendency for followers of one religion not to accept any prophet who comes after the prophet representing their faith and tradition. This tendency occurs even though their holy book mentions the coming of another future prophet to follow the present one. Islam argues that, just as God has sent prophets throughout history, He can appoint another one when and if necessary. Unless of course, God Himself declares in a revelation to an authorised prophet that He will not send any other prophet again.

As a general principle, Muslims recognise all prophets sent by God whether their names are known or not. This recognition includes all the Prophets mentioned in the Bible and, of course, Jesus. Additionally, Muslims recognise all previous revelations of God such as those revealed to Abraham, Moses, David, Jesus and Muhammad. One cannot be a Muslim unless he or she acknowledges all the prophets sent by God: *"The messenger Muhammad believes in what has been sent down to him from his Lord and so do the believers. Each one believes in God, His Angels, His books and His messengers; (they say) we make no distinction between one another of His messengers; and they say: we hear and we obey. We seek Your forgiveness (God's forgiveness) our Lord and to You is the return of all."* [QUR'AN, 2:285]

The Qur'an mentions the names of twenty-five prophets. According to the Prophet Muhammad more than a hundred thousand prophets were sent to humanity during the course of history. We are also told that no prophet was sent between Jesus and Muhammad. The Qur'an says that Muhammad is the last prophet [QUR'AN, 33:40]. There is no need to send another prophet because Islam and its holy book, the Qur'an, will be preserved intact until the Last Day. So far this prophecy has come true. [SEE QUESTION 19 ON HOW THE QUR'AN WAS PRESERVED UNALTERED.]

Muslims neither fully accept nor reject the important figures in other religions with respect to the possibility that they may have been true prophets of God [QUR'AN, 4:163, 165]. This view of recognising all the prophets of prevalent world religions as equally venerable and possibly of divine origin gives Muslims a very tolerant view of other religions and their followers.

In human history, thousands of prophets were sent to all nations at appropriate time intervals. Prophets are the special envoys of God on earth and are supported by giving evidence of a divine source of appointment. Since it is God who appoints prophets, He would expect His creation, humanity, to accept all of them without exception. One's duty is to investigate and verify a claim of prophethood rather than reject it outright. The Qur'an's answer to this attitude is: *"Is it a wonder for people that We have inspired a man from among themselves, saying 'warn mankind and bring unto those who believe the good tidings that they have a sure footing with their Lord?' The disbelievers say, 'This (revelation he brings) is evidently clear sorcery'."* [QUR'AN, 10:2]

Q15

The prophets are seen as an integral part of the Muslim tradition. How would you describe their role in Islam's ethical system?

Prophets have the most difficult job in the world, with no salary. The purpose of their job is to relay a message from the Creator to humans who are not very eager to listen. They are usually subjected to great hardship with no apparent earthly reward. According to Islam, their job description consisted of a diverse set of roles and responsibilities as follows:

- Throughout the course of history, humanity has lapsed into disbelief. Prophets were sent to guide humanity so that people might regain and sustain their belief in the one God.

- The Prophets were sent to remind people of the purpose of their existence, which is to believe and worship the one and only God.

- The Prophets taught people God's laws so that they may live happily in this world and the hereafter.

- Humanity needed leadership in development as well as balance between this world and the next. Prophets provided the much-needed leadership and they brought about important social changes.

- The prophets were God's witnesses on earth so that people would have no excuse when God questioned them in the hereafter.

In addition to the list above, humanity also needs practical models illustrating what God desires in a human being. Prophets have proved to be perfect role models for us all to emulate. All one needs to do to appreciate this is to objectively examine the exemplary lives of Abraham, Moses, Jesus, Muhammad and so on.

As Muslims know the life of Muhammad in more detail than any other previous prophet and, since the general character of all true prophets are essentially similar, Muslims naturally follow the example of the Prophet Muhammad. The Qur'an encourages Muslims to follow his example in the verse, *"Verily in the messenger of God you have a good example for those who look unto God and the last Day, and remembers God much."* [QUR'AN, 33:21] The Prophet Muhammad has also said that he was sent *"to perfect the best of morality and character (ethics)"*. Because of the fact that Islam is seen as a way of life, emulating Muhammad as an example in one's conduct covers the complete set of behaviours (ethics) a person should display in life. There are volumes of authentic reports pertaining to Muhammad's words and actions which sincere Muslims today try to emulate in their daily lives. For Muslims, who could be a better example than a prophet and the Prophet Muhammad in particular? Both friend and foe equally acknowledge the high standards of his moral conduct [SEE ANSWER TO QUESTION 17]. The Qur'an covers passages from the lives of many prophets to provide the reader with some of the fundamental human and social principles working in society.

Being human, we will often falter and sin. How can we follow the prophets if they are so perfect? In Islam, God does not expect people to die sinless. The prophets with their high standards show us what is humanly possible in human spiritual development. In this way, Muslims know they can be better than they are now if they strive to achieve higher levels of being. If prophets commit sins they cannot be guides and good models to emulate. Although prophets do not sin, they can sometimes make errors of judgment in choosing slightly inferior option rather than a superior one. This is called *zelle* in Islamic terminology. Because of their closeness to God, in their eyes these errors are major slips and they turn to God in repentance. In this way, they also show us what to do when we slip.

All the prophets mentioned in the Qur'an were men. Since prophethood is a very dangerous and difficult task, God selected men to fulfil this role. Prophets had to face intense opposition, and psychological and physical torture. They were in danger of attack and had to lead their followers in times of conflict. It is interesting to note that almost always non-believing men led the opposition to prophets. Macho characteristics in these men were very much at the fore. They were extremely unlikely to follow the spiritual leadership of women. In this, I am not saying that women are unworthy of being prophets, but during those difficult times men were more qualified to do the hard job of prophethood.

Although women were not appointed as prophets, the Qur'an mentions two women who received revelation from God. Moses' mother received a number of revelations, while the angel Gabriel visited Jesus' mother, Mary, and relayed some instructions and a revelation from God. The Qur'an also mentions some other men (*Luqman, Khidir, Zul-Qarnayn*) who received revelation but were not prophets. So, Islam recognises that not only prophets, but also other men and women, receive revelation from God.

Q16

What convinces Muslims that Muhammad was the prophet of God and the last prophet?

In the lifetime of the Prophet Muhammad people certainly did not believe in him in a hurry. Muhammad himself said that, apart from his friend Abu Bakr, everyone initially doubted him. Although his first audiences were quite crude by the standards of the 7th century, they were also very smart people and cultured in sophisticated poetry. It was a hard task to convince people that one was a true prophet.

The same reasons that caused people to believe in Muhammad in his lifetime also convince Muslims today that he is the true prophet of God. The evidence of the prophethood of Muhammad falls into three main categories.

1. The strength of his character.
2. The miraculous quality of the Qur'an.
3. Many inexplicable acts that he exhibited.

Before Muhammad declared his prophethood he showed no sign that he would one day claim prophethood. Although he was unhappy about what was happening in society, he was not known to actively involve himself in the affairs of the community, but rather chose to worship and meditate privately on a mountaintop. He was possibly the least expected to become a social and religious activist.

In the case of Muhammad there is no middle ground. He was either a true prophet or a conniving imposter of the worst order. In his youth and adult life, he was known for his truthfulness and honesty, to such an extent that he had the nickname *"Al-Ameen"* meaning "the trustworthy". When he declared his mission no-one could or did accuse him of lying. The rejection of unbelievers usually had other motives. Once, annoyed at seeing someone using deception to call his horse, Muhammad said, *"You should give up*

QUESTION 16

deceiving animals. You should be trustworthy even in your treatment of them!" If he was so sensitive to deception in the most insignificant matters relating to animals, how could he deceive people in the most important matter of religion and truth about God? Two extreme opposites cannot exist in the same person at the same time. If they do, the person would be insane or extremely unbalanced. Muhammad never showed any sign of insanity or unbalance. Thousands of sane people would not gather around him and stick with him if he were unbalanced. He is mostly known for his composure, tranquillity of demeanour and authenticity in his behaviour.

Some orientalists claim that Muhammad was epileptic and had mental delusions that made him believe he was a prophet. This is highly unlikely. How many psychologically disturbed people established permanent world religions? When Muhammad received revelation, he visibly entered into trance and sometimes his body trembled. However, unlike an epileptic, he was totally conscious and was not thrown to the ground shaking uncontrollably. He came out of the trance with the beautifully eloquent words of the Qur'an. Clearly he did not show any symptoms associated with epilepsy.

Some circles also allege that Muhammad was possessed by the devil and that the Qur'an was nothing but the whisperings of Satan. There is nothing in Islam that would please Satan or an evil person. In fact, the Qur'an depicts Satan as an evil being and an enemy of humans. Muslims start reciting the Qur'an, taking refuge in God from the accursed Satan – far from the glorification of the devil.

In contrast with the above repulsive allegations, Muhammad's character and conduct so deeply impressed many people that they were attracted to Islam. They exclaimed, *"He gives as if there is no end. Only a Prophet can be so generous!"* or *"this face is so innocent, it can only be the face of a prophet!"* [SEE THE ANSWER TO QUESTION 17 FOR MORE ON THE CHARACTER OF MUHAMMAD.]

QUESTION 16

In its Arabic original the Qur'an is extremely eloquent. It was this eloquence of the Qur'an, an eloquence beyond human capability, that convinced people to convert to Islam during the time of the prophet. The Qur'an far surpassed the best of poetry that they knew. It is unlike any poetry, prose or essays that we are used to. It is an accumulation and culmination of all these styles into a unique Qur'anic style. In fact the Qur'an itself challenges any reader who does not believe it is from God to produce a chapter that equals it. Many have been unsuccessful in the attempt. Added to this, Muhammad was not known to have composed poetry and he did not even know how to read or write. But he recited the Qur'an with perfect style, grammar, rhythm and choice of words to convey meaning at first utterance and without later editing. It did not take long for astute people who were familiar with poetry and literature to conclude that this was not humanly possible. To this day the Qur'an is a key linguistic reference for Muslim and non-Muslim Arabs alike. To give you an illustration of the sound, consider the following transliteration of the first eight verses of chapter 100.

ARABIC TRANSLITERATION [100:1-8]	ENGLISH TRANSLATION
*Wal **adiyati** dabhan*	By the panting coursers,
*Fal **mooriyati** qadhan*	Striking sparks of fire
*Fal **mooghirati** subhan*	And scouring to the raid at dawn,
Fa athserna bihi naq'an	Then, therewith, with their trail of dust,
Fawa satna bihi cam'an	Cleaving, as one, the centre,
*Innal insana lirabbihi **lakanood***	Lo! human is ungrateful unto his Lord
*Wa innahu ala thzalika **lashaheed***	And lo! he is a witness unto that;
*Wa innahu lihubbil khayri **lashadeed***	And lo! in the love of wealth he is violent.

Even if you do not know Arabic, you can still notice the rhythm in the words shown underlined or in bold font, and see how the

QUESTION 16

sound changes with changes of emphasis in the meaning. This undulating change in the sounds continues to the end of the chapter. When the Qur'an is recited well, Muslims are moved to tears and experience ecstasy, even if they do not understand the meaning.

It is also to be noticed that this superior sound is lost in the English translation, which falls very short in giving the deep meanings conveyed by the original Arabic. The chapter is talking about the suddenness of the Last Day in terms analogous to those describing a raid. It is for this reason that Muslims say that the Qur'an cannot truly be translated.

Apart from the linguistic superiority of the Qur'an, its content also gives the impression that it would have been difficult for Muhammad to compose it himself. The similarity of the stories of the past prophets in the Qur'an and Bible have led some to allege that Muhammad copied the Bible of Judaism and Christianity in the formulation of Islam

The fact is that Muhammad was illiterate. He did not know how to read or write. There were no knowledgable Jews or Christians in Mecca where he grew up. The Bible in Arabic did not exist at the time. His only encounter was a brief hosting by a Christian monk when he was twelve on a trade trip with his uncle. His second journey outside of Mecca was a trade trip to Syria where he was too busy managing a large caravan to have had time to study the religions of Syria. Knowing his lack of contact with Jews and Christians, some Jews in Medina asked him questions that they thought he could not have known in order to corner him. In one instance, Muhammad was questioned about Joseph and his adventures. A whole chapter containing the complete story of Joseph in great detail and eloquence was revealed, startling the questioners.

The Qur'an also includes verses containing many scientific truths which were only discovered in the last one hundred years or so. Muslims argue that there is no possibility that Muhammad could have acquired such knowledge with the limited and false scientific knowledge available at the time, even if he was an educated person. [SEE ALSO QUESTION 7 FOR EXAMPLES.]

We also come across verses in the Qur'an that are critical of Muhammad. For example, the verse, *"God pardon you! Why did you give them leave until those who spoke the truth had become manifest to you and you had known the liars?"* [QUR'AN, 9:43] was revealed when he gave permission to some hypocrites not to join an important expedition. There are other similar verses that criticise some of Muhammad's behaviour and decisions. It is extremely unlikely that an imposter would criticise himself in his own book. On the contrary, to give himself legitimacy, he would glorify himself.

There were also many paranormal events surrounding Muhammad during his mission that were inexplicable by any other causes other than support by God. Islam sees miracles as the temporary removal of natural laws by God to support His special envoy to humanity. Out of more than three hundred authentically reported miracles, some examples include:

- The flowing of water from his fingers;
- The satisfying of large numbers of people with little food;
- Healing the sick;
- Disclosing peoples' secrets that only they could know;
- Predicting the conquest of Constantinople by Muslims;
- The prediction that his daughter Fatima would be the first one to join him after his death (both predictions came true).

Both Muhammad and Muslims consider the Qur'an to be his greatest and living miracle.

What was the personality and character of the Prophet Muhammad?

The Prophet Muhammad had an outstanding character. Reverend Bosworth Smith remarks, *"Head of the state as well as the Church, he was Caesar and Pope in one; but, he was pope without the pope's claims, and Caesar without the legions of Caesar, without an standing army, without a bodyguard, without a palace, without a fixed revenue. If ever any man had the right to say that he ruled by a right divine it was Muhammad, for he had all the power without instruments and without its support. He cared not for dressing of power. The simplicity of his private life was in keeping with his public life."*

He led a simple life and had no worldly possessions other than some essentials when he could have easily lived like a king. His house was a hut with walls of unbaked clay and a thatched roof of palm leaves covered by camel skin. His small room contained a rush mat, a pillow stuffed with palm leaves, the skin of some animal spread on the floor, a water bag of leather and some weapons. These were all his earthly belongings, besides a camel, a horse, a donkey and some land.

Once a few of his disciples, noticing the imprint of his mattress on his body, wished to give him a softer bed but he politely declined the offer saying, *"What have I to do with worldly things. My connection with the world is like that of a traveller resting for a while underneath the shade of a tree and then moving on."*

He enjoined upon Muslims to treat the poor kindly and to help them with alms, charity and in any other way. He said:, *"He is not a perfect Muslim who eats his fill and lets his neighbour go hungry."* He asked, *"Do you love your Creator? Then love your fellow beings first."*

By nature, he was gentle and kind hearted, always inclined to be gracious and overlook the faults of others. Politeness and courtesy, compassion and tenderness, simplicity and humility, sympathy and sincerity were some of the keynotes of his character. Though a virtual head of Arabia and an acclaimed prophet, he never assumed an air of superiority. Not that he had to conceal any such tendencies by practice and pretence. He used to pray, *"O God! I am but a man. If I hurt anyone in any manner, then forgive me and do not punish me."*

He always received people with courtesy and showed respect to young and old and stated: *"To honour an old man is to show respect to God."* On another occasion, he was sitting with his companions when a funeral procession passed him. He immediately stood up in respect of the deceased. His companions stated that the deceased was not a Muslim. He replied: *"Irrespective, he is still a human being".*

He avoided sitting at a prominent place in a gathering, so much so that people coming in had difficulty spotting him and had to ask who was the Prophet Muhammad. He would sit with the humblest of persons saying that righteousness alone was the only criterion of one's superiority over another. He invariably invited people, students, servants or the poorest believers, to partake with him of his scanty meals.

There was no type of household work too lowly or too undignified for him. His wife Aisha has said, *"He always joined in household work and would at times mend his clothes, repair his shoes and sweep the floor. He would milk, tether and feed his animals and do the household shopping."*

He would not hesitate to do the menial work of others, particularly of orphans and widows. Once when there was no male member in the house of the companion Kab Bin Arat who was on an expedition, he used to go to his house daily and milk his cattle for the household.

He was especially fond of children and used to get into the spirit of childish games in their company. He would pick up children in his arms, play with them, and kiss them. When a man said to him that he never hugged and kissed his children, he said, *"God has no mercy on those who have no mercy for others."*

He preached to the people to trust in God. His whole life was a sublime example of the precept. In the loneliness of Mecca, in the midst of persecution and danger, in adversity and tribulations, complete faith and trust in God appears as the dominant feature in his life. However great the danger that confronted him, he never lost hope and never allowed himself to be unduly agitated. Under the intensity of persecution in Mecca, his uncle Abu Talib requested him to abandon his mission, but he calmly replied, *"Dear uncle, do not go by my loneliness. Truth will not go unsupported for long. The whole of Arabia and beyond will one day espouse its cause."* When the attitude of the Meccan opposition became more threatening, Abu Talib again begged his nephew to renounce his mission but he replied, *"O my uncle, if they placed the sun in my right hand and the moon in my left, to force me to renounce my work, verily I would not desist therefrom until God made manifest His cause, or I perished in the attempt."*

The Prophet Muhammad was known as a truthful person, so much so that even after he proclaimed his prophethood, his enemies could not accuse of him of lying. His nickname before his prophethood was *Al-Ameen*, meaning "the trustworthy". During the hard years of persecution and oppression in Mecca, the leaders of the harsh opposition decided to murder him to solve the issue. They had collected a large sum of money as reward for the assassins. However, they could not trust each other with the money and entrusted it to Muhammad, the very person whom they were going to murder.

He was not only trustworthy towards people, but even warned people against deceiving animals. Once, annoyed at seeing someone calling his horse using deception, he said, *"You should give up deceiving animals. You should be trustworthy even in your treatment of them."*

The Prophet Muhammad asked people to be just and kind. As the supreme judge and arbiter, as the leader of men, as a reformer and apostle, he always had to deal with people and their affairs. He often had to deal with mutually opposed and warring tribes when showing justice to one carried the danger of antagonising the other, yet he never deviated from the path of justice. In administering justice, he made no distinction between believers and non-believers, friends and foes, high and low. The Jews, in spite of their hostility to the Prophet, were so impressed by his impartiality and sense of justice that they used to bring their cases to him, and he arbitrated among them according to Jewish law.

Once, in the hustle of a crowd, he accidentally pushed a man with a stick, causing a slight abrasion. He was so sorry about this that he told the man that he could have his reprisal, but the man said, "*O messenger of God, I forgive you.*"

Muhammad asked people to shun notions of race, family or any other form of superiority based on mundane things and said that righteousness alone was the criterion of one's superiority over another. His chief assistant in the mosque was a black African named Bilal at a time when blacks were considered inferior and deemed worthy of being only slaves.

The Prophet not only preached to the people to show kindness to each other but also to all living beings. He forbade the practice of cutting the tails and manes of horses, of branding animals on any tender spot and of keeping horses saddled. If he saw any animal over-loaded or ill-fed he would pull up the owner and say, "*Fear God in your treatment of animals.*" He stated at another time, "*Verily, there is heavenly reward for every act of kindness done to a living animal.*"

In short he was a human among other humans with no special distinctions. Once, a group of men came to his wife Aisha sometime after his death and asked what was the character of the Prophet

Muhammad like. She replied *"don't you read the Qur'an? He was the walking Qur'an"* – embodiment of all the teachings of the Qur'an in human form.

So much can be said about the life and character of Muhammad. For those who would like to find out more about his life, I recommend the book *Muhammad* by Yahiya Emerick and those who want to find out more about various facets of his character, I recommend *The Infinite Light: Prophet Muhammad* by M. Fethullah Gulen.

Q18

Can you explain the background to the Qur'an? We understand that Islam acknowledges four inspired books – the Qur'an, the Laws of Moses, the Psalms of David and the Gospel of Jesus. Are books other than the Qur'an read by Muslims and studied by scholars?

Unlike the Torah, which was revealed on tablets to Moses in one session, the Qur'an was revealed orally over the 23 year mission of the Prophet Muhammad. The revelation was usually tied to certain events, the questions of believers or non-believers and on needs that appeared as early Muslim society developed. Sometimes a few verses, at other times whole chapters, were revealed in a variety of ways [QUR'AN, 42:51].

Those people who witnessed the Prophet Muhammad when he received revelation say that he would be conscious throughout and start sweating even if it was a cold day. In his own words, the Qur'anic revelation come to him in four ways.

1. It sometimes came to him in a trance together with a ringing sound. Muhammad said that this was the hardest way of receiving revelation.

2. Sometimes revelation was given to him in his dreams.

3. On some occasions, revelations were implanted in his memory.

4. On other occasions, Archangel Gabriel would visit him in human form (sometimes visible to others) to deliver Qur'anic passages.

For the background on how the Qur'an was collected into a book refer to my answer to QUESTION 19.

It is an essential part of Islam that Muslims are required to believe in all the prophets and the revelations sent to them throughout human history. Muslims believe that the Qur'an is the final version of God's revelation to humanity, confirming what was revealed before [QUR'AN, 5:45]. It is also a fact that Islam acknowledges the four inspired books – the Qur'an, the Laws of Moses, the Psalms of David and the Gospel of Jesus. [ALSO SEE MY ANSWERS TO QUESTIONS 14–15 ON ISLAM'S VIEW OF PROPHETS AND REVELATION.]

Since the Qur'an essentially contains truths of the previous revelations, *"None of Our revelations do We abolish or cause to be forgotten, but We substitute something better or similar: Do you not know that God has power over all things?"* [QUR'AN, 2:106], average Muslims see no need to study the books that preceded it. The perspective of a Muslim is that whatever is true in other religions was revealed by God and is retained in the Qur'an and whatever has been added or altered by humans is omitted or corrected by the Qur'an.

The Qur'an and narratives about the Prophet Muhammad contain a great detail about Judaism and Christianity. There is a chapter named after Mary. Moses' story is the most quoted story in the Qur'an. Muslims know more about Judaism, Christianity and important figures in those traditions than many non-Muslims realise. Muslims also get daily advice and wisdom from the Qur'an, and from the sayings and the example of the Prophet Muhammad.

Nevertheless, ordinary Muslims who have the time and inclination, as well as scholars who are interested in comparative religious studies, read the present forms of the Bible, Torah or any religious text of traditions other than Islam.

Muslims say that the Gospel and other revealed books have lost their authenticity. Could this have also happened to the Qur'an?

Unlike other revealed books, the Qur'an still maintains its authenticity. It is as fresh as if it had been revealed yesterday. The authenticity of the Qur'an is a historical fact. In its original Arabic form, millions of current copies of the Qur'an around the world are exactly the same. No-one can show a copy of the Qur'an from the past or present which differs even slightly from other copies.

Even though Muslims take comfort in the Qur'anic claim that it is under the special protection of God [QUR'AN, 15:9], they have been very careful to preserve the Qur'an themselves, starting with Muhammad himself. The Qur'an was preserved in three different ways in the lifetime of the Prophet Muhammad:

- Written records
- Systematic memorisation
- Control mechanism

Since the Prophet Muhammad was illiterate, he had up to forty official scribes. The gradual revelation of the Qur'an over 23 years meant that the Prophet did not know when he would receive new revelation. Consequently, he would always have a scribe ready alongside him. When a new revelation was received, Muhammad would recite it to the scribe, who wrote it down on a parchment, a scroll of leather or whatever suitable material could be found. He would also mention the verse number or what part of the Qur'an the revelation belonged to. Muhammad then asked the scribe to read it back to him in order to check and correct it in case there were errors made in the writing process. Later, written passages of the Qur'an would be taken to the mosque for others to memorise and produce copies. Today, some of these original parchments are displayed in the Topkapi Museum in Istanbul, Turkey.

From early times, Muhammad asked his companions to memorise the passages of the Qur'an which had been revealed to him. As a result, hundreds of people knew the complete book by heart. Moreover, every Muslim had memorised significant portions of the Qur'an. The educational campaign of Muhammad also ensured that many people learnt how to read or write and consequently wrote parts of the Qur'an for their personal records.

Even still, there was the possibility that people might make mistakes in the memorisation and copying process. This possibility was eliminated by a control mechanism of the public checking of the Qur'an. Every year in the month of Ramadan, the Prophet Muhammad would recite the whole Qur'an to an audience of all the Muslims, who in turn would check his words against their written copies and what they knew by heart. In the last Ramadan before his death, this control recitation was done twice in a row. The tradition of reciting the whole Qur'an in Ramadan and the memorisation of the whole Qur'an continues to the present day, and hundreds of thousands of Muslims know the whole Qur'an by heart.

After the death of the Prophet and those of a significant numbers of memorisers, the first caliph Abu Bakr established a committee under the chairmanship of the chief scribe of the Prophet, Zayd bin Sabit, to collect the Qur'an into a single volume. Although many people, including Zayd, knew the whole Qur'an by heart, the objective criterion of *"citing at least two written records for every verse"* was applied. This process took place transparently in public in the mosque. Thus, the complete Qur'an was established in book form within a few years of Muhammad's passing away.

Later on, as the Muslim world grew to include non-Arabic nations, new converts began to argue about the the correct way of pronouncing the Qur'an. People started to write personal copies of the Qur'an with the different ways of spelling some words. About twenty years after the Prophet, upon the insistence of the companions of the Prophet, the third Caliph, Othman, decided to reproduce copies of the Qur'an from the original book written at the time of Abu Bakr. Seven copies of the Qur'an were reproduced from the original volume and sent to major Muslim capitals. This copying was done by a committee, again led by Zayd bin Sabit. The text of the Qur'an was also written more strictly to allow only the Meccan dialect so as to standardise its pronunciation and dialect in order to prevent difficulties or misunderstandings faced by non-Arabic speaking Muslims. He also stipulated that all subsequent copies of the Qur'an were to be produced from these copies. Two copies of the seven, one in Istanbul and one in Tashkent, survive to our time.

Does the Qur'an contain more about God and humanity and their relationship or law?

The Qur'an is a book of law, a book of prayer, a book of wisdom, a book of worship, a book of prophecy, a book of history and a unique Holy Book, comprising many books in one, in which Muslims find wisdom and solutions for their spiritual and human needs.

The Qur'an is a book of 604 pages, 114 chapters and over 6200 verses. Chapters and verses vary in length. The chapters are not like the ones we come across in regular books. In fact, the Qur'an is not organised like a conventional book at all. It is not divided into sections or specific parts that deal with one subject matter at a time. Rather it is an integral book where all subjects and meanings centre around a profound meaning and axis that permeates every chapter and verse of the book. **This axis is the calling of all humans to the belief and worship of one God using their reason and free will. Although God has created all people as His servants without asking them first, He is inviting humanity to accept this honourable role of servanthood willingly. At the same time informing humans of the transience of this worldly life together with life's happiness, tribulations and the permanence of life after death**. In a way, the Qur'an is composed to constantly remind the reader of this message, irrespective of the immediate subject matter of discussion.

The Qur'an has some very unique characteristics. When a person reads it you get the feeling that it is custom-written for you alone. Irrespective of your education level, you feel that it relates to you better than anyone else. You never get the impression it was revealed fourteen centuries ago. Perhaps, it is more relevant today than ever before in a world of spiritual deprivation.

Nevertheless, the Qur'an essentially focuses on four main subjects:

1. Monotheism: The Qur'an describes God, His existence and His unity. In doing so, it directs the attention of its readers to observe and reflect upon natural phenomena. The absolute authority of God is demonstrated in human history and the universe.

2. Prophethood: The Qur'an describes the need for prophets, their responsibilities and struggles in the cause of faith in the one God. It does not tell the stories of the prophets at great length, but rather highlights the vital details and aspects of their stories that point to the essential principles of life and humanity. The real heroes of the stories are not really the prophets but the principles that are in line with faith and the correct behaviour of model individuals faced with familiar human conditions. For example, in the story of Abraham, the real players are monotheism and polytheism and the conflict between them in human history.

3. Resurrection: The Qur'an proves the existence of resurrection by directing our attention to the continued resurrection that happens around us in nature. It describes in vivid detail life after death. It directs human attention to the permanence of life in the hereafter. The Qur'an gives glad tidings for people who recognise God and do good deeds and warns those people who take no heed of the justice of God.

4. Justice: The Qur'an describes justice, in the form of balance and harmony, seen in the universe. It asks humans to synchronise with this harmony by finding a wholesome balance within and with the social and natural environment. Every commandment of God contained in the Qur'an directs us to find the *Sirat-al Mustakeem* (the straight and balanced path) in our personal and social life. The legal verses in the Qur'an fall under the theme of

QUESTION 20

"justice". The Qur'an has no more than 80 verses that can be categorised as strictly legal. It seeks to highlight principles of law rather than its detailed codification.

Chapter 3

Judgment Day and Life after Death

The mystery of life after death has been the main focus for almost all religions. Even if a religion does not teach of a life in another realm, it teaches the perpetuity of existence by reincarnation. Longing for a perpetual life seems to be the greatest human need we have and the most fundamental trait the Eternal One has ingrained into our natural disposition.

Islam gives a definite answer to the mystery of life. It teaches that there will be a life after death and humanity will be resurrected, entering a new existence after a cataclysmic Last Day, which will be the end of the universe as we know it. Islam gives a vivid picture of how we will give an account of our lives in the hereafter and of the places of reward and reprimand.

Q21

**Will there be a physical resurrection?
If so, will the body be as it was during the earthly life?**

Muslims are required to believe in an eternal life after death. According to Islam, humanity was sent to this world to read and reflect upon the signs that God has placed in nature and the universe, in order to realise that He exists. This realisation, in turn, leads to knowing the character and qualities of God. A person's knowledge of God has the natural consequence of producing a desire to please God in worship. Serving God in worship will lead to wanting to contribute to the lives of other people through social service. As a result, a person will attain human development and perfection, raised on top of the tripod of knowledge, worship and service.

The earthly life is a place of testing to see if we will live up to this purpose or not. As the natural outcome of this test, we will be resurrected from death for a second, eternal life in order to go through a process of review and, depending on our record, either receive a reward or be reprimanded. One of the recurring themes in the Qur'an is a preparation for this inevitable resurrection. Just as our birth was not in our hands, our resurrection will not be under our control.

As in every tenet of Islam, we are not expected to believe this blindly. God has placed many signs that infer resurrection in our personal life, in nature and in the universe.

God has given humans the need to sleep and dream every day. During sleep the body does not move and is in a state of unconsciousness. Yet, we dream during sleep and can be in wonderful places or have nightmares. Among the other purposes of sleep, it is designed to show us that resurrection is a reality and we are shown a glimpse of it every night.

QUESTION 21

Seasons and the changes observed in the environment indicate resurrection. For example, a tree appears to be reduced to its skeleton in winter only to be revitalised again in spring. In a sense this is a resurrection. The repetitive turning of the seasons shows this sign to all human generations.

Sometimes in arid terrains the earth and its environment appears to be dead with no sign of plant or animal life. With a good rainfall the dead landscape comes back to life with many species of plants and animals. *"So consider the signs of God's mercy; how He gives life to the earth after its death. Indeed, it is He Who gives life to the dead, for He is powerful over all things."* [QUR'AN, 30:50] Such resurrection is to be seen in the case of Lake Ayer in Australia, which is usually totally dry but rejuvenates after rare rainfalls. Within a week many birds, fish, animal and plant life spring up almost out of nowhere.

It is easy for God to resurrect the creation. In fact, it is relatively easy for a trained army to gather at the sound of a horn after they disperse for a break. Similarly, resurrection after death is much easier than the first creation. The Qur'an declares, *"And he puts forth for Us a parable and forgets his own creation. He says: 'Who will give life to these bones when they have rotted away and became dust?' Say! He (God) will give life to them Who created them for the first time! And He is the All-Knower of every creation!"* [QUR'AN, 36:78–79] With this line of reasoning, the Qur'an is telling the reader that when one witnesses the creation, the possibility of resurrection cannot be in doubt.

Belief in resurrection rests on belief in God. For example, the perfect balance and subtle artistry in all things in nature show the imprint of an infinitely Wise and Just Artist, God. However, we see that absolute justice is not fulfilled in the human domain. Hence, there must be another realm where absolute justice will prevail.

We do not need faculties such as love, intellect, free will, self-awareness, etc., to physically survive on this planet. Animals exist without them. Just as our characteristics in the womb are evidence that we are designed not to live in the womb but to roam on earth, the extra faculties we have now show that we are yet to live in another realm where they will be put to full use.

The final resurrection, according to Islam, will be physical. We do not know in detail what our physical composition will be. Descriptions in the Qur'an and the sayings of the Prophet Muhammad indicate we will have a similar external body appearance as we do in this life, but it may be different or even grotesque depending on what kind of life we lived on this earth.

Q22

Is judgment in the hereafter according to our actions or intentions? What is the basis of judging an act to be good or bad? On what fundamentals will God judge us? Are good deeds and bad deeds judged and treated equally?

In the hereafter, the fundamentals of judgment will be faith and good works done with a sincere intention. According to the Prophet Muhammad, God will look only at deeds when a person passes the test of faith. *"Actions are judged according to intentions. Whatever someone intends to do, he gets its reward,"*[5] declared the Prophet in one of the most famous narratives. It is very clear according to this saying that intention is the key in the judgment process, as it is in the processes of modern law.

The literal meaning of intention is a tendency or inclination of the heart towards a purpose. In some cases, intention may be enough to gain a reward even though the intended action is not performed because of an unforeseen obstacle. In other cases, intention may increase the reward for a good deed. Even though this worldly life is not enough to gain Paradise, the intention of worshipping God for as long as one lives is a key factor in God granting eternal bliss. Muhammad has also declared: *"The intention of a believer is more rewarding than his actions."*[6]

In Islam, intention turns everyday actions into acts of worship that gain rewards. Actions also gain worth according to the underlying intention. For example, we normally get no reward for staying hungry throughout the day. However, if it is done for the sake of God it becomes a religious act of fasting, which is a valuable form of worship. Studying to acquire knowledge for the sake of God

---

5 Bukhari *Bad'u l-Wahy*, 1; Muslim, *Imara*, 155; Abu Dawud, *Talaq*, 11.
6 Majma'al-Zawaid, 1.61, 109.

also becomes an act of worship. This notion can be extended to such a degree that, according to *Imam Shafi*[7], even the sleep of a student of *ilm* (knowledge, science) becomes an act of worship for as long as there is purity of intention.

Sincere intention is extremely important in Islam. The cornerstone of good actions is undertaking them only for the sake of God. If rewards are expected in the hereafter, sincere intention should underscore every action. Just as it is not possible to get any heavenly reward for an apparently good deed when the underlying intention is bad, it is also not possible to expect a reward for evil deeds citing good intentions.

Good deeds and bad deeds will not be weighted equally. According to the Qur'an, "*He that does good shall have* **ten times** *as much to his credit: He that does evil shall only be recompensed according to his evil: no wrong shall be done unto (any of) them.*" [QUR'AN, 6:160] This verse highlights the fact that in Islam the compassion of God comes before His justice and God's bias towards the salvation of humanity. The door to forgiveness is also wide open for all repentant souls.

How do we know when something is good or evil? Since it is impossible for the human mind to encompass the infinite variability of the human condition or the infinite possible combinations of the visible or invisible consequences of all actions, there has to be an overarching intelligence to decide what is good and what is bad. Therefore, the authority of judging something good or evil sits only with God in His infinite Knowledge and Wisdom. In Islam, the Will of God is reflected for humanity in the Qur'an through His messenger Muhammad. This is always so, provided that the revela-

---

7 *Imam Shafi* is a distinguished Muslim jurist who lived in the 3rd century after the Prophet Muhammad.

QUESTION 22

tion has not been corrupted over time [SEE QUESTION 19 FOR THE AUTHENTICITY OF THE QUR'AN].

Human reason, in the case of good and evil, can be used to understand the wisdom of God and confirm His injunctions. Assertions of good and evil are usually self-evident, so one does not really have to labour a great deal to understand His wisdom. Who can argue that justice, charity, chastity, integrity and forgiveness are not good? On the other hand, who would disagree with the fact that lying, stealing, gambling, killing and slandering are intrinsically evil or have evil consequences?

Does being a Muslim guarantee Paradise on the Day of Judgment? Will a Muslim be punished in Hell if he lives a bad life?

No-one, including Muslims, is guaranteed Paradise on the Day of Judgment. What is important is not one's title, but what is in one's heart. We would not know for certain that people have true faith in their heart and intentions unless their actions are pure and sincere. According to Islam, all actions are judged according to intentions. The Prophet Muhammad said that even he was not guaranteed entry to Paradise.

According to the Qur'an, anyone who has faith in God, the angels, the prophets, revelation and resurrection, coupled with good deeds and good intentions, will go to Paradise. "*...Whoever, whether male or female, does an atom's weight of good and is a believer, all such shall enter into Paradise...*" declares the Qur'an [40:40]. The main agent of qualifying for Paradise is the special grace and favour of God. God, as the Creator and Owner of the universe and hereafter, has the right to send anyone to Paradise as He wills. One should also bear in mind that God is Just and is free from tyranny.

There are certain offences that God would find unforgivable if not repented. Rejecting belief in God and associating God with partnership are two of the most abominable crimes in Islam. On the Day of Judgment we are accountable to God for our deeds. "How good was this person in following the guidelines of God?" is a question that every person will face.

Just as there is a consequence if one does not follow the laws governing this life, there is a consequence if one does not follow the guidelines and laws set by the Governor of the Universe, God. Hence, a Muslim is accountable for his or her deeds. A form of punishment may be incurred for a period of time to be decided in the Supreme Court of the Hereafter.

God gives us the glad tidings that our sins will be forgiven when we show sincere repentance directly to God and to God alone. On the other hand, God does not forgive acts of transgression on the rights of other people. People are expected to settle their affairs before death. God will settle any unsettled transgressions in the hereafter. Some people may find that their good deeds are transferred to their victims. If no good deed is left the sins of victims will be passed to the offender.

It is alleged in some circles that Islam places great emphasis on the "fear of God". This is simply not the case. On the contrary, there is greater emphasis on the mercy and grace of God. Yes, there are verses that warn people of a punishment if no heed is taken. However, the Qur'an says, *"Why should God punish you if you have thanked and believed in Him? And God is All-Appreciative, All-Knowing."* [QUR'AN, 4:147]

Since the Qur'an wants to address all humanity it fashions its arguments in all possible forms. While some people are positively influenced by the promise of eternal bliss in Paradise [QUR'AN, 20:118-119], some poor performers are swayed by warnings of a reprimand [QUR'AN, 2:206]. Highly spiritual individuals are attracted to a more personal relationship and they could only be content with God alone [QUR'AN, 18:28], whereas the knowledge and greatness of God render astute thinkers awestruck [QUR'AN, 18:51].

The Qur'anic verse [9:72], *"God has promised to believers, men and women, gardens under which rivers flow, to dwell therein, and beautiful mansions in gardens of Eden Paradise. But the greatest bliss is the Good Pleasure of God. That is the supreme felicity,"* is an example of both a positive incentive of a reward in Paradise and a higher form of influence of the love of God. This higher form of being is best expressed by an early female Muslim spiritual leader, Rabi'a al Adawiya (d. 796) who said, "*O God! If I worship You in fear of hell, then burn me in it; and if I worship You in hope of heaven, exclude me from it; but if I worship You for Your own sake, do not withhold from me Your everlasting beauty.*"[8]

The position of a Muslim is one of balance. The desired state of being is one between *hope* and *concern*, with a bias towards *hope* since according to Muhammad God's compassion comes before His punishment. While *hope* gives people the motivation to continue on the path of belief and wholesome goodness, *concern* prevents people falling into complacency.

---

8 Emerick, Yahiya, *The Complete Idiot's Guide to Islam*, Marie Butler-Knight, United States (2002) p. 340.

Q24

Many Muslims are aware that there are strict guidelines to follow. Is there a punishment if you do not act according to the rules outlined? Does judgment, punishment and reward start immediately after death?

Muslims' strong commitment to the practice of Islam gives the impression that Islam sets many strict guidelines. In reality though, prohibitions and obligations in Islam are exceptions. The guidelines of Islam provide a set of boundaries around a wide circle of free acts, sufficient for all tastes and the satisfaction of lawful needs and pleasures. For instance, Islam does not encourage or force Muslims to be vegetarians as in some Eastern religions, nor does it require the strict supervision by clergy for food to be lawful and edible as in Judaism. Islam allows the consumption of all foods and beverages, with the exception of mind-altering intoxicants, pork, the meat of carnivorous animals, blood, unhealthy meat and the meat of animals which are sacrificed in the name of idols.

In Islam, as in other religions and systems of law, the purpose of injunctions is the well-being of individuals and society. In order to achieve the fruits of a law there have to be rewards and punishments. Rewards encourage people to follow the law, while the threat of punishment acts as a deterrent, encourages order, obedience and compliance and prevents the transgression of another's rights.

Let us imagine there is a law that one cannot drive over 70 km/hour without speeding fines for offenders of this law. Would it be possible to influence behaviour of *all* drivers and guarantee that there will be safe driving for all? Of course it would not be possible. While most people do not need the enforcement of speeding fines to behave correctly, a minority will make driving a dangerous experience for us all unless they are checked by the threat of heavy fines. The speeding fine policy is not designed purely to punish people, but rather for their greater safety. Once the policy of fining is set, it has to be enforced. Lack of enforcement would not only render the law futile but would also lead people to lose their trust in the authorities, who would in turn lose their power of influence.

Similarly in Islam, sins and punishments will be written upon the sinner, and spiritual merits will be recorded for the worshipper and follower of obligations. It should be noted that God neither needs our worship nor our obedience; it is we who need them in order to attain spiritual development and to stop transgressing the rights of others, resulting in balanced individuals and a happy society.

Physical punishments and rewards do not start after death since they depend on the judgment of God on the Day of Judgment, which will be after the collapse of the universe, which is a place of testing. Nevertheless, the Prophet Muhammad informed us that some kind of spiritual reward and punishment will be impressed on the person in the grave before resurrection and on the Day of Judgment in the form of a good or bad welcome to show whether one's place is in Paradise or in Hell. The period of spiritual existence from death to resurrection is called the *barzakh*, meaning partition or transition [QUR'AN 23:99–100].

One of the great aspects of Islam is the endless chances for repentance and forgiveness for wrongful acts. Sincere repentance expressed directly to God, and countering wrongful acts with good deeds and acts of worship and charity, tilt the balance towards reward and forgiveness rather than punishment. The Qur'an states, "*Say: Oh My servants who have transgressed against themselves by committing evil deeds and sins! Despair not of the mercy of God: verily God forgives all sins. Truly He is Oft-forgiving, Most Merciful*" [QUR'AN, 24:53].

Q25

How are believers who sin a lot and non-believers who do good deeds to be judged on the Day of Judgment? According to Islam, can a non-Muslim go to Paradise?

The Day of Judgment will be the time when the absolute justice of God will be realised. God revealed in the Holy Qur'an that, *"Whosoever does good equal to the weight of an atom shall see it and whosoever does evil equal to the weight of an atom shall see it."* [QUR'AN, 99:7–8] So everyone, Muslim or non-Muslim, will face the consequences of their beliefs and actions.

Being a Muslim does not guarantee paradise or salvation. A person has to have sound faith and is expected to do good deeds as well. On the Day of Judgment people are not expected to appear in the Supreme Court of God spotlessly clean and with no room for error. A preponderance of goodness is sufficient for salvation. A Muslim has a balanced attitude towards salvation. While there is concern about the possibility of failure, there is also a bias of hope that God will show His grace and mercy. Lack of certainty concerning one's end ensures that a Muslim stays consistently virtuous throughout his or her lifetime.

According to Islam, the recognition and worship of the one true God, belief in resurrection, in all the prophets, in revelation and in doing good deeds ensures salvation. According to the Qur'an, a believer is not necessarily a person who believes in Islam. The definition of a believer is more generic. One has to be a *Mu'min* (believer) before he or she can be a *Muslim* (practitioner of Islam). A *Mu'min* can be found amongst the ranks of other religions. The Qur'an, for example, says that not all of the people of the book (Christians and Jews) are alike; there are some amongst them who fall into the above definition of a believer, *"and whatever good they do nothing will be rejected of them…"* [QUR'AN, 3:113–115] The Qur'an also gives good news to people of other religions, "*Lo! those who believe, and those who are Jews, and Sabaeans, and Christians whosoever believes in God and the Last Day and does right there shall no fear come upon them neither shall they grieve.*" [QUR'AN, 5:69] Some Muslim scholars interpret "Sabaeans" to include all the major religions other than Judaism and Christianity.

Moreover, actions will be judged according to intentions and the reward will be according to the intention. Actions that are sincere and performed with the intention of obtaining God's pleasure and acceptance are valued the most. If a believer or a non-believer performs a good deed in expectation of rewards and benefits other than God's reward in the hereafter, accordingly he or she will not be rewarded by God. His or her reward will be in the present lifetime according to what the person intended. "*Those who deny Our Ayat (signs and revelations) and the meeting in the Hereafter, their works are fruitless. Do they expect to be rewarded with anything except what they used to do?*" [QUR'AN, 7:147]

The Qur'an tells us that no-one will receive any injustice in any way on the Day of Judgment. The final outcome for a person depends on the opportunities for finding the truth he or she had in this life and how well he or she took advantage of those opportunities. The Qur'an says that God gives people opportunities once or twice a year to turn to Him [QUR'AN, 9:126].

A person has the responsibility to recognise the mission of all the prophets, including the final Prophet of God, Muhammad, if they have a chance to find out and investigate this final message. If a person has not heard about the Prophet Muhammad's name and mission and yet believes in one God and does good deeds, we expect the person to be saved by the grace of God. However, people are responsible to God when they realise the value and truth of the Holy Prophet Muhammad's message. If a person then rejects it, he

QUESTION 25

or she is said to be a *kafir* or a "concealer of truth". The word *kafir* is often mistranslated as "infidel".

We leave the final judgment to God for He has absolute compassion and justice and He is free from tyranny. Ultimately, judging people is the role of God, not the role of mere humans.

If a child dies, does she end up in heaven or hell?

In Islam, the age of legal and religious responsibility comes with puberty or the age of 15, whichever comes first. Children before this age have not developed sufficient knowledge and experience to differentiate between what is right and wrong so they cannot be held responsible for their actions. Similarly, mentally disabled people are similarly free from religious responsibility.

Making a person accountable before the age of puberty or condemning them to hell would certainly be unjust, both in the light of reason and with regard to the mercy of God. Before this age a person does not have the mental capability to understand the implicit concepts of religion. How can we expect such a person to grasp faith consciously as Islam requires? In the religious sense, Islam does not accept the concept of Original Sin [SEE ANSWER TO QUESTION 9 FOR MORE ON ISLAM'S DIFFERENCES WITH CHRISTIANITY]. A baby comes to the world pure and without the burden of anyone's sins on its shoulders. Hence, there is no condemnation of babies if they die at an early stage of life.

Moreover, the Prophet Muhammad said that every person is born with a Muslim *fitra*, that is, with a natural disposition to believe and submit to God. He went on to say that the parents of children then convert or influence them to other religions through conditioning and education. It is for this reason that a person who comes back to Islam is called a "revert" instead of a "convert". This notion also supports the Muslim belief that if children die before the age of puberty they go to Paradise regardless of what religion their parents may have attached to them.

When people reach puberty they complete their physical and mental development. Adolescents start asking questions such as *"Why am I here?"*, *"Where do I come from and where am I going?"*. They now have the mental capacity to understand God and believe in Him. Puberty also signals the emergence of certain emotions that truly test our behaviour. If a person dies at a time after puberty, he or she will be accountable for their beliefs and actions [SEE QUESTION 25 FOR MORE ON JUDGMENT].

Q27

If someone is a really good person, but an atheist, can he be saved on the Day of Judgment?

Atheism can be defined as absolute non-belief, that is the acceptance and conviction that a Creator for the universe does not exist. On the assumption that God exists in reality as Islam would argue, then atheism becomes a serious spiritual crime for which no good act in the world can compensate. Atheism is an act of absolute injustice and a transgression against the rights of creation and God because:

- Atheism denounces creation, alleging it to be without worth or meaning. Just as denying the existence of Leonardo da Vinci would reduce the Mona Lisa to its mere material worth, atheism reduces the value and art in all that exists to almost nothing. Therefore atheism is an insult to the whole of creation.
- It is a denial of the manifestation of the Divine Names and Attributes mirrored in all created things.
- It is a rejection of the witness of countless beings of the existence and unity of God.
- It alleges that God lies while enjoying the life and countless blessings that God has provided.

By virtue of condemning all beings, the universe and God to death and eternal non-existence, atheism becomes an immense act of collective spiritual murder of all beings in the universe. In law, a murder, which takes a second to commit, is given the punishment of a lifetime prison sentence or death. Since an atheist commits such countless crimes every second of his or her lifetime, the only fitting verdict for the crime of atheism is eternal punishment.

Furthermore, an atheist also rejects the existence of a life in the hereafter and intends to receive the benefits of good deeds only in this life. Accordingly, the benefits and rewards will only be granted in this lifetime. God is just and free from tyranny. So, the treatment of an atheist will also be just. It would not be justice if all those who believed in God and did good deeds received the same treatment as the ones who continuously rejected God. No-one can be more merciful and gracious than God.

If, as the atheists proclaim, "there is no God", then they have nothing to worry about. However, if God truly exists as the Qur'an proclaims, then atheists will be in a lot of trouble. A mighty gamble indeed. On the other hand, believers in God are in a win/win situation. If God truly exists they will be rewarded for their faith in the hereafter. If not, they still lead a life of contentment and goodness.

Q28

Is the final destination eternal?
Will those who go to Hell stay there forever?

In short, the answer is yes. Both Islam and Muslim reasoning do not accept reincarnation or eternal non-existence. In Islam, this world is like a field in which to plant the seeds of a good life based on belief in one God.

According to Islam, out of His grace God will favour an eternal life of bliss for a righteous believer. One who enters Paradise will live a very happy life, free from suffering, pain, sadness or death. God will be pleased with the person, who will have a chance to see God living there forever [SEE QUESTION 30 FOR MORE ON PARADISE].

God has described certain images in the Qur'an to bring the unseen beauties of Paradise nearer to our comprehension, *"But those who believe and do good deeds, We will admit them to gardens (Paradise) in which rivers flow, lasting in them **forever**..."* [QUR'AN, 4:57]

Nearly all societies and religions have a concept of a place where those people who seem to get away unpunished for their atrocities and crimes on earth are punished. The Qur'an paints a picture of Hell as the place where justice, not realised on Earth, is fulfilled. Those people who end up in Hell due to non-belief will stay there forever [SEE QUESTION 27 FOR MORE]. Yet again, only God would know what He will do with those people eventually. He is never unjust in His retribution.

Hell, in Islam, is also a place of purification. On the Day of Judgment, everyone will receive a copy of their life record. The judgment of the believers will be according to this record. If the merit points attributed for good deeds (at least 10 or more to every good deed) end up being less than the negative points for unrepented bad deeds, the person will be cleansed in Hell for a time to be determined by God. According to this simple formula a person really has to be 90% "bad" to end up in Hell. Provided the person had faith in God, at the end of this temporary sentence, the individual would be released to dwell in Paradise forever. The Prophet Muhammad said that the last person to leave Hell will receive four times the wealth and delights of a king ruling over the whole earth.

Q29

What is the description of Hell? Are there angels in Hell? What will be Satan's role in Hell?

Is it at all possible for an earthly government not to have laws and regulations to ensure the happiness and general well being of all of its citizens? The answer can only be no. We clearly see that great social problems and human rights violations occur when there is no stable government or rule of law. One of the consequences of having such a system is to punish those who overstep the boundaries set by the law. Similarly, the Governor of the Universe will also have general laws and regulations for existence and for human beings and some sort of system of reward and punishment for those who follow or go against the principles of divine law. We also see that in the human domain; very good people die without receiving their due reward and evil persons die without receiving due justice. Hence, Heaven and Hell must exist and there must be another realm where justice will be fulfilled. This is the realm of the hereafter.

The Prophet Muhammad tells us that God's compassion comes before His punishment. God does not want anyone to end up in Hell. For this reason, He has warned people through revelation and the prophets to take the path of belief and righteousness. He has also depicted vivid pictures of Heaven and Hell to influence some hard-line people into goodness. For example, in the Qur'an [78:21–27], Hell is described as follows: *"When the Blazing Fire is kindled to fierce heat; truly Hell is as a place of ambush for the transgressors a place of destination: they will dwell therein for ages. Save a boiling fluid and a fluid, dark, murky, and intensely **cold**, A fitting recompense (for them). For that they used not to fear any account (for their deeds)."* Hell is not only an extremely hot place but it also has very cold compartments.

When the deserving end up in Hell, they will be completely isolated from everyone else. The Qur'an says that the people will

QUESTION 29

ask God to be sent back to earth so they could demonstrate that they can be believers. The Qur'an answers that they will be the same regardless. The conversation of people in Hell and the contrasting conversations of people in Paradise are given in vivid detail.

Punishment in Hell will be according to the crimes committed. While the lightest punishment is the putting on of red-hot iron shoes, the most intense punishment will be at the lowest level of the seven levels for hypocrites (pretending to believe) and atheists.

Hell is not the headquarters of Satan. He does not have a special throne where he conducts his evil plans. Contrary to the perceptions of many people, neither does he have a duty to perform in Hell. Rather, he is also appropriately punished for rebelling against God and leading many people astray. There are special angels in Hell with a disposition suitable for serving in such an environment. They are guardians of Hell, mercilessly performing a given set of tasks.

How can a merciful God bear to punish His weak creatures? A woman asked this question of the Prophet Muhammad in a gathering. She had just instinctively snatched up her wandering child, who was about to place its hands in the fireplace. Muhammad cried softly, bowing his head forward. He said that God does not like to punish. He is forced to punish those who continuously reject Him and commit evil actions in spite of clear warnings and guidance. After all, wouldn't the mother also punish her child if the child did something wrong?

Could you describe Paradise from an Islamic point of view? Will I be able to see my loved ones in Paradise?

Many verses in the Qur'an and many narratives from the Prophet Muhammad colourfully describe Paradise. The Qur'an states, *"But those who believe and do good deeds, We will admit them to gardens (Paradise) under which rivers flow, lasting in them forever..."* [4:57] and *"Be quick in the race for forgiveness from your Lord, and for a Garden whose width is that (of the whole) of the heavens and of the earth, prepared for the righteous."* [3:133]

When, with a small study circle, Muhammad became quiet and said, *"...Paradise and Hell-fire were displayed in front of me on this wall just now and I have never seen a better thing (than the former) and a worse thing (than the latter)."* At another occasion, he is reported to have said, *"He who would get into Paradise (would be made to enjoy such an everlasting) bliss that he would neither become destitute, nor would his clothes wear out, nor his youth would decline."* The Qur'an remarks similar characteristics in verses 20:118–119.

In Paradise we will have perfect bodies at the peak of adulthood. There will be no old men or women. Babies who died as infants will be the children of Paradise. There will be no vice or anything forbidden. People will live in spacious places as families. Both males and females will have mates especially created for them in Paradise. A vibrant community of people will get together and remember the happiness and challenges of their earthly life.

Above all rewards, the ecstasy of seeing God and His beauty will be beyond measure. Muhammad said that living in Paradise for an hour is better than living on earth like a king for a thousand years and seeing God for an hour is better than living in Paradise for a thousand years.

QUESTION 30

Muhammad told us that the experience of Paradise is beyond imagination and unlike anything that we have encountered on this earth. In another narrative, he says that *"no eyes have ever seen and no-one ever conceived of"* the delights waiting for us in Paradise. The Qur'an also says, *"No person knows what is kept hidden for them of joy as a reward for what they used to do"* [32:17]. All the physical pleasures and descriptions of Paradise are only given with reference to the things we know in this universe so we can get a glimpse of it. It is like the preview of the real thing in terms we know and understand.

Laws of existence will also be different in Paradise. The sequence of cause and effect that we are so accustomed to in this universe will not necessarily continue in the hereafter. Whatever we wish or desire will materialise in front of our eyes without an apparent cause. In the verse mentioned previously [QUR'AN, 4:57], the Qur'an tells us of rivers flowing underneath majestic palaces, almost describing a suspended setting with no gravitation.

Once a man burst into tears in front of Muhammad. When he questioned him why he was crying, the man said that whereas Muhammad is a prophet, he was but an average Muslim. Surely, they will be at different places even if he ends up in Paradise. *"But"* the man continued, *"I cannot bear to be without you. That is why I am crying."* Muhammad wiped away his tears and said. *"Don't worry, a person will be with his loved ones in Paradise."* The difference will be in the way one perceives and takes pleasure in the experiences of Paradise. The more a person has developed his or her spiritual faculties, the more benefit he or she will get from Paradise and from observing God. This is similar to the difference in the pleasure an architect would get out of observing the Blue Mosque or the Opera House compared to that of a person that knows nothing about architecture.

PART II

LIVING ISLAM

Chapter 4

Personal Practice and Spirituality

All religions provide a regimen of exercises, meditations and charitable works to foster spiritual awareness and development. By following such a regimen, responsibility for one's own actions is kindled.

Islam is not different in this goal of developing the person. It offers a unique blend of knowing the divine and the self, a deep spiritual journey and healthy social activity. It seeks to disclose the human faculties that are innate in each individual.

Q31

How does a Muslim's spiritual life interact with his or her belief? If one does not pray is he or she still considered a Muslim?

Belief penetrates not only the spiritual life of a Muslim, but also has a positive impact in all aspects of his or her life. Islam considers life to be a matter of balance rather than separate compartments.

The Qur'an constantly encourages its readers to examine the universe and nature. In a way, the human disposition has been designed with a curiosity to investigate and an ability to read the book of the universe. Such mental endeavour will result in the realisation that there must be a Supernatural Being that we Muslims call God. The continued venture of reading the book of the universe leads to knowledge of God and how He compassionately looks after the whole creation including humanity. Since a human loves the one he or she knows, knowledge of God leads to love of God, which in turn translates into a tendency to please God in the form of worship. Over time a worshipper goes through a process of spiritual development and ends up as a refined person wanting to help and contribute to the lives of others. Social contribution and activism become a feedback mechanism that keeps a person balanced and enables him or her to advance in virtue.

Hence, in Islam, belief, spirituality and action are intertwined as three entities that strengthen one another. It is for this reason that Islam enjoins a Muslim to establish a direct spiritual connection with God. The Qur'an teaches us that God is closer to us than life supporting arteries and expects men and women to foster a reciprocal relationship with God. Along with daily prescribed prayers, the Prophet Muhammad encouraged Muslims to have an awareness of God's presence. The Qur'an tells us that remembrance of God is the greatest form of worship [QUR'AN, 29:45]. It also informs us that true

QUESTION 31

spiritual satisfaction and human fulfilment is found only in the remembrance of God, "... *for without doubt in the remembrance of God do hearts find satisfaction.*" [QUR'AN, 13:28].

A non-practising person is still considered to be a believer and a Muslim. However, he or she is on the borderline of faith and lacks the protection that spiritual practice offers. At the very least, a chance for spiritual reward and fulfilment is not exploited.

Q32

**What is the daily life and practice of a Muslim?
How does Islam influence the daily life patterns of Muslims?**

The everyday lifestyle of a practising Muslim is essentially no different to that of any other average person. Just like everyone else, Muslims go to work to earn a living or study at an educational institution to build a career. They get married and have children. They enjoy time spent with family and friends over a barbecue. In addition to this, a practising Muslim is conscious of God and His presence in their everyday social and natural environment.

Spirituality is integrated into the daily life of a practising Muslim in the form of daily prescribed prayers called *salat* [SEE QUESTIONS 36 TO 39 ON *SALAT*]. She normally wakes up before sunrise to offer the dawn prayer, starting the day with the remembrance of God, the cause of her existence. In between work, study or other daily activities, she takes a break two more times at noon and in the afternoon to praise, glorify and exalt God in a meditative mode, in order to connect with the divine and remove herself from the hustle and bustle of life. Another session of prayer is offered in the evening and before going to sleep at night.

In daily interactions with others she treats people with elegance and courtesy while displaying high standards of integrity. She tries to stay away from wrongful acts. If and when she does wrong, she turns to God immediately in apology and repentance.

Being a Muslim in everyday life manifests itself in three progressively higher states of being:

1. In addition to basic daily activities, she is in a constant mode of learning. She does her best to follow daily worship, stay away from wrongful acts and treat others well. She is thankful for the goodness she receives and patient and resilient when facing hardships and trials.

QUESTION 32

2. In addition to observing the above activities, a higher state of being is to constantly try, with no hidden selfish motives, to contribute to the lives and development of other people.

3. The highest level of being is to be an individual among others while at the same time being constantly connected to God through a conscious awareness of Him. While she is dealing with money or customers, the beating of her heart sounds the remembrance and praise of God. The Qur'an tells us that remembrance of God is the greatest form of worship: "*...and remembrance of God is the greatest (thing in life) without doubt...*" [QUR'AN, 29:45]. As a result, she has found inner peace and contentment.

In a predominantly non-Muslim culture the practice of daily religious duties sometimes places a Muslim in conflict with her work or social environment. See the answer to QUESTION 89 for more on how a Muslim deals with the challenges of a non-Muslim or secular society.

Could you describe public worship and private worship?

Public worship comprises all expressions of worship that involve a group of people in a congregation or an individual performing acts of worship in view of God and others. Private worship, on the other hand, may be defined as the acts of goodness and spiritual merit that are performed in the sight of the Creator alone.

Both public and private worship have their unique advantages and, in some cases, disadvantages. Public worship has the benefit of positively influencing other people to also perform acts of worship. It also has a synergistic effect of producing greater spiritual yield, multiplying the positive elements of joint worship for everyone involved. For example, those Muslims who regularly pray in a mosque with a large congregation develop an inner drive and desire to continue the prayers, whereas those who pray privately at home most of the time may experience a certain sluggishness in their prayers. Praying publicly in a mosque also connects the community together, and thus delivers many social benefits. Conversely, with some individuals the public expression of worship may result in pretence. Private worship, on the other hand, offers a sincere and close relationship with the Creator, but without the beneficial effects of communal influence.

In Islam, both forms of worship are encouraged in a balanced manner in order to maximise their benefits and restrain possible negative effects on the spiritual development of an individual or the society as a whole. Both forms of worship are acceptable as indicated by the verse, *"Those who patiently persevere, seeking the countenance of their Lord; Establish regular prayers; spend, out of what We have bestowed for their sustenance, **secretly and openly**; and turn off evil with good: for such there is the final attainment of the (eternal) home."* [QUR'AN, 13:22]

QUESTION 33

The balance is ensured by promoting public worship of the five pillars of Islam while at the same time encouraging people to keep private certain optional acts of worship. Since the five pillars are enjoined on the whole community, public promotion is both necessary and beneficial. There is no pretence since everyone is expected to fulfil the obligation. Because only a few take up optional worship and it is usually an indication of higher levels of spiritual development, there is a chance that pretence and feelings of spiritual superiority may result if optional worship is displayed publicly. Hence, all optional acts of worship should be done privately to maintain sincerity of action. As reported by his wife Aisha, Muhammad led the brief congregational prayers in the mosque, but also spent hours in privately worshipping God during the quiet darkness of the night. Similarly, he asked all of his followers to join the daily congregational prayers in the mosque, at the same time as he also encouraged certain individuals to practise nightly private vigils for higher spiritual development.

How are the five pillars of Islam important to a Muslims ethical system? Please give an example.

In the words of the Prophet Muhammad, the practice of Islam is summarised in "five pillars", which are listed as follows.

1. Creed (*Shahada*): The verbal commitment and pledge that *"there is no deity but the One and Only God and that Muhammad is the Messenger of God"*, which is considered to be the Creed of Islam. A person becomes a Muslim when, having felt the truth of Islam in the heart, he or she openly professes this creed in front of witnesses.

2. Prayers (*Salat*): The performance of the five short daily prayers required of Muslims.

3. Fasting (*Saum*): Fasting is a month-long abstinence from food, liquids and intimate intercourse (between married couples) every day from dawn to sunset during the month of Ramadan.

4. Purifying Alms (*Zakat*): This is an annual payment of a small percentage (usually 2.5%) of a Muslim's excess wealth, which is distributed among the poor, needy and other rightful beneficiaries.

5. Pilgrimage (*Hajj*): The performance of pilgrimage to Mecca is required once in a lifetime if physical and financial means are available. *Hajj* is partly in memory of the trials and tribulations of Prophet Abraham, his wife Hagar and his eldest son, the Prophet Ishmael.

To appreciate the relationship between the five pillars and the ethical system of Islam, we need to first look at how human behaviour affects society.

Human beings have been given certain emotions and powers such as anger, intellect and desires (sexual desires, hunger, etc.) to sustain their life on earth. These emotions and powers are limitless in their ability to motivate a person to find a level of balance and in due process unleash human potential and development. There is a desirable level of balance of these emotions among countless possible deviations. Since we all need to live together to meet our needs, there is a danger that individuals who have not been able to attain a balance in these emotions will transgress the rights of others in either a small or a significant manner. Hence, there must be law and a complementary ethical system to achieve safety and justice in a civil society. The establishment of laws and ethical systems are not enough to ensure that people actually follow them, nor is it practical to constantly police the actions of every individual. Hence, it is necessary to develop one's conscience to ensure that transgressions in human relations are minimised and order, harmony and justice in society are achieved. The only way in which this can effectively be achieved is when the society is made up of individuals who believe in an afterlife. One's place in that afterlife is positively or negatively influenced by one's actions and in an All-Seeing God who is recording their actions for an inevitable assessment of life. In such a society, an individual has an internal drive to check his or her own excessive acts and behaviour. Such a belief only exists in religions such as Islam and can only be strengthened and maintained through regular worship.

This is where the five pillars of Islam enter. Uttering the creed of Islam is the sign of faith, committing a person to be accountable to God on the Day of Judgment. Meditation and remembrance of God during the five daily prayers remind the person that God is Ever-Present and All-Seeing, greatly reducing the chance that he or she will commit misconduct and wrongdoing. Fasting not only strengthens the will power of the individual, but also makes it easier for the practitioner to resist the temptation to transgress the rights of others. Purifying alms forms a bridge between the rich and the poor, removing much social dissension and the causes of transgression. Finally, Pilgrimage moves people to higher levels of human appreciation, with an unmatched experience of universalism, enabling them to value humanity much more than any other act possibly can.

From an ethical perspective, not only does Islam as a religion set lofty standards of ethics, it also minimises human motives for transgression by equipping individuals with a mental and spiritual competence and empowering them to overcome negative tendencies.

How do Muslims worship and when do they worship?

In Islam, worship is a three dimensional phenomenon offered to God with the primary aim of pleasing Him and the resultant aim of achieving spiritual development.

1. The first dimension is the quantity and variability of practising *active worship*. Fasting, alms giving (*zakat*) and prescribed prayers (*salat*) are different types of worship that require some form of action by the practitioners, *"who believe in the Unseen, and perform As-salat (prayers) and spend out of what We have provided for them."* [QUR'AN, 2:3]

2. The second dimension is *passive worship*, which involves abstaining from acts that are damaging to one's mind, spirituality, assets, family or life, such as gambling, consuming intoxicants, sexual promiscuity or slandering people.

3. The third dimension is the development of a direct personal relationship between God and a Muslim. This is measured by the degree of closeness to God and how much a person remembers and communicates with God at a personal level. This dimension is important as it provides depth and quality to the other two dimensions, *"…Verily, in the remembrance of God do hearts find rest."* [QUR'AN, 13:28]

In addition to these three dimensions of worship, I could also talk about three different forms of worship and prayer:

1. Daily prayers (*salat*). In Islam, the meaning of worship is this: the human being, as a servant of God, being aware of his defects, weakness and poverty in the Divine presence, prostrates himself in love and wonder before the perfection of God's Lordship, Might and Compassion. Daily prayers are an expression of our surrender to God. [SEE QUESTION 36 FOR MORE ON *SALAT*]

2. Supplication (*du'a*). In addition to the daily prayers, a Muslim is encouraged to communicate with God in spoken language and ask for God's support in personal and spiritual life. The Qur'an says *"And when My servants ask you (O Muhammad) concerning Me, then (answer them), I am indeed near. I respond to the invocations of the supplicant when he calls on Me. So let them obey Me and believe in Me, so that they may be led aright"* [QUR'AN, 2:186]. Although God responds to all prayers, out of His wisdom He does not always grant our requests, as they may be harmful to us. This is similar to the situation when a person goes to the doctor and asks for a prescription and the doctor prescribes some other medicine, as the doctor best knows the disease and the condition of the person suffering from it.

3. Remembrance (*Zhikr*): This is the silent or voiced chanting of God's names and attributes or glorifying, praising and exalting God. *"Say: Call upon God, or call upon Rahman: by whatever name you call upon Him, to Him belongs the Most Beautiful Names. Neither speak thy Prayer aloud, nor speak it in a low tone, but seek a middle course in between"* declares the Qur'an [17:110]. Muslims who follow a spiritual path to God (Sufism) focus more on this form of worship.

All three forms of worship are important in Islam. There is a rich tradition of supplications reported from the Prophet of Islam. His wife Aisha reported that anyone who saw him would think that he was in a constant state of supplication. He implored God when mounting a horse, after a meal, when entering the house and so on. Consider this example, *"O God, I ask You for steadfastness in my affairs. I ask You for resolution in guidance. I ask You for gratitude for Your bounties and acceptable service to You. I ask You for a truthful tongue and a sound heart; and I seek refuge in You from the evil of what You know, and I ask You for the good of what You know and I ask for Your forgiveness for what You already know. Surely You are Knower of the Unseen."* [TIRMIDHI]

A Muslim's worship spans his or her whole life. While certain acts of worship are made on a daily basis, others may be done only once in a lifetime. Performing pilgrimage to holy lands is required to

QUESTION 35

be done once in a lifetime for those rich and healthy enough to make the journey. *Zakat* (Alms) is the payment of 2.5% of a person's excess wealth to certain categories of people such as the poor and needy. It is paid once a year. Fasting is done for one month every year while prescribed prayers are done five times a day. These are what we call the "pillars of Islam". Collectively, they are divinely prescribed practices to ensure physical, mental, spiritual and social development and the wellbeing of a Muslim.

Q36

Why do Muslims pray five times a day? What is the meaning of prayer? How do you pray and in what direction and style?

Each particular prayer (*salat*) is made for glorifying, exalting and praising the Lord. The words *subhan-allah* (Glory be to God), *Allahu akbar* (God is the Greatest) and *al-hamdu li-llah* (All praise be to God) are uttered with the heart, tongue and body during a prayer session, totally engaging the person in worship.

Prescribed prayer in Islam is such that it thoroughly engages a person mentally, socially, spiritually and physically. As part of the prayer a Muslim worshipper recites from memory passages from the Qur'an; utters phrases of glorification, exaltation and praise, and goes through a set of movements. The movements in a prayer have significant purpose and meanings [SEE ANSWER TO QUESTION 37 FOR MORE ON THE MOVEMENTS]. The worshipper also goes into a meditative state she neither pays attention to the environment nor speaks with anyone during the prayer.

The five times of worship are the early morning, noon, afternoon, evening and at nightfall. These are not only significant times for a person during the day, but they also represent the five most significant milestones in one's lifetime, ranging from birth to adult life, old-age and death, when all trace of one's having been in the world is lost.

The spaced repetition of prayers at these five times also provides a conscious way of positive self-conditioning that results in a constant awareness of God, significantly reducing the committing of bad deeds.

To pray five times a day may appear excessive, but collectively they take less than about 40 minutes to perform. Muslims who have developed a habit of prayer do not see this as a burden. On the contrary, they give a small portion of their daily time back to God

QUESTION 36

knowing that He has bestowed twenty-four hours in a day on them. Prayer is an opportunity to be in the direct presence of, and in communication with, God without any intermediary.

All Muslims face in the direction of the *Ka'bah* when they are praying. This does not mean that they worship the *Ka'bah* or that they think that God is within the *Ka'bah*. It simply indicates the direction of worship [SEE ANSWER TO QUESTION 54 ABOUT *KA'BAH*].

The physical movements in the prayer appear strange. What is the purpose behind these movements?

Prescribed prayer (*salat*) in Islam is an integral form of worship that totally immerses a person within a unique combination of mental, social, spiritual and physical engagement. As part of the prayer, a Muslim worshipper goes into a state of meditation and neither pays any attention to the environment nor speaks with anyone during the prayer. She recites passages from the Qur'an from memory and contemplates their meaning, utters phrases of glorification, exaltation and praise of God while spiritually feeling the near presence of God, and goes through a set of movements such as lifting both hands up to shoulder height, standing up with hands beside the body, bowing down, prostrating and sitting. These movements are made shoulder to shoulder in a congregation, and the movements are synchronised.

The movements in prayer have significant purposes and meanings. They are the physical expressions of glorifying, exalting and praising God. For example, when the person is standing upright and makes the intention of praying to God alone, she begins by saying "*God is the Greatest*" whilst at the same time lifting both hands up to shoulder height, meaning that the world and worldly affairs are thrown behind and she is alone in the court of God. When the worshipper bows, she lowers her "self" in the court of God and by doing so glorifies God. When the worshipper prostrates, she lowers the "self" to the lowest point in the court of God and displays the ultimate level of physical glorification of God.

Physical movements for a Muslim in prayer also display progressively increasing levels of submission to God. In the standing-up position, with the hands together in front, the worshipper is as if saying "*my hands are tied, I am ready to submit to You*". Bowing is a higher level of submission. Breaking the defence mechanisms of the

QUESTION 37

"self", it is as if he is saying *"I bow down only to you, I cannot see what's in front of me. My God, I have submitted myself to You."* The prostration is the ultimate level of submission. It is as if the worshipper is saying, *"my God, I am lowering my head to the same level as my feet. With respect to You I have made myself as nothing. I am completely defenceless against Your will. Even my self does not stand between You and me."*

Expressing one's limits and weaknesses and recognising the greatness and glory of God is the essence of worship and the means of getting spiritually close to God. Whoever sees himself as above everyone and everything else can never develop spiritually. Hence, movements in the prayer break delusions of self-glory and open the door to spiritual enlightenment.

What are the benefits of the prescribed prayers?

Daily-prescribed prayer (*salat*) is the cornerstone of religious practice in Islam. The Prophet Muhammad was very attentive to his prayers and strongly encouraged Muslims to perform them. He said, *"salat (daily prescribed prayers) is the (central) pillar of religion"* [TIRMIDHI, IMAN 8]. Prescribed prayers offer many benefits in the personal development of a Muslim:

- Remembrance of God during daily prayers enables a person to feel the Divine presence and, as a result, directly develop a closer relationship with God. The Prophet Muhammad said, *"a person is closest to God at the moment of prostration"*.

- *Salat* is the best form of worship [SEE QUESTIONS 36–37]. Therefore it leads a person to find a spiritual groove in life and feel the spiritual contentment of living up to the purpose of his or her creation, which is to know and worship God.

- It raises an awareness of being in the presence of God, motivating the mind to seek God and hence prevent the committing of wrongful acts.

- All enjoined prayers are performed in groups with shoulders touching each other, thus building social cohesion and solidarity. Friday, *Eid* (festive) and Ramadan prayers are especially performed in congregations. This way of praying also promotes the direct communication of Muslims with each other.

- Focus and meditation during prayer clears the mind. Breaking for prayer at key times during the day prevents stress.

- Ablution with water before the prayer cleans the external limbs of the body. It also removes the static electricity of the body and provides relief and comfort, as water is known to be a soothing element.

- The physical movements during prayer stretch every muscle in the body and provide vital movement in the joints to help prevent diseases of the joints in old age.

In addition to these benefits, *salat*, together with the other practices of Islam, enables a Muslim to reach higher levels of being and hence tranquillity in this world and the next. Through spiritual struggle and development, a person goes through three levels of being:

The Commanding Self – This is the animal in all of us that needs to be tamed. The human animal self is quite different to those of real animals. While a cow would be contented after a good meal of grass in the meadows and a lion satisfied with only one killing of zebra, the human animal self has no limit in its desires and powers of destruction. This inherent nature of "self" might seem to be against us but in fact it has good consequences. While the Creator has created the human self so that we can survive in this world, He did not set any boundaries to emotions so that the door to human progress and development is never closed. Otherwise, there would be no difference between humans and animals, which have a fixed level of being. The goal is not to totally blunt our desires, which is impossible, but to balance and channel them according to the purpose for which they were originally created. A person who is at this level of being is a slave to insatiable desires guided by immediate pleasure and disregarding the pain and burdens that inevitably follow. He thinks he has complete freedom, but he is a slave to many masters (desires, fear, fame, wealth, people in higher places and so on). His attitude is that "life is too short to waste, I must enjoy it while I can." According to Islam, a person in this state will never find contentment, just as a person will never quench his thirst by drinking salty seawater. The human "self" rests between our spiritual being and physical existence. A purified "self" can act as an instrument of spiritual enlightenment.

The Accusing Self – The Qur'an [9:126] mentions that people who are at the level of the commanding-self, that is oblivious to God, receive a number of reminders to nudge them out of their forgetfulness. These are normal events that we all encounter in life, such as a car accident, a dying relative or a word said by a friend. They trigger certain questions, such as, "I am made up of flesh and atoms, yet I can feel and learn. Who am I then? Why am I here? Where do I come from and where am I going?" After gaining an awareness of God and seeing the need to enter a path of spirituality, a person commits to a way of life (or religion) and tries to control his or her actions for the better. Since he has not yet mastered his own helm, he stumbles along the way. Blaming himself for not being true to his commitment, he learns from the experience and resolves to renew his commitment. This struggle (*jihad*) towards the ultimate goal continues this way until the person finds rest.

The Restful Self – Through resilience and persistence, there comes a time when he succeeds in finding heartfelt peace and tranquillity. He now knows for certainty that there is God and understands who God is. All the truths of belief become clear in his consciousness and heart. He also understands that when he dies he will unavoidably return to God. He realises that by being a servant of God he gains real freedom from the multiplicity of masters racing to control him. His attitude becomes "life is too short to waste, I must collect as much yield from the fertile soil of life (in good deeds and spiritual closeness to God) and leave a lasting legacy." This enlightenment leads to a complete surrendering to God, willingly looking forward to a time to meet God. In this state of being, Rumi called his own death the "wedding night", which is the time to meet with the beloved God. At this point in time, the restful soul gets a divine invitation: "*O, the one in complete rest and satisfaction, come back to your Lord, well-pleased and well-pleasing to Him.*

QUESTION 38

Enter you, then, among my honoured servants and enter you in My Paradise."
[QUR'AN, 90:27–30]

In addition to these three levels of being, Sufi literature talks about another four layers (the inspired self, the pleased self, the well-pleasing self and the pure self) relying on the verse above and other similar verses. Some spiritual masters also talk about negative levels of self. It is beyond the scope of this book to go into further detail on this subject. For more information, I recommend the *Key Concepts of Sufism* by M. Fethullah Gulen.

How important are daily prayers to a Muslim and what role do they play in one's morality?

There is a direct relationship between daily prayers and one's morality. Just as prayer should lead to good character, similarly the level of one's character becomes a measure of the quality of one's prayer.

In Islam, daily prayers have a deep influence on one's conduct in life. The Qur'an says, *"Recite that which has been revealed to you of the book and establish regular prayer (salat), surely prayer keeps one away from indecency and evil…"* [QUR'AN, 29:45]. A person who stands in God's presence five times a day, renewing his or her commitment to God, would surely watch what he or she did in the times between prayer. When a person is confronted with an opportunity to do wrong or has an immoral inclination, the person would think, *"I have just had a strong spiritual connection with God, how can I even think about it?"* Or if the time to prayer is close, the person would possibly think, *"I will be standing before God in a few minutes, how can I face God if I do this?"* In this way, a Muslim is conscientiously prevented from doing wrong and stays on the straight path (*sirat al-mustaqim*). The deeper the relationship with God, the more profound is its effect.

Looking at the issue from the opposite angle, we could measure the degree of intimacy of a Muslim's relationship with God and his or her sincerity in prayer by the level of his or her character and morality. Signs of elevated morality in a Muslim are indicative of the quality of that person's daily prayers. Similarly, if a person is visibly displaying immoral behaviour, the spiritual connection during the prayers would not be very strong.

Thus, moral conduct and daily prayer reinforce one another. While prayer should improve one's morality, the moral character of a person is the litmus test for the quality of worship. In the words of the Prophet Muhammad, the aim of Islam in the personal sphere is to perfect one's character through balanced personal development. It is for this reason that he said, "*Salat (daily prayers) is the (central) pillar of religion.*"⁹

---

9 Tirmidhi, *iman*, 8.

When is a person required to start to pray? What is the age of religious responsibility?

Islam enjoins its followers to pray regularly as a spiritual activity to develop a person's spirituality. This development requires that the exercise be spaced at intervals and take the same form. Therefore, prayer in Islam is spaced at five time intervals during the day and consists of standard parts. The form of worship is exactly prescribed. As I explained in my answer to QUESTION 35, there is a clear distinction between the prescribed prayers (*salat*) and supplication (*dua*) in Islam. While *salat* refers to a uniform expression of worship composed of certain rites, *dua* refers to communicating with God in a more personal manner.

Each and every Muslim is enjoined to perform the prescribed prayers. However, a person must meet three conditions before they will be considered responsible enough to observe all their religious obligations. Firstly, he or she must be a Muslim. It would be ineffectual for a non-Muslim to observe prayer and practise the religion without first and foremost professing the essence of prayer. Secondly, he or she has to be intelligent and of full mental capacity. Children, as well as people with intellectual impairments, are recognised as not being fully aware or capable of understanding the significance of Islamic religious obligations. Lastly, and flowing from the second condition, he or she must have reached an age of physical and mental maturity that is substantial enough to bear the responsibility of prayer.

Islam acknowledges that sufficient mental and physical capacity has been reached by the age of puberty. For females, this is reached with the onset of menstruation, usually between the ages of 9 and 15. For males, the age of responsibility occurs when ejaculations begin, commonly between the ages of 12 and 15. In either case, the age of 15 is the upper limit.

QUESTION 40

Anyone who does not meet the specified criteria will not be held accountable for their religious obligations. Before the age of puberty children are considered sinless and innocent, and hence a child will go to Paradise if death occurs before the age of puberty irrespective of what religious background the child comes from.

What preparations take place before worship and why?

Islam places great emphasis upon keeping oneself in a state of physical and spiritual cleanliness. The Qur'an states, "*Surely God loves those who turn to Him again and again, and He loves those who purify themselves…*" [QUR'AN, 2:222] The Prophet Muhammad said that, "*the key to Paradise is prayer and the key to prayer is purification…*" Physical purification of the body and the place of worship is a necessary condition for prayer. This is also the reason why Muslims take their shoes off when entering a mosque and, in the majority of cases, their homes.

A Muslim is required to be in a constant state of full body ablution (*ghusl*), which needs to be refreshed after sexual intercourse and menstruation. This consists of cleaning the internals of the mouth and nose; and showering the whole body in water. This is similar to the ritual of baptism, but is done privately in one's bathroom.

Standard ablution (*wudu*) is required before all prayers and needs to be refreshed after sleep and any waste is excreted from the body. The Qur'an specifies the manner in which this ablution is to take place: "*O you who believe! When you rise up to prayers, wash your faces and your hands as far as the elbows and wipe your heads and wash your feet to the ankles; and if you are under an obligation to perform a total ablution, have a bath…God does not desire to put on you any difficulty but He wishes to purify you and that he may complete His favour to you so that you may be thankful…*" [QUR'AN, 5:16] This specific description of the manner and reasons why ablution are to be performed add weight to its importance.

While the primary purpose of both forms of ablution is physical cleanliness, they have mental and spiritual dimensions as well. The Prophet Muhammad said, "*the person who has not performed ablution,*

QUESTION 41

does not remember God in doing it (prayer)...", meaning that spiritual closeness to God should start with ablution even before the prayer. The ablution serves to focus one's heart and the mind on the significance of the worship about to be performed. Washing the face, feet, hands and forearms also removes static electricity in the body and thus relaxes the person for prayer. A Muslim is required to keep his body, his clothes, and in fact the whole of his or her environment, clean at all times.

What are the main acts of charity one must perform in Islam? What are their main benefits?

Islam gives charity (*sadaqah*) its broadest definition. It starts with the giving of a small rate of obligatory alms and extends to good deeds towards people, kindness towards animals and refraining from committing evil acts. In the words of the Prophet Muhammad it even extends as far as giving a simple smile.

Islam enjoins Muslims to pay the obligatory *zakat* or purifying alms. The obligation only commences if a person has growth-based assets (money, gold, shares, etc), in excess of his basic living expenses, with a total above a certain minimum threshold. So *zakat* is paid only from the excess wealth a person possesses. In the case of money, the rate of *zakat* is 2.5%. Once collected by the government or charity organisations, *zakat* can only be potentially handed out to eight categories of people, such as the poor, needy, people in debt, the destitute traveller, and so on [QUR'AN, 9:60]. A person can also give the *zakat* personally to rightful beneficiaries.

Although God is the only Sustainer of life on earth, He does not directly hand out sustenance into the hands of those He has created. The Divine Will is to foster movement and activity within life. The main driver of motion is the activity to earn one's living. In this way, the exhibition of God's works of art can be discovered and viewed by as many as possible of those He has created. Life also becomes more interesting and enjoyable for all the living. Divine Wisdom has also made us depend on each other so that human progress and development can be stimulated. One consequence of this scenario is that the acquisition of wealth is amassed disproportionately by individuals, yet God provides enough sustenance on earth for everyone. Since it is a basic human right to have minimum living standards of food, clothing and shelter, the rightful portion of the poor is included within the excess wealth of every one of us. Consequently, Muslims are enjoined to give *zakat,* which is called the "purifying alms", not just as charity but also as the rightful portion of the less fortunate.

Another trademark form of charity occurs during the second festive season, *Eid-al-Adha,* on the Muslim calendar that coincides with the time of Pilgrimage. Those Muslims who have the means above a minimum threshold are required to purchase an animal and dedicate it to God, symbolically representing personal submission as depicted in the attempt of Abraham in sacrificing his son Ishmail. *"It is not their meat nor their blood, that reaches God. It is your piety that reaches Him…"* warns the Qur'an [22:37]. One-third or more of the meat of the animal is given to the poor in the community. Today, this Islamic practice is a major form of food charity, where organisations collect money equal to the cost of a sheep and send the total to poorer Muslim countries.

Fitr is another form of charity paid at the end of Ramadan and before the *Eid-al-Fitr* festivities (end of the fasting month of *Ramadan*) commence. This charity ensures that no member of the community is left out of the enjoyment that comes with the communal festivities.

Another type of charity is *karzh-i-hasn* or a "beautiful loan" [QUR'AN, 2:245]. This is an interest free loan given to a needy Muslim without expecting anything in return from anyone other than God.

The fifth form of charity in Islam is every other optional act of tangible and intangible giving. *"The best form of sadaqah (charity) is for a Muslim to acquire knowledge and then to teach that knowledge to his or her Muslim brothers and sisters"* [10] said Muhammad. On another occasion,

---

10 Ibn Maje, *mukadimah,* 20.

when he said, *"every Muslim is required to give charity"*, his companions questioned, *"O prophet of God, what should one do if one cannot find anything to give in charity?"* Muhammad replied, *"He works with his own hands and uses the earnings for himself and in charity."* They asked, *"what if one cannot do this?"* He replied, *"one should help a needy person who cannot do his or her own work."* When they continued, asking, *"what if one cannot do this?"*, Muhammad replied, *"one does good deeds and refrains from evil deeds, this is a charity to one's own self."*[11] Consequently, for a Muslim, the whole of life becomes an act of charity.

The history of Islam shows that there were periods when poverty was totally eradicated in Muslim lands through this culture of charity. So much so that they did not have any poor citizens to give alms to and directed charity to neighbouring Christian countries. Compassion of the rich for the poor and respect of the poor for the rich underscores the social fabric of a Muslim society.

---

11 Bukhari, *zakat*, 30.

Why do you fast for a whole month in Ramadan? How can you not eat or drink for a whole day?

What might appear to an outsider to be a self-inflicted ordeal, fasting is a profound act of worship for a practitioner. It engenders a deep experience of self-sacrifice in order to discipline the never-ending desires of the human self. It is a way to personally feel the suffering the poor and needy go through in their daily lives.

A fasting day begins with an early morning meal (*sahoor*) before dawn. Practitioners abstain from food, drink and sexual activity with their spouse from dawn until sunset while they are involved in normal daily activity. At sunset the fast is broken with a break-fast meal, usually sharing the joy of eating with invited guests, friends and family members. In the evening, Muslims can go to the mosque for a special prayer (*tarawih*). The daily cycle is repeated consecutively for a whole month, at the end of which the Muslim community celebrates a three-day festival (*Eid al-Fitr*). This celebration is a personal celebration where it symbolically represents the victory and control one has attained over his or her human self. It is also a communal celebration where people exchange visits and gifts.

According to Islamic teachings, one way in which God exhibits the perfection of his Lordship, Grace and Mercy is through the creation of this world as a table of blessing. He has placed all kinds of blessings and sustenance on that Divine table for us to take advantage of, yet most people forget the fact that the ultimate source of all sustenance is God Almighty and credit transient causes as the source of the blessings. Islam says the causes only act as delivery agents for the Divine. During Ramadan, believers show a collective act of worship in the presence of the mighty and universal Mercy as they wait for the Divine invitation to attend the table of blessings at the break-time of the fast. Therefore, fasting establishes a link between the Sustainer and humans, which reaches a climax just before the break of the fast. It is for this reason that the Prophet Muhammad said, *"God will not reject the prayer of a fasting person made just before the break of the fast."*

For the sustenance that God cultivates on earth for humans, the only price He wants and expects is the price of thanksgiving. True thanksgiving is to know that all sustenance comes directly from God, to acknowledge its value and to feel our need and dependence on that sustenance. Fasting is the best way to show this true and sincere thanksgiving, since most people know the value of, and need for, food and water when they experience hunger and thirst. Because a Muslim fasts for the sake of God, he or she acknowledges that the sustenance we may take for granted actually comes directly from God.

There is also a moral dimension to fasting. It serves as a way to regulate one's own behaviour and bad habits. *"Whoever doesn't give up lying and acting on lies during fasting, then God has no need for him to give up food and drink,"* remarked the Prophet Muhammad. Fasting has many benefits for a practising Muslim and the Muslim community:

1. The greatest benefit of fasting is that it is the best form of exercising will power. As it lasts for one month, self-control becomes a habit.

2. It triggers spiritual growth as fasting reminds the self that God is its true owner and that it does not have absolute sovereignty.

3. Fasting reminds the human self (*nafs*) that it is weak and poor and how much it is dependent on God to provide basic needs, opening the door for connecting with and submitting to God.

4. Hunger through fasting gives the spirit a chance to be freed from the dominance of the physical body and to develop.

5. Through fasting, the wealthy experience what it means to be hungry and not able to buy food. Therefore the wealthy will be

more inclined to give charity when they fast. This builds up a relationship between the wealthy and the poor resulting in social cohesion.

6. In Ramadan, there is a high level of interaction between Muslims since they invite each other to break the fast and see each other in the mosque every evening for special Ramadan prayers, thus cementing community ties.

7. By fasting for thirty days, Muslims learn to control their eating habits. Furthermore, one month of fasting rests our digestive system and especially the liver. This recuperation benefit is only achieved if all bodily intake is stopped for a prolonged period during the day.

Muslims generally start to fast after the age of ten. After the first year of orientation, fasting becomes a habit and Muslims actually look forward to the time of fasting and the community spirit it cultivates.

Why do Muslims make pilgrimage to Mecca? What is its significance?

Those Muslims who are financially able are required to make the journey to Hajj, the Pilgrimage, at least once in a lifetime, as it is one of the five fundamental pillars of Islamic practice. *Hajj* consists of visiting and circling the *Ka'bah* [SEE QUESTION 53 FOR MORE ON THE *KA'BAH*], being present in the plains of *Mount Arafat* and performing specific rites during the period from the 8th to 13th Dhu'l Hijjah, the twelfth month on the Islamic calendar. Both the *Ka'bah* and *Mt Arafat* are in Mecca, Saudi Arabia. Pilgrims also visit Medina, where the first Muslim community was established. The Prophet Muhammad's first mosque and his grave are also located in Medina.

Muslim Pilgrimage has profound meanings for the relationship of a believer with God, humanity and the universe.

All creatures of God worship and praise Him in the language of their natural disposition. The Qur'an declares, *"All that is in the heavens and on the earth extols and glorifies God, for He is the Tremendous, the Wise."* [QUR'AN, 57:1] Just as this occurs individually, when each creature displays the wonders of its Creator's art and lives in accordance with the purpose for which it was created, it also occurs collectively. Animals migrating in their millions and plants blossoming in the springtime can be given as examples of such collective worship. Muslims also obey the call of God by turning up in millions at the time of the *Hajj*.

The central aims of worship (exalting, glorifying and praising God) are realised individually and collectively during the Pilgrimage. Muslims exalt God by turning up in large numbers, in a way saying, *"You are greater than my self and above the whole of humanity; here we are ready to worship you collectively"*. They glorify God by going around the *Ka'bah*, as if saying, *"just as we are all going around the one*

149

and only Ka'bah, the oldest place of worship on earth, we only obey You the Absolute One worthy of worship. Your Divinity and Your call are sufficient for us to come to You". They praise God by assembling in the plains of *Mt Arafat*.

An act of worship observable in the universe is that every entity orbits around a central point. Electrons orbit the nucleus in an atom; the earth and planets orbit the sun, the solar system orbits around the Milky Way and so on. Muslims join in this mode of worship and synchronise with the universe and all existence by circling the *Ka'bah* as a place symbolising the worship of the one and only God.

The Muslim Pilgrimage is more than just a matter of connecting with the historical legacy of Islam, but is rather a way of establishing a connection with the monotheism symbolised by Adam and Abraham respectively and its human legacy.

Muslims believe that the *Ka'bah* was the first place of worship built by the first human and the first prophet, Adam. It was later rebuilt on the same foundations by Abraham and his son Ishmail and declared as a shrine dedicated to monotheism. Abraham called on people to make pilgrimage to the site. Before the days of Islam, the Hebrew Bible confirmed the existence of this pilgrimage to Mecca (or Beca). Psalm 84:4–6 says, *"O Lord Almighty, my King and my God. Blessed are those who dwell in Your house; they are ever praising You. Blessed are those whose strength is in You, who have set their hearts on pilgrimage. As they pass through the Valley of Beca, they make it a place of springs; the autumn rains also cover it with pools."* Thus, when Muslims circle the *Ka'bah*, they are affirming their commitment to God and to monotheism. As people from all races and nations gather at the spiritual epicentre of the world, the *Ka'bah*, they are affirming their common paternal ancestry with Adam and their spiritual ancestry with Abraham.

The climax of Pilgrimage occurs at the plains of *Mount Arafat*, about twenty kilometres outside of Mecca. All pilgrims have to be present at this location at the same time, simulating the day of resurrection. Everybody wears the same simple garment and supplicates to God with no distinction of race, status or wealth.

It is believed that Adam and Eve both repented to God for their "sins" and received forgiveness at this location. Muslims hope for similar forgiveness when they collectively petition God for forgiveness for the sins they have committed in their lives. Although God cannot be compelled, taking the time to travel thousands of kilometres just to ask for forgiveness collectively is a compelling reason to grant forgiveness. In the words of the Prophet Muhammad, a sincere pilgrim comes out of the experience of Pilgrimage washed of his or her sins and becomes as clean as a newborn baby.

Q45

From the perspective of a person who has experienced the *Hajj* (Pilgrimage), what was it like?

Together with my mother, I performed the Pilgrimage in 2001. It was the most unforgettable experience of my life. It is a total human experience. I became fully engaged in the experience of being a pilgrim.

You cannot help but have a physical involvement in the Pilgrimage. The rites of Pilgrimage involve a lot of walking. At the end of about four weeks of daily activities, you come out a fit person. My mother had knee problems prior to her travel. Towards the end of the Pilgrimage, her condition was cured thanks to lots of walking.

You are fully engaged spiritually in the experience of Pilgrimage. Visiting the holy grounds, attending the prayer sessions with thousands of other people greatly boosts one's spirituality. Hardly anyone would not be moved to tears at the collective supplication at *Mount Arafat*.

I must admit that I did not expect the experience of circling the *Ka'bah* would be as spiritual as it turned out. When I first entered the main courtyard housing the *Ka'bah* on an overpass, I was struck by the river of people walking under me between two hills reportedly walked by Hagar, the wife of Abraham, in search of water. The sight of the *Ka'bah* for the first time was awesome. My heart started to beat faster at the spectacle and the sheer number of people. My expectation in circling the *Ka'bah* was not great. I was going to do it because it is a requirement of the Pilgrimage, but when I was actually circling the *Ka'bah*, I felt as if I was near the epicentre of a spiritual storm.

Ali Shariati expresses very well the essential experience of the rite of circling the *Ka'bah*: *"As you circumambulate and move closer to the Ka'bah, you feel like a small stream merging into a big river. Carried by a wave you lose touch with the ground. Suddenly, you are floating, carried on by the flood. As you approach the centre, the pressure of the crowd squeezes you so hard that you are given a new life. You are now part of the People; you are now a man, alive …The Ka'bah is the world's sun whose face attracts you into its orbit. You have become part of this universal system… You have been transformed into a particle that is gradually melting and disappearing. This is absolute love at its peak."* [12]

You are engaged in the experience mentally as well. A pilgrim's mind is totally removed from business and other worldly commitments or worries. This removes stress to a great extent and provides the effect of real recreation. I felt that I entered another world for one month. Before I went on Pilgrimage, I was losing hair in some spots in my beard. Doctors attributed this to stress. I can tell you that the hair grew back during the Pilgrimage without any medication.

You are also engaged socially. Most Muslims only see and talk to Muslims from their own country. An Indonesian Muslim may never get a chance to see another Muslim from a different national and cultural background. As a result, a person may not even know that Muslims exist in Africa, China, America, etc. Only the experience of the Pilgrimage makes a person realise that Islam is truly a universal religion. Malcolm X, who was a prominent figure in America's Nation of Islam during the early 1960's, shed his extreme views about "white people" after the experience of pilgrimage. He was transformed when he performed his pilgrimage. Michael Wolfe, the writer of The Road to Mecca, said in a CNN documentary about pilgrimage that he really "got it" (Islam) after the experience of pilgrimage, even though he had been a Muslim for two years.

---

12 Shariati, Ali, *Hajj* (trans. Laleh Bakhtiar) (Teheran, 1988), pp. 54–56.

QUESTION 45

As a result of the intense experience, emotion and benefits of the Pilgrimage, most people have a great desire to go back. Sometime in the near future, I hope to go one more time with my wife.

What are the responsibilities of men and women in this religion?

I will answer this question from the perspective of the spiritual status and religious responsibilities given to men and women. I will address the roles of women in the social context in my answer to QUESTION 76.

In Islam, women were not an afterthought in the scheme of creation. *"O mankind! Reverence your Guardian-Lord, who created you from a single human self* (nafsin wahidatin) *and created from it (the same essence), his partner. And from them twain scattered (like seeds) countless men and women. Revere God, through whom you demand your mutual (rights), and (reverence) the wombs (that bore you), for God ever watches over you."* [QUR'AN, 4:1] This verse is the opening verse of the Qur'anic chapter entitled "Women" (*Nisa*). It is a reminder to both genders to realise they are both created from the same human essence and therefore men and women should respect each other's rights.

The Qur'an tells us that God does not distinguish between people, irrespective of their race, gender or social status. The only criterion of superiority, as far as God is concerned, is one's level of spiritual development and awareness of God. The Qur'an says, *"O humankind! We created you from a single (pair) of a male and a female, and made you into nations and tribes so that you may know each other (not that you may despise one another). Verily the most honoured of you in the sight of God is the most righteous of you. And God has full knowledge and is well acquainted (with all things)."* [QUR'AN, 49:13] In Islam, oneness of humanity is a fundamental teaching.

Islam goes a step further and transcends the gender dichotomy and sees both men and women as human beings complementing each other in their natural disposition, just as God has intended: *"The Believers, men and women, are protectors of one another…"* [QUR'AN,

155

9:71]. In this perspective, neither men nor women have any important advantages or disadvantages. Each gender has strengths and weaknesses. Only the communion of the two would produce a complete realisation of full humanity.

One of the first revelations of the Qur'an is that women are enjoined to seek knowledge together with men. The Prophet Muhammad said that gaining knowledge is incumbent upon every Muslim, whether male or female, and that injunction was put into full practice at the time of the Prophet. Women were heavily involved in the great educational campaign in Medina. The Prophet's wife Aisha was a foremost authority in the Qur'anic commentary, law and prophetic narratives. She transmitted 2210 narratives from the Prophet Muhammad.

Islam gives equal religious responsibility to both men and women. Therefore, both have the same capacities for spiritual development, *"For Muslim men and Muslim women, for believing men and believing women, for devout men and devout women, for patient men and patient women, for humble men and humble women, for charitable men and charitable women, for fasting men and fasting women, for chaste men and chaste women, and for men and women who engage in the praise of God – for them God has prepared forgiveness and a great reward."* [QUR'AN, 33:35] It is interesting how the words "men" and "women" are repeated for each religious injunction or good attribute to get the point across that all men and women are equally required to adhere to Islam's teachings. This verse also concisely lists attributes towards which all Muslims should aspire.

Islam also expects men and women to share the responsibility of establishing a peaceful, safe and just society. The Qur'anic verse [9:71] mentioned above continues to read, *"…they enjoin what is just, and forbid what is evil: they observe regular prayers, practise regular charity, and obey God and His Messenger. On them will God pour His mercy: for*

God is Exalted in power, Wise." This duty requires that women should also be socially active alongside men.

As a result of these duties, successful practitioners are given the good news that both men and women will equally receive the final reward, "...*Whoever does an atom's weight of good, whether male or female, and is a believer, all such shall enter into paradise...*" [QUR'AN, 40:40]

It is clear that Islam gives equal responsibility and religious roles to both men and women. Women are not excluded from society and receive the ultimate reward in Paradise along with men, provided they believe in God and do good deeds.

Many Muslims see Muhammad and God as role models and figures, which Muslims are to follow. Do you agree and why?

The Prophet Muhammad said, *"wear the character of God."* Obviously, this does not mean that in Islam God is a human being to be emulated. On the contrary, God is a transcendent reality and unlike any of His creatures [SEE ANSWER TO QUESTION 2 MORE ABOUT THE CONCEPT OF GOD]. However, the way God designed the universe and the way He governs it reflects something of His divine qualities and character. For example, when we observe the natural environment, we notice that a perfect balance prevails throughout the universe. The amount of oxygen in the atmosphere remains at the same level even though oxygen is constantly converting to carbon dioxide and vice versa. Numerous other examples could be given to show that there is a constant act of balancing in the universe. Since it is God who set up this balanced system and maintains it [QUR'AN, 55:7], we conclude that God is The Just (*Al-Adl*) and that acting justly is part of God's "character." Therefore Muslims are asked to act justly in the Qur'an [55:8–9]. In this way, Muslims are expected to *"wear the character of God"* as encouraged by the Prophet Muhammad.

The Prophet Muhammad also said, *"I have been sent to perfect the best of morality and character."* When people asked his wife, Aisha, what the character of the Prophet was like, she said, *"Don't you read the Qur'an? He was a walking Qur'an."* Muslims hold Muhammad to be the perfect human model and the model given by God, as expressed in the Qur'an. Therefore, one of the most fundamental roles of Muhammad, and of all the prophets, was to put into practice the principles of religion so that people could actually see that it is practically possible to live the ideals of religion in both the social and private spheres of life.

QUESTION 47

Both friend and foe have acknowledged the high standards of the Prophet Muhammad's character. My answer to QUESTION 17 gives a glimpse of his character. All Muslims are encouraged and expected to follow his example (*Sunnah*) in living Islam and perfecting their character. The shortcomings you might see in some Muslims are a reflection of their own limitations and weaknesses, not a reflection of the character of Muhammad.

Your sacred book, the Qur'an, is essential in outlining the role of Muslims' ethical system. What are the fundamentals that make up the ethical system and which one is most important to you?

In QUESTION 20 we discussed the four main themes in the Qur'an, one of which is justice. The ethical system is a component of justice. There are four fundamentals in the ethical system of Islam, all of which are important and complement each another:

1. Finding a wholesome balance in one's emotions and character.
2. The moral conduct of the individual.
3. Social justice.
4. Active promotion of virtue and the prevention of vice.

All individuals come to this world with seed-like faculties waiting to be developed. Since our emotions have no limit, we need to strive to find a wholesome middle ground (*sirat al-mustaqeem*) to realise our humanity and find a restful state of being. Good behaviour, which is the cornerstone of ethics, will only emanate from individuals with such internal balance.

The word *adab* is mentioned in the Qur'an as signifying a discipline of the mind or every praiseworthy discipline by which a person is trained in any excellence. Good morals and good manners are stated as the true test of an individual's excellence. The Qur'an states, "…*The noblest of you in the sight of God is the one who is the best in conduct…*" [QUR'AN, 49:13] This is further affirmed by the Prophet Muhammad when he said, "…*The best of you are those who have the most excellent morals…*" This is so because it is only when individuals excel in ethics that they do not harm themselves and others in society, which leads to practical social justice underscored by peace and happiness for all.

One of the most important fundamentals of ethics in the Qur'an is the way one treats one's family – parents, children, spouse. A Muslim is also enjoined to take care of the disadvantaged members of the community – the poor, needy, elderly, orphans and disabled. As the Qur'an states, *"…Righteousness is this: that one should believe in God…and give away wealth out of love for Him to the near of kin and the orphans and the needy and the wayfarer and the beggar…"* [QUR'AN, 2:177] This recognises a fact further elaborated in the Qur'an [49:10] that Muslims are brethren, members of one body and parts of one structure (*ummah*) and therefore must provide help for one another and practise acts of kindness. The Prophet stated, *"…God has no mercy on him who has no mercy for others…"* Charities and *zakat* in particular extend the theme of social justice into action.

The fourth component of the ethical system of Islam is the principle of *"promoting virtue and goodness and the prevention of vice."* The Qur'an [3:104] states, *"And from among you there should be people who invite to good and enjoin what is right and forbid the wrong and these are those who shall be successful."* According to Islam, this principle is an important element of a healthy society with a sound ethical system. The Qur'an also describes how previous nations and civilisations perished due to the moral decline of the masses and lack of social activism to reverse the decline. The practice of the Prophet and generations of Muslims who followed has been to personally help and advise individuals and to emphasise education and a public awareness of the perils of vice rather than imposing certain laws on people.

Muslims hold and practice many traditions (e.g. Pilgrimage). How important are they in a Muslim's life and what overall impact do they have on Muslims?

The Arabic word for "religion" is "*deen*", which also means "a way of life." So, Islam is not only a spiritual path leading a person to higher levels of being but is also a way of life, providing balanced guidelines for every human need and situation. When Islam first appeared in Arabia, it not only transformed religious beliefs and practices there, but also the everyday way of living for individuals. It came naturally that the Prophet commented on the behaviour of people to develop a highly sophisticated but yet practical etiquette. Instead of gulping down water the Prophet recommended it be drunk slowly, that hands should be washed before and after eating, to brush the teeth, bath regularly and smell nice. These are but some of the manners and grooming introduced by the Prophet in the 7th century world. Traditions, especially those reported from the Prophet, served to give Muslims a common identity for centuries in populations of diverse demographic, cultural and racial background.

The fundamental practices of Islam, termed the pillars of Islam, have the greatest impact for the practising Muslim. With the profession of the *shahadah* (the creed of Islam) in front of witnesses, a person recognises the one and only God and Muhammad as a true Prophet of God and hence becomes a Muslim. This public acknowledgment commits a person to a lifelong process of learning, spiritual development and community involvement, conducted at one's own pace.

While the daily prayers bring a person closer to God they also engender humility in a person by the physical act of prostration. A humble Muslim realises the value of the basics of life through the month-long fast. More importantly, he or she realises the hardships that the less fortunate go through every day. Coming out of Ramadan with strengthened will-power and a spirit of compassion, a Muslim is more inclined to pay *zakat* alms to the poor and needy.

Such development over years reaches its climax with pilgrimage. The oneness of God and the oneness of the message of God resonate with the realisation of the oneness of humanity. Islam truly leaves a lasting positive impression on the life of a practising Muslim.

Muslims have strong connections to their religious heritage and customs. Do you agree with this statement and why?

In his farewell speech during his first and last pilgrimage, the Prophet Muhammad outlined very important principles to more than a hundred thousand Muslims. Many historians consider this speech to be the first Declaration of Human Rights in history. In this speech, he strongly recommended that a Muslim should hold tight to two things – the Qur'an and the Sunnah (his example). He warned them that they would deviate not only from religion but also from their newly found social success if they did not adhere to the ideals and principles embodied in these two sources. It is for this reason that Muslims have always had a strong connection with their religious heritage.

Muslims believe the Qur'an is the final word of God. They take it as an instruction manual for human beings and societies. They have a high level of trust in its authenticity [SEE QUESTION 19]. The example of Muhammad, the living and practical reflection of the Qur'an, is also preserved with great accuracy in *hadith* books. Collectively, Muslims have a strong conviction that the Islam they know and practice is the one given by God to Muhammad. This perspective, coupled with the admonition of Muhammad to hold onto the Qur'an and Sunnah, provides a strong attachment to Islam by practising Muslims.

When we examine the corpus of narratives from the Prophet, we realise that Muhammad commented on every aspect of life. He educated his followers in topics ranging from how to run a state to table manners. A wide spectrum of life ranging from personal hygiene to international relations is covered by Prophet Muhammad's example. Although it is not compulsory (but highly recommended) to follow the Prophet Muhammad in everything,

Islam became not only a belief system but also a practical system of life for Muslims.

Eager Muslims in the early centuries of Islam lived Islam to the point that existing cultures were significantly altered and Islam became the culture of society as a whole, thus generating a unique Islamic Civilisation transcending all local cultures. QUESTION 64 explains the line of demarcation between culture and religion in Muslim society.

If one has committed sins and wrongdoings in one's life, how is this seen and what effect does it have on a Muslim's morality?

Islam lays out clearly which actions are good and which actions are frowned upon. Although there is no list of "Ten Commandments" or "Seven Deadly Sins", there are similar counterparts in Islam. Personal integrity, charity, honesty, compassion and self-control are virtues that are encouraged. Idolatry, gossip, slandering innocent people, murder, theft, disobeying parents, giving false testimony and sexual promiscuity are sins in Islam.

One of the fundamental concepts in Islam is that human beings are essentially good. Humans are also given the freedom to choose their actions. It necessarily follows that a number of choices must be available for humans to choose from. Choices can be clearly good or evil or else they fall within a wide grey area of uncertainty. Muslims are encouraged to rely on their conscience as a guide in the grey area of life. When a man asked the Prophet Muhammad what a sin was, he answered, *"Give up something when it bothers your conscience."*

Freedom of choice also requires that an intention must be present before a choice is made. Therefore, individuals following a moral code revealed to them by God are judged by their intentions and not just their actions. An unintended sinful action may not be deemed punishable if it is not accompanied by an impure intention. This is very similar to the concept of *mens rea* (the guilty mind) in criminal law.

A Muslim should consider a sinful act as a dangerous deviation from the balanced state of being. The Prophet Muhammad said that every wrongful act places a black dot on one's otherwise clear heart. If these black dots are not cleared, in time the whole heart becomes black, rendering it opaque to goodness and faith.

The conflicting feelings of guilt and the persistence of the sinful act over a long period of time does not produce a healthy state of being. In order to relieve the painful feeling, a person (unable to stop the sinful act) may interpret a minor hint against the tenets of faith as major evidence and lapse into disbelief. The individual may rationalise in his mind that if, after all, God does not exist, there is no reason to feel guilty. So he looks for an excuse to reject God. However, the feeling of unsatisfactoriness (guilt) is necessary for us to question our actions and effect change for the better. Without this feeling we can never improve as a person.

Islam deals with this paradox through the system of repentance, in which a person faces himself honestly and resolves to change and get rid of the guilty feeling. When a few Muslims came to the Prophet Muhammad complaining about their inability to lead perfect lives, the smiling Prophet said, *"If you never sinned and repented, God would have created another being who would do so,"* indicating that our sinful nature is intended in our design. But why?

Without the capacity to sin, the option to commit a sinful act makes no sense. And without the option to commit a sinful act, we cannot talk about freedom of choice. It is this freedom and our choice for goodness despite the possibility of evil that makes human activity extremely valuable. We cannot talk about a very accurate computer as a "truthful" computer because it is programmed to always give the right answer. However, we say that a person is 'truthful', because she chooses to stick to the truth, even though it was possible that she could have easily chosen to lie. She becomes virtuous, while the computer simply does what it is supposed to do.

Furthermore, the only possible way to consistently achieve human improvement is through erring and taking corrective action. It is simply not possible to continually improve ourselves without failures or sins. From time to time we get stuck at a particular level,

QUESTION 51

with no improvement. Failures or sins, coupled with the resolve to change for the better (repentance), trigger the inner impetus for further development. This is the principle used in making steel. The repetitive actions of heating, beating and dipping in cold water create the hardness of the steel. Trials in life and inner struggles cause a person to develop spiritually and to become an integrated being.

Where there is freedom of choice, some people will inevitably make wrong choices. In Islam a sin is considered to have occurred when a person knowingly harms himself or some other part of creation. Since not everyone could know what is harmful, the Qur'an acts as a guide for a Muslim, directing his or her behaviour towards useful actions and away from the harmful.

Muslims follow a process of repentance to ensure the clearing of the heart and neutralising the damaging effects of the sinful acts on the immediate environment. This is a four-stepped process as follows:

- One should feel remorse for the sinful act in one's heart [QUR'AN, 9:118].
- One should verbally ask for forgiveness from God [QUR'AN, 7:149].
- One should resolve not to commit the sin again [QUR'AN, 4:18, 20:82].
- One is to compensate for the sinful act by performing a good act and if possible attempt a reconciliation with the people involved [QUR'AN, 13:22].

Repentance in Islam is not a sacrament. It is a matter between the individual and God and does not require a third party to endorse it. Then how does a Muslim know he or she is forgiven? The Qur'an says that if the process of sincere repentance described above is followed then one should know he or she is forgiven and should move on. "*God accepts the repentance of those who do evil in ignorance and repent soon afterwards; to them will God turn in mercy: For God is full of knowledge and wisdom.*" [QUR'AN, 4:17] QUESTIONS 22–24 provide more information on this subject.

Some Muslims have a beard and some don't. Why is this the case?

Growing a beard for Muslim men is considered as a Sunnah practice, one of the verbal and active traditions deriving from the Prophet Muhammad. The Prophet Muhammad encouraged Muslim men to grow a beard, which is a natural male characteristic. At the same time, in line with the general Islamic principle of having a pleasant, tidy and clean look, he instructed his followers to make sure the moustache was short and above the lips and that the beard was trimmed, brushed and no longer than a fistful.

In order to understand why some Muslims grow a beard and others don't, we need to examine how one should understand the Sunnah and its implementation. The Sunnah of the Prophet Muhammad has four varying levels of importance in the religious context which therefore demand varying levels of responsibility from Muslims. Moreover, all Sunnah should be based on proven narratives from the Prophet Muhammad collected in *hadith* books.

1. Some aspects of the Sunnah are very strong, such as the building of a mosque for the Muslim community if no mosque exists and the recitation of *azan* (the call to prayer). A Sunnah that falls into this category is termed a "sign of Islam" in a land and is placed at a higher level than individual obligations. These Sunnah are few in number but are incontestable and cannot be changed in any way.

2. The practices of the Prophet that related to worship constitute the second level of Sunnah. The Qur'an enjoins Muslims to make *salat* (prayer) but does not prescribe exactly how this is to be done. Similarly, it enjoins Muslims to pay *zakat* (alms), but does not detail exactly how this is calculated or what assets are applicable for *zakat*. We learn the complete picture of the Islamic practice from the

QUESTION 52

Prophet himself. This is to be expected, since the Qur'an points out that all the Prophets received, "...*the Book and Wisdom*..." [QUR'AN, 3:81], the "Book" being the revelation and "Wisdom" being the practice of the revelation and explanations of its teachings. Moreover, if the revelation detailed everything it would render it hard to record and preserve and pass on to future generations. There are, for example, optional Sunnah prayers around the five daily prayers. To wake up for an early morning breakfast (*sahoor*) before dawn on a day of fasting is also considered as Sunnah. These are described in the books of Islamic jurisprudence, and to change a clear practice of the Prophet related to worship is considered as innovation (*bid'a*) and strongly discouraged by the Prophet himself. Muslims are highly advised to follow this type of Sunnah to complete their worship.

3. The third category of Sunnah covers moral conduct and the model deportment (*akhlaq*) of the Prophet, who said, "*I was sent to complete the perfect akhlaq (moral conduct)*". Muslims are expected to follow the Prophet's exemplary behaviour and virtuous character [SEE ANSWER TO QUESTION 17 FOR EXAMPLES OF HIS CHARACTER]. This aspect of the Sunnah is very important for Muslims, especially at our time when there is an observable gap between the actual behaviour of Muslims and the model lived by the Prophet.

4. The fourth category of the Sunnah is called *adab* (etiquette/ manners) and it covers the Prophet's habitual actions in everyday life, whether in speaking, dressing, appearance, eating, sleeping, etc. When the Prophet established the first community in Medina, he found people had few manners. They would gulp water, eat food with all ten fingers, dress untidily and grow facial hair with long moustaches over their lips and long scruffy looking beards. Naturally, he showed a good example in everyday manners and encouraged people to follow it. Behaviour that opposes this category

of Sunnah is not defined as opposed to Islam, but is recommended as optional good conduct.

Although all Muslim scholars are in consensus that growing the beard is a practice of the Prophet and the norm to be encouraged for all Muslim men, there is difference of opinion as to where it sits in the above-mentioned categories. Some see the beard as a visual sign that a person is a Muslim, and therefore for them it falls in the first category as an obligation for all men. Others say that it is part of one's personal appearance, and therefore falls in the category of the habitual Sunnah. Growing the beard is therefore optional for them.

Regardless of what a Muslim might think, those who grow a beard do so to follow the example of the Prophet in their physical appearance or to differentiate themselves as Muslims. Those who do not grow the beard do so either because they are not practising Muslims or choose not to practise an optional part of the Sunnah in their unique personal circumstances.

Chapter 5

Spirituality in a Mosque

The whole earth is a place of worship for Muslims. The Qur'an includes other places of worship, for example, churches and synagogues, as places where God is abundantly remembered [QUR'AN, 22:40]. *Therefore, Muslims can pray on any clean ground, including churches and synagogues.*

In this chapter, you will find more about the holy places of Islam, mosques, congregational practices and the spiritual experience of a Muslim in a place of worship.

What are the sacred places of Islam?

There are three tiers of sacred places for Muslims: the whole earth; places of worship and in particular three main mosques; and cities significant in the history of monotheism and the early development of Islam.

The Prophet Muhammad said that he is to be distinguished from previous prophets in the way the whole earth is granted as a place of worship. He said (as narrated by Jabir), "...*I have been granted five things which were not granted to any one before me... and for me the earth has been made a mosque and a means of purification; therefore if prayer overtakes any person of my congregation, he should say his prayers (wherever he is)...*" Therefore a Muslim may pray at any place, as long as he or she is facing the *Ka'bah* located in the Mosque of Sanctuary (*Masjid-al Haram*) in Mecca. You might have seen a group of Muslims laying a mat and lining up to pray in the park. This public expression of collective or individual prayer is perfectly normal for Muslims throughout the globe. The concept of the whole earth as a place of worship has the extended meaning that for Muslims the earth and land are sacred. For as long as Muslims are free to live their religion in any corner of the earth, it can be figuratively considered as a Muslim land.

In the second tier, all places dedicated to the worship of God such as mosques or prayer halls are also sacred in Islam. Sometimes the figurative "house of God" is used to refer to a mosque in Muslim terminology and literature. This labelling simply means that a mosque is a place dedicated to the glorification, praise and worship of God. Since the inside of a mosque is a "holy ground", Muslims take their shoes off when entering. Taking off the shoes also ensures the place of prostration is clean of any physical impurities.

QUESTION 53

In Islam, there are three holy cities – Mecca, Medina and Jerusalem – and three mosques – the Mosque of Sanctuary, the Mosque of the Prophet and the Sacred Mosque, which are the mosques in the three holy cities.

■ **Mecca and the Mosque of Sanctuary:** Mecca was established as a settlement when Abraham left his son Ishmael together with Hagar in the valley of Beca, where they rebuilt the *Ka'bah* as a centre for monotheism. It later became a bustling city for traders. The mosque where the *Ka'bah* is located is called the Mosque of Sanctuary. The present capacity of this mosque is in the vicinity of one million people [SEE QUESTION 54 FOR MORE ON *KA'BAH* AND ITS SIGNIFICANCE]. The Prophet Muhammad was born in Mecca and received his first revelation in a cave on the outskirts of the city. Mecca is also the Pilgrimage centre of the Muslim world [SEE QUESTIONS 44–45].

■ **Medina and the Mosque of the Prophet:** In the year 622 (Common Era), escaping the persecution in Mecca, Muslims and the Prophet Muhammad migrated to Yathrib, a city about 450 kilometres north of Mecca. The first Muslim society and polity was established in Yathrib, which came to be called the City (*medina*) of the Prophet. In time, the name Medina stuck. The Prophet Muhammad built the first mosque of Islam in Medina and next to it a few small rooms where he resided together with his family. He passed away in one of these rooms and was buried where he died. The building was extended many times in history, with the most recent extension being made a few decades ago. The present mosque can accommodate about 250,000 worshippers at the same time.

■ **Jerusalem and the Sacred Mosque (*Masjid-al Aqsa*):** Jerusalem is the name derived from the Arabic phrase *Dar-ussalam* meaning "the place of peace". It is the city where many prophets recognised in Islam served their missions. These include Abraham, John the Baptist, Jesus, Solomon, David and many more. Muslims believe that in a miraculous night Journey [QUR'AN, 17:1] the Prophet Muhammad travelled to Jerusalem and led a prayer session to the spirits of all the prophets in the Sacred Mosque. This mosque also served as the first direction for prayer (*qiblah*) for Muslims during the first fifteen years of Muhammad's mission.

In addition to these cities, Karbala, where the Prophet's grandson Hussain was martyred and buried, is an especially sacred place for Shiite Muslims. Another city held in high-regard by Shiite Muslims is Najaf, where the fourth caliph and the Prophet's son-in-law, Ali, are buried [SEE THE ANSWER TO QUESTION 66 FOR MORE ON THE DIFFERENCES BETWEEN SHIITE AND SUNNI MUSLIMS]. Both cities are located in present day Iraq.

Q54

What is the *Ka'bah*? Do Muslims worship the *Ka'bah*? Why do Muslims face in the direction of the *Ka'bah* when praying?

The Arabic word for *Ka'bah* simply means "cube". It is a simple cube-shaped stone-bricked structure, measuring about 10 by 11 metres and covered with a heavy black cloth. It is located in the middle of the Mosque of Sanctuary (*Masjid-al Haram*) in Mecca, the birthplace of the Prophet Muhammad. *"God has made the Ka'bah, the Sacred House, an asylum of security for mankind..."* explains the Qur'an [5:97].

The *Ka'bah* is considered to be the first shrine in the history of mankind to be erected for the worship of the one and only God. *"Verily! The first House (of worship) appointed for mankind was that at Mecca, a blessed place, a guidance to the peoples"* [QUR'AN, 3:96]. In addition to some reports that the *Ka'bah* was built by the first human and prophet, Adam, the Qur'an [2:127] talks about the *Ka'bah* being erected again by Abraham and his son Ishmail. Ishmail was also to be the first prophet sent to the people of the Arabian Peninsula. The Prophet Muhammad's lineage goes back to Abraham through Ishmail and his sons.

In the early years of Islam, Muslims faced in the direction of the Sacred Mosque (*Masjid-al Aqsa*) in Jerusalem. In Medina, the direction of worship was changed by a verse of the Qur'an [2:144] to the direction of the *Ka'bah*. Since then, Muslims have always faced in this direction (called *qiblah*) to pray. When Muslims pray they form circular rows all around the world similar to ripples in a pond of water. At the level of a mosque congregation, facing in one direction brings order and harmony to the act of worship. At the global level, facing the same direction unites Muslims in the shared act of worshipping one God. Some people have suggested that in every second of the day, there's at least one person praying and facing Mecca.

The *Ka'bah* does not have any divinity nor is it believed that it is part of the Divine. Muslims certainly do not worship the *Ka'bah*. However, it is believed that it marks the location of an important spiritual axis that extends in both directions across the universe. The physical building itself is a historic structure and an important heritage of monotheism. The *Ka'bah* has been the spiritual epicentre for humans for thousands of years.

Some allege that Islam came from a pagan tradition. They cite the *Ka'bah* as evidence, in that the pre-Islamic pagan society used to venerate and pay pilgrimage to it. It is correct that before Islam pagan Arabs made pilgrimage to the *Ka'bah*. They also filled it with 360 idols. However, this does not mean that Islam is a product of idolatry. Muslims find this allegation ridiculous, since Islam is opposed to just about everything that pagan idolatry stood for. Although Meccans worshipped idols they also believed in an unreachable God called "Allah". They also remembered and held in high esteem Abraham and Ishmail. Belief in a supreme God and the *Ka'bah* as a place of pilgrimage were all remnants of the original religion of Abraham.

I have said in many places in this book that Islam does not claim to be a new religion. The primary mission of Islam was to reform religion itself by removing superstitious ideas about God and to bring religion back to its pristine form of believing in and worshipping one God as one human race. Since none of the ancient religions changed completely, it is natural that some of their true aspects need no alteration. In a similar way, the *Ka'bah*, which was originally dedicated as a centre of monotheism, changed over time and became a centre of idolatry. Islam brought it back to its intended past function. Also the pilgrimage initiated by Abraham was changed over time to include many strange practices, such as circling the *Ka'bah* naked. Islam also refined this ancient practice of monotheism back to its proper essentials.

QUESTION 54

As another independent source of information, the Bible also makes reference to the importance of Mecca and the tradition of paying pilgrimage there: *"O Lord Almighty, my King and my God, Blessed are those who dwell in Your House; they are ever praising You. Blessed are those whose strength is in You, who have set their hearts on pilgrimage. As they pass through the valley of Beca, they make it a place of springs; the autumn rains also cover it with pools"* [PSALMS 84:4–6]. The valley where Mecca stands is called the Valley of Baca.

What are the main features of a Mosque? Does the architecture have any symbolical meaning?

The Arabic word for mosque is *masjid,* a place of prostration. A mosque is a gathering place for worship, meditation and learning. Every mosque has five standard functional features:

1. The *mihrab* is a niche on the front wall, where the *imam* (prayer leader) stands to lead the daily prayers. It indicates the direction of the *Ka'bah* in Mecca which according to Islamic belief is the oldest place of worship in human history. The niche serves to reflect the voice of the *imam* back to the congregation, since the *imam* faces the same direction as the congregation.

2. The *mimbar* is the raised pulpit with several steps used by the *imam* to deliver Friday sermons to the gathered congregation. It enables the congregation and *imam* to see each other.

3. The internal courtyard is the open space where people offer their prayers. Since Muslim prayers are composed of certain movements that include prostration, there is no furniture in a mosque other than some chairs for the elderly and disabled [SEE QUESTION 37 FOR THE EXPLANATION OF MOVEMENTS IN THE PRAYER].

4. One or more external towers, which are called *minarets,* are used to call people to prayer by reciting a special passage called the *azan* [FOR MORE ON THE *AZAN* SEE QUESTION 61].

5. Since Muslims need to cleanse themselves prior to a prayer, an area is reserved for ritual ablution away from the main prayer area.

In addition to these features, some mosques have a separate pulpit called the *kursi* for informal lectures and sermons and in order not to unnecessarily occupy the *mimbar,* sometimes referred to as "the Prophet's pulpit".

QUESTION 55

Since Muslims consider the mosque as "holy ground" and prostrate during prayers, cleanliness within the mosque is very important. Muslims do not wear shoes in a mosque nor eat or drink there, so as to maintain a clean environment.

The simple mosque built by the Prophet Muhammad consisted of four walls and a date-leaf roof supported by timber columns. Over time, as Islamic civilisation developed and Muslims got richer, Muslim architects turned every functional feature of a mosque into an art form. The features of a mosque and its architecture gained a certain symbolism in line with the development and sophistication of Islamic art and architecture. It is important to note that the symbolism of the structure comes from the architect or the artist, not necessarily from the religion itself.

One of the most celebrated Muslim architects of the 17th century, the architect Sinan, explained in his biography how multiple meanings were attributed to the same structure following the arts of his time. For instance, the Suleymaniye mosque in Istanbul is built on the model of the *Ka'bah* in Mecca. The main pillars represent the major ancient civilisations in the pre-Islamic period, because each pillar was brought from the relics of a different civilisation such as Egypt, Babylon and Rome. The dome represents Islam, which rises on the past legacy of humanity. The interior of the mosque is paradise. The fountains of paradise are represented by a fountain used for ablution. The colours from the coloured glass of the windows symbolise the wings of the angels in paradise. Another dimension of meaning is that the four pillars represent the four Rightly-Guided successors (Caliphs) to Muhammad while the dome represents the Prophet himself. Similarly, while the dome represents the declaration of faith, the four supporting columns represent the remaining four pillars of Islam.

The use of the dome, which was adopted from Byzantine architecture and widely used by the Seljuk and Ottoman architects, come to symbolise a typical Muslim mosque. The functional purpose of the dome is to provide a vast open space without breaking it with pillars. It also serves to provide acoustics and natural ventilation. The shape of the dome also reflects the perfect balance of Islamic monotheism. The dome's exterior, which extends to the infinity of heaven, is the same shape as the interior, thus reflecting the ideal conformity of the inner and outer aspects of a Muslim.

In a mosque, the domed structure, the simplicity of the internal features, the beauty of the natural motifs in the wall decorations and the internal cleanliness create a spiritual and peaceful atmosphere that lifts the heart and spirit.

Why aren't there any pictures or images inside the mosque?

The absolute unity of God being the most important tenet of Islam, its essence is the concept of monotheism. Muslims believe that the transcendence of God cannot be adequately expressed by any image. For Muslims, not only does figurative art violate the unity and divinity of God, but also distracts a worshipper from the transcendence of God. Therefore you will not find statues or icons of God in Muslim mosques.

Islam was revealed in order to replace the worship of idols. The Prophet Muhammad explained that one of the causes of ancient idol worship was the custom of placing images of national heroes, holy people, kings and so on in places of worship. Over time, the original reasons for installing the images were forgotten and people came to associate divine attributes with the persons the statues represented. For this reason Muslims do not carve statues or paint pictures of Muhammad.

In Islam, God is totally unlike His creation [QUR'AN, 112:4]. This is similar to the artist being different to his works of art or an author being completely different to the book he has written. Muslims argue that the universe is a work of art, and the Artist cannot be in the universe. Creation is a book, the Author of which, God, is unlike anything we are familiar with in the universe. Moreover, God created space and time and therefore these two defining dimensions of physical existence do not bind God. Any attempt to represent such a transcendence reality is bound to fail and therefore is a blasphemous act.

Furthermore, placing statues and images in a place of worship distracts the worshipper from the transcendence of God. If there were statues or pictures of God, people, especially children, would imagine God in the image of those pictures, again opening the door for people to develop false perceptions about God.

In some religions images are used in places of worship to help a person have a personal relationship with God. Islam argues that we don't need to bring God to ourselves. He is already closer to us than our jugular veins [QUR'AN, 50:16]. By focusing on the qualities and divine names of God rather than on what God might look like, Muslims get a better feel for God and see His presence in everyday life, nature and the universe, without feeling the need to see a physical image [SEE QUESTIONS 2–5].

What significance does the mosque have for a Muslim and what is its role in Muslim society?

Mosques are places where individual and congregational prayers can take place. It is the place where members of the community can hold social and religious services.

Although Muslims can pray in any clean place, Friday congregational prayers can only be performed in a mosque. For Muslims, the building of a mosque for the purpose of divine worship is an event worthy of divine recognition. *"...Whoever builds a mosque, desiring thereby God's pleasure, God builds for him the like of it in paradise..."* said the Prophet Muhammad. In stating, *"and the mosques are for God..."* [QUR'AN, 72:18], the Qur'an gives them significance and an exalted position above any other man-made construction. Hence, Muslims have always established mosques wherever they have settled in sufficient numbers. The existence of a mosque in a land has come to symbolise the existence of a Muslim community and the freedom to practice Islam openly. Once a mosque has been erected, it can no longer be used for any other purpose.

The first thing that the Prophet did after his migration to Medina was to establish a mosque for the city. Next to the mosque a school functioned as a centre for learning. The mosque in Medina was used for all the social and administrative affairs of the people. It was the place where Muhammad led prayers, taught Muslims, listened to people, met foreign delegates and held public meetings. In addition to the main mosque in Medina, around forty other mosques were established in towns and the provinces during the lifetime of the Prophet. The multi-faceted function of the mosque continued throughout history and the mosque became a complex where all the educational (schools, universities), social (charities), physical (hospitals, baths) and spiritual needs of a community are met. Today, all mosques fulfil some or all of these functions. Although not compulsory, marriages and funeral prayer services also generally take place in a mosque.

Perhaps, most importantly, congregational services in the mosque demonstrate the unique force of Islamic prayer in unifying the human race, since all Muslims stand shoulder to shoulder before their Creator regardless of racial or social distinctions.

Q58

Could you outline the prayer service in a mosque? What exactly goes on in a mosque? What are the ceremonies held in a mosque? Why do men and women worship separately? What language is used in prayer services?

All of the three types of Islamic worship, *salat* (daily prescribed prayers), *du'a* (supplication) and *zhikr* (remembrance), occur in a mosque [SEE THE ANSWER TO QUESTION 35 FOR A DESCRIPTION OF THESE TYPES OF WORSHIP]. While each can be done individually, daily-prescribed prayers are generally done in a congregation in a mosque or in any other suitable place. Muslims numbering three or more always pray together, even if they are at home or out in the park.

The language of *salat* is in Arabic, while *du'a* could be in any language that a worshipper speaks and understands. *Zhikr* consists of chanting short Arabic phrases of praise, exaltation and glorification of God openly or quietly. It also involves repeating the names of God many times, like a mantra, while keeping God in one's awareness.

During a prayer session, the congregation lines up in tight rows behind a person who wears the title of *imam* only during the prayer. Everyone in the congregation, including the *imam*, face the *qiblah*, which is the direction of the *Ka'bah* in Mecca and marked by a small niche (*mihrab*) on the mosque wall. The rows are tight as people make sure that the shoulder of one touches the shoulder of the next person. The Prophet Muhammad said, *"Make sure your shoulders are touching so that the devil does not walk between you."* His reference was to the devil of pride, social status, wealth and any thought of racial superiority, practically demonstrating the oneness of humanity in Islam. Children are scattered among the congregation or next to their family members, depending on their age.

Because of the physical closeness and the act of prostrating during the prayer, ladies usually line up at the back of men purely for their comfort and to ensure that all can have maximum spiritual focus. In some mosques, gallery levels are reserved for ladies or the room is split in half to accommodate men and women. Although this is usually done to give more space and comfort to men and ladies, no such practices existed at the time of the Prophet Muhammad. Incidentally, in the Mosque of Sanctuary in Mecca, the normal arrangement is not possible near the *Ka'bah* because of the sheer number of people and the circular rows. Consequently, men and women pray in mixed rows. Having said that, I should stress that the purpose of prayer in mosque is not to facilitate social interaction with men and women, but rather is to reinforce one another's spiritual journey to get closer to God.

For those who may think that praying in separate rows is segregation for women let me tell you an anecdote. I was asked to talk about Islam to a group of about one hundred High School students in Sydney. During the discussion, their teacher suddenly asked them to do the movements of the Muslim *salat* together. But he lined them up in mixed rows. Even though these kids were not Muslim, it was noticeable that girls did not want their shoulders to touch those of the boys and they could not prostrate because there were boys behind them. At this point, I asked them wouldn't it be better if you lined up the rows as the Muslims usually do. All the girls agreed to my proposition.

Once everyone is lined up for *salat*, the whole congregation goes through the movements of the prayer [DESCRIBED IN QUESTION 37] in unison. While the *imam* recites passages of the Qur'an on behalf of the whole congregation, the normal phrases repeated in personal prayers are also quietly repeated by each individual at every stage of the prayer.

QUESTION 58

In a mosque there are other services offered in addition to the daily prayers. All Muslim men must attend congregational prayer at noontime on Friday, while attendance for women is optional. An obligation for both men and women to attend would be a hardship for families with children. In addition to the Friday congregational prayer the *imam* delivers a Friday sermon. Funeral prayers are also done in a mosque, coinciding with daily prayer times when there is a congregation in the mosque. Although the wedding ceremony is not a sacrament in Islam, it is also usually performed in a mosque.

In addition to the main function of the mosque as a place of worship, the mosque also functions as a community centre for learning, charitable and social services [SEE QUESTION 57].

Q59

What is the role of the *imam* in the mosque? What hierarchical position does the *imam* hold in a mosque? Does Islam have a clergy? Is there only one *imam* in a mosque? Can a woman lead the prayer or become an *imam*?

The word *imam* literally means a person "standing in front". In religious terminology, it denotes the person who leads prayer in a congregation of Muslims. The *imam* also usually delivers the Friday sermons. Since Islam has no sacraments, such as marriage, baptism, confession, etc., that can only be performed under the supervision of anointed people, an *imam* does not need to be anointed to perform religious duties.

In the time of the Prophet Muhammad, he led all the prayers in the mosque. When he was sick or out of town, he always appointed a person who knew the Qur'an well from amongst his companions to lead the prayers temporarily. He also appointed *imams* to lead prayers in other mosques established during his lifetime. The appointment of Muhammad was never understood to be an anointment. It was simply understood as an assignment to fulfil a role.

After the Prophet, Muslims usually preferred people who had good Qur'anic and scholarly knowledge to act as a semi-permanent *imam* in the mosque. Full-time, paid *imams* came much later, when endowments (*vaqf*), which built and maintained mosques, also selected the *imams*. A grand mosque with a large congregation had more than one *imam*. During the time of the Ottomans, the Sultan, who usually approved the local selection, would appoint the *imam*. The *imam* had some legal, social and religious duties in the precinct that he served.

In some countries with a Muslim majority, such as Turkey, a department of religious affairs exists. This department has *imam* personnel and an administrative hierarchy. Secular regimes or

QUESTION 59

military dictatorships usually established these departments to have some control over religion. Shiite Muslims usually have a hierarchy of clergy that ranges from a *Grand Ayatullah* to a *mullah*. They are considered to be the learned class of Shiite Muslims. At present there are very few Muslim countries (Bosnia is one example) where religious leaders have complete independence.

Today, in most of the mosques that exist in Western countries, the mosque administration appoints its own *imam*. If the full time *imam* does not exist or is absent for a particular prayer service, the usual practice is a democratic one. Any Muslim who knows the Qur'an well and knows how to lead a prayer (this criteria covers almost all practising Muslims) is usually invited from among the congregation to lead the prayer.

Since there is no "church" establishment in Islam, usually mosques are built by rich individuals and non-profit-making organisations. When a person funds a mosque, he or she dedicates it to God for community use and relinquishes ownership forever. Consequently, every mosque is independent. In theory, there is no limit to the number of mosques that can be built in any one area. In Australia, migrant communities funded the establishment of the mosques. The consequence of this is that a particular ethnic community becomes the dominant part of the congregation. Nevertheless, a Muslim goes to any mosque to pray that is at a convenient location and a place where he or she can benefit the most.

Although, there are no clergy in Islam, the Prophet Muhammad said that the *ulema* (learned scholars) were heirs to Islam. Learned men and women, who focused on religious learning and teaching, have always been the benefactors of Islam. A passing of knowledge from teacher to student in the form of a diploma (*ijazah*) was the means of guaranteeing scholarly legitimacy. The best of scholars who mastered all the Islamic sciences were called *mujtahids*, and could interpret Islamic law through deductive reasoning. A *mufti* was a person who gave religious rulings in a local area. Today Muslims coming from diverse educational backgrounds are increasingly involved in religious learning and teaching.

A woman can lead the prayer in a congregation of women. Since a woman cannot practically stand before men in prayer, as explained in the previous question, women do not lead a congregation made up of men and women. Women usually bypass the intermediary step of the *imam* role and go to higher scholarly roles. In Islam, both men and women can take religious leadership roles provided they prove their knowledge and spiritual insight. A process of selection by the people works here. There were great women scholars and spiritual leaders in the past, such as Aisha, Muhammd's wife, and Rabi'a al Adawiya (d. 796) who passed on their knowledge and spiritual insights to men and women alike.

Can an *imam* get married in Islam? Are *imams* celibate? What do you have to do to become an *imam*? Is there a training school for religious leaders in mosques?

In Islam, the only criterion that qualifies a person to lead prayer is to know enough passages from the Qur'an and to know how to lead a prayer. This just about qualifies every practising Muslim as an *imam*. Two or more Muslims can make up a congregation in any place. Worshippers usually select someone to lead the prayer session. Almost every mosque has an appointed full-time or part-time *imam* who leads the prayers and is in charge of religious teaching. In larger mosques, such as the ones in major Muslims countries, where tens of thousands of people form the congregation, more than one *imam* may be appointed as the need arises.

In appointing a full-time *imam*, the management committee of a mosque looks for evidence of religious acumen and some form of higher education in religion. Most universities in Muslim countries have schools of theology where people develop their learning and receive academic qualifications. Some of the most notable universities are the International Islamic University in Malaysia, the prestigious Al-Azhar University in Egypt and the Divinity School in Marmara University in Turkey.

Imams do not need to be celibate. In fact, Islam views sexual activity within marriage as a blessing of God to be cherished and not as an obstacle to ascent in the ranks of spirituality. For Muslims the important thing is not to denounce the world and its pleasures totally but not to have any real attachment to them. This is best illustrated in the example of the Prophet. He was married yet he said, *"What have I to do with worldly things? My connection with the world is like that of a traveller resting for a while underneath the shade of a tree and then moving on."*

Islam does not have separate expectations for the "average Muslim" and those who elect to practice at a higher level. Rather, the injunctions of the Qur'an apply to all Muslims equally. The personal practice of the Prophet has shown an optional path to those who want to go a step further in their spiritual and personal development. Nevertheless, there have been and still are few spiritual leaders (B. Said Nursi, d. 1960, is one example) who have chosen to be celibate or delayed their marriage in order to dedicate their life to the service of God.

What is the significance of *azan* (the Muslim call to prayer)? Is it allowed to be read aloud in non-Muslim countries? What is the role of the *muazzin* in the mosque?

One of the first things a non-Muslim traveller to a Muslim country notices is the echoing of the call to prayer at regular intervals during the day. Muslims announce the time of daily prayer by reciting a special call named *azan*, consisting of announcing the greatness of God, the creed of Islam, as well as inviting people to prayer. *Azan* is always recited loudly in Arabic, irrespective of the country in which it is performed. The Arabic original and its translation are given below.

Arabic Transliteration

Allahu Akbar, Allahu Akbar
Allahu Akbar, Allahu Akbar
Ashadu an la ilaha ill Allah
Ashadu an la ilaha ill Allah
Ashadu anna Muhammadar Rasulullah
Ashadu anna Muhammadar Rasulullah
Haya alas salah, Haya alas salah
Haya alal falah, Haya alal falah
Allahu Akbar, Allahu Akbar
La ilaha ill Allah

English Translation

God is the greatest, God is the greatest
God is the greatest, God is the greatest
I declare there is no deity but God

I declare there is no deity but God
I declare Muhammad is the Messenger of God,
I declare Muhammad is the Messenger of God
Come to prayer, come to prayer
Come to success, come to success
God is the greatest, God is the greatest
There is no deity but God

When the Prophet Muhammad built the first mosque in Medina after the migration from the oppressive city of Mecca, the question of how to inform people of the time of gathering for prayer arose. The Prophet consulted his companions, as was his usual habit in matters of public importance. While some suggested they should ring a bell like the Christians, others suggested blowing a horn like Jews or beating drums, and so on. No-one was satisfied by these suggestions. It had to be unique to Islam. The Prophet prayed for guidance over this issue. A few days later, a companion ran to the mosque and told the prophet that he saw a man calling some phrases in a loud voice asking people to come to prayer. After listening to these words, Muhammad said that the dream was from God and asked Bilal to go up the mosque wall and call these words. After hearing these words others came in saying that they heard these words in their dream. In this unique way, the *azan* became the Muslim call to prayer.

The person who recites the *azan* and a second reminder call just before the congregational prayer starts (*iqamah*) is called a *muazzin*. The *muazzin* acts as an assistant to the *imam*. As in the case of the *imam*, usually someone from the congregation assumes the role, although most mosques have a default person or a *muazzin* appointed by the management of the mosque. Usually someone who has the best voice is selected to be a *muazzin*.

QUESTION 61

The *muazzin* of the Prophet Muhammad was Bilal, a black African ex-slave with a beautiful voice. Bilal converted to Islam as a slave and suffered torture at the hands of his non-Muslim owner. Abu Bakr, bought and freed Bilal to end his persecution. Bilal carried out the role of "Muazzin of the Messenger" for more than ten years until the death of the Prophet. Out of sorrow, he vowed never to call *azan* again.

Azan is called out to the public from a tower called the *minaret*. Although the shape of the minaret changes from culture to culture and with the architectural style deployed in the mosque, the shape of "l" and "the pen" was used in a widespread manner by the Ottomans. This shape symbolised the importance Islam laid on the acquisition of knowledge and the unity of God. Knowledge and wisdom are especially important in Islam, since the first revelation to Muhammad was the commandment "to read" [QUR'AN, 96:1]. The Prophet also said that the gaining of knowledge is an obligation for all Muslims, both male and female.

Both *azan* and the *minaret* are counted among the key signs for the existence of Islam and Muslims in a land. In countries where Muslims form a minority, *azan* is not allowed to be called publicly on a daily basis. The building of *minarets* is allowed in most countries after some initial hesitation. Muslims also do not push to get permission to publicly call the *azan* in order not to disturb the non-Muslim residents near a mosque. Therefore, the role of the *muazzin* is less prominent in mosques outside of Muslim countries.

In Australia, the local government in Wollongong has allowed the Illawarra Mosque to call the *azan* for the Friday noon prayer. While recognising that the public recitation of the *azan* five times a day will disturb the majority of non-Muslims, it would be a good gesture of tolerance if local councils or governments were to allow the *azan* to be recited for the Friday noon prayers only.

Q62

Why does the Friday prayer have to be performed in a mosque? Why is Friday the holy day? If a person does not live near a mosque, how do they pray on Friday?

At the very least, Muslims are asked to come to the mosque once a week for the Friday noon prayer. This is obligatory for men but optional for women. "*O you who believe! When the call is proclaimed to prayer on Friday hasten earnestly to the Remembrance of God, and leave off business: That is best for you if you but knew!*" declares the Qur'an [62:9]. One of the first actions of the Prophet Muhammad when he migrated to Medina was to establish the Friday prayers. For Muslims, being able to perform the Friday prayer as a community is a symbol of religious freedom.

While all other prayers can be offered in any clean place on earth, the Friday prayer has to be performed in a mosque or a place dedicated to prayer. This is to ensure that once a week all Muslims get together to hear a sermon (*khutba*) delivered just before the shortened congregational prayer. The preacher usually starts with passages from the Qur'an and gives a short talk addressing the problems and affairs of the community. Muslims also feel the experience of belonging to a worldwide community focusing on God during every 24-hour period.

The significance of Friday lies in that there is an hour on Friday where God is said to accept any prayer. But we are not told when the exact hour is during the 24-hour period. In this way, Muslims are encouraged to spend as much of the day as possible in prayer, worship, mediation and reflection. The Prophet said, "*The best day on which the sun rises is Friday. On it Adam was created, on it he was expelled (from Paradise), on it his repentance was accepted, on it he died and on it the Last Hour will take place.*" Friday is also a festive day when Muslims celebrate the week and meet with each other at home or the mosque. The Prophet asked people to wash themselves and put on the finest fragrances and come to the mosque in their best clothes.

If a person cannot make it to prayer on time or does not live near a mosque, they just perform the regular noon prayer instead. Three or more Muslims living in the same area usually hire a hall to perform the Friday prayer as a congregation.

Chapter 6

Communal Experience of Islam

Although all religions have a level of community attachment, the sense of belonging to a Community of Believers (ummah) *is perhaps strongest in the case of Islam. All Muslims belong to a transnational community in an egaliterian brotherhood. "O mankind! We created you from a single (pair) of a male and a female, and made you into nations and tribes, that you may know each other (not that you may despise each other). Verily the most honoured of you in the sight of God is (he who is) the most righteous of you. And God has full knowledge and is well acquainted (with all things)" declared the Qur'an* [49:13] *fourteen centuries ago.*

Islam is a private and a public religion at the same time. It announces its creed five times a day in the call to prayer. Muslims stop their daily activity to pray five times a day, wherever they are. You cannot help but notice the scarf on a Muslim woman, fasting people in Ramadan and the spectacular Pilgrimage every year. Islam is very much in the social sphere for these reasons. In this chapter, we will look at the communal and the cultural experience of Muslims.

Q63

There seem to be different versions of Islam in various countries. Why is this the case? Are all Muslims of Arabic origin?

Only about 20% of about 1.2 billion Muslims around the world are from an Arabic background. Muslims are a majority in 56 countries, while there are small or significant minority Muslim populations in almost all countries around the globe. The largest Muslim country is an Asia-Pacific country, Indonesia. There are millions of Muslims in China and Islam will soon be the second largest religion after Christianity in the United States. Islam is truly a global religion.

Since the birth of Islam in the 7th century CE, it has drawn people from all races. The early Muslim believers who gathered around the Prophet Muhammad were from many tribes and races. The first person assigned to the duty of calling Muslims to prayer was Bilal, a black African. Islam attracted such people because of its universal message of the "oneness of humanity". Islam teaches that no-one is superior to any other except in their goodness and piety [QUR'AN, 46:13]. Therefore, all Muslims feel a level of attachment to the global community (*ummah*) of Muslims.

Irrespective of which Muslim country one may travel to in a vast region spanning from North America to the Philippines, the core of Islam, the essentials of faith and personal practice, serve as the same common denominator for all Muslims. All Muslims believe in one God; they all have the same version of the Qur'an; they believe in the Prophet Muhammad as the messenger of God and believe in the permanence of life after death. The five pillars of Islam are also essentially the same for all Muslims. Nevertheless, there is an observable variation in the way Islam manifests itself in the visible spheres of culture and society. A number of factors cause the variation:

QUESTION 63

1. The inherent flexibility of Islam, allowing varieties of cultures to flourish.
2. Difference in the level of development between Muslim countries.
3. Influences from other neighbouring cultures.
4. Differing historical experiences and attitudes.

Islam does not promote communities to be rigid and clones of one another. It sets the fundamental principles that should shape a society rather than a detailed set of complex prescriptions and rituals. For example, Islam asks men and women to cover certain parts of their bodies, not the fashion to be followed [SEE QUESTION 81 ABOUT WHY MUSLIMS ARE REQUIRED TO COVER THEIR BODIES]. Consequently, different styles of clothing have developed in different parts of the Muslim world. Similarly, Islam only requires a legal wedding ceremony and a public announcement in the case of a marriage. Therefore the customs of marriage differ widely from country to country. Sometimes even different provinces of the same country have developed a variety of marriage celebration styles.

The level of development of a country also impacts on the general character of a society and how Islam shapes it. For example, the marked differences between Afghanistan and Turkey may be partly attributed to the state of war-torn, underdeveloped Afghanistan and that of westernised and developed Turkey. And compare how women are treated in the two countries.

Sometimes neighbouring cultures can also influence a Muslim country, causing it to wear a distinctive look in comparison to other Muslim countries. For example, in Pakistan, the bride's family is expected to provide the groom with a car, furniture and sometimes a house, as is the custom in the neighbouring Hindu culture.

The historical experience of a nation can also influence its attitudes and how religion is perceived. Influenced by their experience in leading a multicultural empire, the Ottomans have always understood Islam as a tolerant religion. On the other hand the Shiite Muslims of Iran have a legacy of rebellion and a sense of being outcast that have shaped their attitudes for centuries.

All of these factors and others have meant that around the same core of religion and practice of Islam, rich cultural experiences have also flourished, giving an outsider the impression that Islam is practised differently in various Muslim nations.

In Islam, where does culture begin and religion stop?
You seem to make a distinction between Islam as a religion and Muslim culture, but isn't a society's culture inevitably shaped by religion?

Culture is a set of communal habits that shape everyday life in a society. Just as it is not possible to have an individual without a set of habits, it is not possible to have society without a culture. Just as some people knowingly keep doing the wrong things due to the compulsion of a habit, so too, people in a society may knowingly do the wrong thing because of bad communal habits that create a compelling force in spite of the teachings of religion.

By our very nature, we are created to develop habits, which bypass our freedom of choice and the space between the social and personal stimuli and the responses we give to those stimuli. Ninety-five percent of what we do each day is a result of our habits. Good habits are so because they conserve energy and time, but bad habits become destructive when we allow them to develop and linger on. Similarly, communal habits that determine the character of a culture conserve social energy. Culture easily shapes the behaviour of individuals without the necessity of having to educate and convince all the time. Just as in the case of bad individual habits, bad cultural habits also cause problems for all of society.

Habits in individuals are acquired over time through a conscious or unconscious conditioning produced by repetition. People get used to smoking over time even though the first few experiences of smoking are usually uncomfortable. Also habits do not go away overnight and it requires conscious alternative conditioning to break them. Similarly, cultural habits also develop over time and it becomes hard to change them when and if change is required.

When Islam first appeared on the historic scene, it changed the culture of the entire Arabic society for the better. It also had a similar impact on other cultures as it expanded. Since the early expansion was rapid around the epicentre of Mecca, the final cultural equilibrium that settled in at distant parts of the vast Muslim world has not always been the ideal cultural norm of Islam. Therefore, some cultural elements prior to Islam lingered on for centuries. One example is female circumcision, which continued to occur in Somalia, Sudan and some other African countries, both Muslim and non-Muslim. Although Islam does not require females to be circumcised, in these regions it stayed on as part of the culture.

In Islam, there is a clear line of demarcation between Islam and culture. The sources of Islam are clear – the Qur'an and the example of the Prophet. However, Islam and Muslim scholars also recognise culture (*orf*) as an important element of a society and consider it in formulating legal solutions when the religious sources do not give a directive on a particular matter.

I said earlier that culture has good elements. Let me give you an example. If you travel to a village in rural Turkey and knock on the door of a house and say you are the "guest of God", they will welcome you, give you the best room of the house to sleep in and feed you with the best food they have available. Hospitality has become a characteristic feature of Anatolian culture. Few people know that this tradition was developed over time as a result of the Prophet Muhammad's recommendation that every guest is a guest of God and it is the guest's right to receive offerings and not be turned away.

A cultural custom becomes dangerous when people forget how the custom connects with their religion. Loss of this connection can alter the good communal habits that have developed because of religious teachings. Let me give you an example of a cultural element that altered in this way in spite of Islam. In marriage, Islam requires the bride to receive a marriage gift called *mahr*, which is chosen by the bride herself. In some cultures, such as the Turkish, it was not considered honourable for a woman to negotiate the amount of *mahr* by herself. Also some men promised the marriage gift and did not pay it after the marriage took place. Male family members felt they had to step in to protect the bride. So, the leading male family member started to negotiate on her behalf and made sure that the *mahr* was received before marriage. Over time, however, opportunistic male family members started to keep the money. This practice spread and lingered on until the 20th century. It took a lengthy educational campaign to change it.

Islam shapes a culture for the better, but sometimes people forget the connection of cultural norms to their Islamic roots, either out of ignorance or a lack of historical awareness. When this happens, bad cultural habits can develop in spite of Islam. The solution is nothing other than effective and complete education.

Is Sufism Islamic? Is it considered to be another sect of Islam or just another religion?

Sufism is neither a stand-alone religion nor a sect in Islam, but a discipline that focuses on the spiritual aspects of Islam. Sufism does not belong to just one Muslim orientation, but exists in all Muslim countries and societies. However, not everything that goes on under the name of Sufism can be attributed to Islam. In order to judge whether something is Islamic or not, it must be evaluated against the well-established criteria of the Qur'an and the application of Islam (*Sunnah*) in the example of the Prophet Muhammad. Sufism is no different. A certain Sufi practice or custom clearly not in line with the set criteria would be judged as un-Islamic. On the other hand, if it is in agreement with the criteria it would be judged as perfectly Islamic.

Sufism can be divided into two broad categories. The first category is the genuine and authentic *tasawwuf* (Sufism), which is undoubtedly in perfect agreement with Islamic standards. The second category is pseudo-Sufism, which includes the practice of cultic rituals contrary to the mainstream practices of Islam. Muslims generally frown upon this pseudo-Sufi aberration of Sufism that merges some flavour of Islam with speculative mysticism or Neo-Platonism in its practices. The Sufi orders that fall into the second category are not considered to be in line with Islam.

Much of the confusion with regard to Sufism stems from the fact that some non-Muslim enthusiasts treat Sufism and some Sufi masters without paying attention to their strong Muslim identity. For example, Rumi (*Maulana Calal-addin Rumi*), a strong Muslim and devout follower of Muhammad, has been depicted in the West as a mere poet and a humanitarian and his path is reduced to the spectacle of whirling dervishes. Rumi was followed by millions of

Muslims in his lifetime and since. He made a strong contribution to the development and continuation of Islam in Ottoman lands for centuries.

Sufism was born in the early development period of Muslim society as a reaction to increased wealth, the over-indulgence of rich Muslims and the over-emphasis of jurists in following the rules of Islam. Concerned individuals felt that the pure message and the spirituality of Islam were in danger of being lost. They started to renounce the world and live austere lives to show a good example to other Muslims, just as the Prophet Muhammad did in his lifetime. Instead of wearing fine silk, they wore simple wool garments. The word Sufi actually comes from the word "wool" in Arabic. They focussed on the individual and collective chanting of God's names and attributes to cleanse the heart and reach a constant state of awareness. When spiritual geniuses attracted students and followers, Sufi orders (*tariqas*) were established. Sufism enjoyed a mass following and acceptance when Al-Ghazali showed that law and spirituality could be merged once again as the Prophet did by his example.

Sufism is a lifelong process of spiritual development and has been described differently by famous Sufi masters. Junayd defines Sufism as a method of realising a "self-annihilation in God" and "permanence and subsistence with God". Shibli summarises it as having a constant awareness of God or always experiencing God's presence, so that no worldly or otherworldly aim is even entertained. Abu Muhammad Jarir describes it as resisting the temptation and bad qualities of the carnal self and acquiring admirable moral qualities. All these definitions could be summed up in the broad definition that Sufism is to live a life centred on the awareness and love of God, leading to an experience of faith in spiritual delights, having attained almost angelic qualities and conduct as a result of freeing oneself from human vices, weaknesses and inherent limitations. The difficulty in defining Sufism with words is that it is a lived and practised phenomenon rather than a theoretical discipline.[13] When expressed and practised in this manner, *tasawwuf* (Sufism) is not only an authentic Islamic discipline but is also the essence of Islam as a practical and spiritual reality.

The Muslim world benefited a lot from Sufism. At a time when scholars were busy with their academic work, the Sufis educated and organised the Muslim masses and established a strong civil infrastructure. Sufis travelled far and wide and spread Islam to many parts of the world. They organised charities and mobilised people in the self-defence of their homes against foreign attack.

---

13 Gulen, Fethullah, *Key Concepts in the Practice of Sufism*, The Fountain (1999), p. xiv.

Q66

In Christianity there are various denominations, each expressing their faith in different ways. Is Islam similar? What are the differences between Shiite and Sunni Islam?

Because of the unique disposition of every one of us, it is inevitable that there will be different interpretations of religion. In spite of this fact, Islam has certain unique advantages in comparison to other religions.

1. Irrespective of what orientation Muslims may have, the Qur'an is the ultimate reference accepted by all. Since the Qur'an has never changed from the time of the Prophet, authentic Islam has always been with us to the present time.

2. The essentials of faith, the five pillars of Islam, are also the same for 98% or more of the 1.2 billion Muslims on earth. These tenets are clearly outlined in the Qur'an. The differences are usually in peripheral issues and the way the social application of Islam evolved differently across the demographic and cultural landscape of the vast Muslim world.

3. The objectivity and genius of early Muslim scholars preserved the *Sunnah*, which includes what the Prophet said, what he did and those actions that he permitted or disallowed. These scholars undertook rigorous critical evaluation and the filtering of these traditions.

4. Islam is a living religion. The practices of Islam were well-established at the time of the Prophet and continued to be practised in personal and communal spaces in a continuous manner up to the present day.

The result is that authentic Islam is preserved and the great majority of Muslims in the world follows this authentic and mainstream Islam. The Muslim world has three main orientations:

a) Sunni: Constituting about 85% of the Muslim world, Sunnis are in the majority. The title "Sunni" comes from the word "Sunnah", meaning "the followers of the example of the Prophet".

b) Shiite: Making up about 13% of Muslims, those of Shiite orientation form an important minority. Most of Iran and minority populations in its neighbouring countries are of Shiite orientation. The title "Shiite" refers to followers of Ali, the son-in-law and cousin of the Prophet Muhammad.

c) Gulat: Forming about 2%, this includes many diverse and small minorities who have developed extreme doctrines that cannot be supported by the Qur'an or the teachings of the Prophet.

The polarisation between the Sunni and Shiite Muslims did not occur over theological differences; but arose over the question of who should lead the Muslim world after the death of the Prophet Muhammad. When the Prophet Muhammad passed away Muslims in Medina elected Abu Bakr as the political and military leader of the community. Abu Bakr was the father-in-law and a close friend of the Prophet, who appointed him to lead the prayers when he was sick. Abu Bakr was also known for his sagacity and piety. Being the caliph, his position had a religious significance as the head of the *ummah*, the worldwide community of Muslim believers. However, a small band of people was of the opinion that the leadership should have been on hereditary lines rather than through an election. Since the closest relative of the Prophet was Ali, who was married to the Prophet's only surviving child Fatima, Ali should have been elected as the Caliph. Dissension grew within this band as Ali was passed over two more times. Ali eventually became the fourth Caliph in 656 CE. The Shiites were still a political faction, when Ali's rule was short lived. The struggle for leadership that started between the sons of Mu'awiya and Ali was marked by the tragic martyrdom of Husayn (the second son of Ali and the grandson of the Prophet), at

Karbala in 680 CE. After the fall of the Umayyads and the disappointment of the Shiites when the Abbasid Caliphate did not appoint a descendent of Ali, the Shiites turned inward and developed certain philosophies to give meaning to all that had transpired in the first century of Islam.

I should point out that all Muslims were concerned about these events and abhorred the perpetrators of the oppression and injustice inflicted on some members of the family of the Prophet. However, a group of Shiites who held extreme love towards Ali and the family of the Prophet responded strongly to these events, causing the polarisation in the Muslim world.

Although both Sunni and Shiite Muslims accept and use the same Qur'an, believe in the same essentials and practice the five pillars of Islam, the Shiite partisan paradigm caused them to develop additional beliefs and practices in accordance with their interpretation of Islam.

1. Leadership: In the Sunni orientation, the Caliph or the Imam (leader of Muslims) is elected from among the Muslims on the basis of his competence and leadership. Apart from the Prophets, everyone is fallible. In the Shiite orientation, on the other hand, the Fourteen Pure and Perfect Ones (Ali, Fatima – Ali's wife and Prophet's daughter – their two sons Hasan and Husayn, and nine other Imams) are all infallible. The Caliph should be a direct descendant of the Prophet.

2. Sources of Law: While both the Sunni and Shiite accept the Qur'an and the Sunnah of the Prophet as inspired, authoritative textual sources, the Shiite maintain their own collections of the traditions, which include not only the Sunnah of the Prophet but also those of Ali and the Imams. Shiites also do not accept any narratives from the majority of the companions of the Prophet because they believed that those companions did not support Ali.

3. Intercession: For Sunnis, God and human beings have a direct relationship. Pious scholars with wisdom and knowledge are not intermediaries but simply scholarly interpreters of the religion. For Shiism, Ali and the other Imams were divinely inspired models, guides and intermediaries between God and the believers.

4. Holy Days and Celebrations: Along with those holy days that are celebrated by Shiite and Sunni alike, Shiite also celebrate the birthdays and mourn the anniversaries of the deaths of the Imams. Husayn's martyrdom at Karbala and the associated remembrance and ritual re-enactment of the tragedy form a cornerstone of personal and communal identity.

5. Ritual Practices: Sunni practice is centred on the five pillars of Islam and the associated practice of the Prophet. In addition to daily prayers, Shiism has developed dramatic recitations, passion plays and street processions centring on the tragedy of Karbala.

Sunni orientation is the common denominator in the whole Muslim world, while the Shiites add some beliefs and practices derived from their deep love of the Prophet Muhammad and his family. The Sunni orientation centres its practice on the Qur'an, the prophethood of Muhammad and his role as a person epitomising the ideal model presented by the revelation of the Qur'an, hence God. The Shiite orientation, on the other hand, centres on the Qur'an, the personal aspects of the Prophet and loyalty to his family.

Could you explain the Qur'anic or *Shariah* law?

Shariah is an Arabic word meaning "the path" to be followed. Literally it means "the way to a watering place". In its broadest definition, *Shariah* consists of a set of laws, which are composed by human deductions from the two main sources of Islam, the Qur'an and the Sunnah (Prophet Muhammad's sayings or *hadith*[14], his actions and those things he sanctioned). Islam provides guidelines in the relationship between humans and God, human relationship to the universe and the relationship between humans in a society. *Shariah* usually refers to the latter, and hence we can define *Shariah* as the social reflection of Islam.

While comparative legal systems contain a constitution that appoints a sovereign, and law-makers who are empowered to enact new legislation, Islam says that all humans are essentially limited to comprehending the human being and life in its totality. At least, it is highly probable that the legislation and the rule of those with authority can be biased and influenced by political lobby groups or by their human weaknesses and desires. Therefore a set of timeless,

---

14 The Arabic word *"hadith"* means a "spoken word" or a "saying". In the Islamic context, it refers to the recorded sayings of the Prophet Muhammad. The books in which these are compiled are called *"hadith* books". There are six popular collections of authentic *hadith*. These are the Bukhari, Muslim, Abu Davud, Nisai, Tirmidhi and Ibn Maja collections. Among these the Bukhari and Muslim collections have a special place because of the tough criteria that they have applied to objectively prove a narrative to be authentic. For example, for Bukhari to accept a narrative as authentic, there had to be evidence that consecutive people on the chain of the narration have lived at the same time period and that they have seen one another. This was one among the 10 criteria he applied. There are over 9000 narrations when all six collections are combined, not counting the repetitions. Considering that this selection is done from a pool of more than 100,000 narrations, Muslims have a high level of trust in their authenticity.

self-evident and universal principles independent of human intervention, is needed in law to ensure that no transgressions of human rights are made. For example, the "right to live" is one such principle. Who can argue against the "right to live" and who can say that it is only applicable at certain times? Since God has designed and created humans, He is in the best position to educate us about the principles of life, so that no-one transgresses the rights of the other. Therefore, God alone has the right to set the principles of justice.

The Islamic commandments and prohibitions that form the core of *Shariah* centre on the protection of five principal human rights: freedom of the mind (speech and belief); the right to life; the right to own personal property, the right to reproduce; and the right to lead a healthy life (both mentally and physically).

Despite the fact that Islam recognises the Divine authority, there is an inherent flexibility in Islamic law. In the strictest sense, the Qur'an contains no more than about eighty legal verses out of more than 6200 verses. The Prophet Muhammad established the first constitution in human history in consultation with the people of Medina (Muslim and non-Muslim citizens). This document shows that human beings are empowered to self-govern provided they are in tune with the principles set out in the Qur'an. One such principle is the strong emphasis on justice that underscores the character of the *Shariah*. The Qur'an states, "*God commands you to give over the public trusts to the charge of those having the required qualities and to judge with justice when you judge between people*" [QUR'AN, 4:58].

Shariah has been both a common source of law and ethics for Muslims for more than a millennium, across a population of diverse political, demographic, cultural and racial backgrounds. Muslims enjoyed the benefits of a legal system of a high order 1400 years before the developed countries. Islam established the concept of the "rule of law" in theory and in practice throughout the vast Muslim world. In Islam, the notion of the "rule of law" gains a second dimension. It not only means that law applies to everyone equally, but it also means that law-makers are also equal to us all, since they are not totally sovereign and cannot go beyond a set of unchanging principles. This gives law a stronger foundation [QUR'AN, 4:135].

The rule of law was so firmly established at the time of the Prophet that the crime rate was almost negligible, even though there wasn't a police force. A Jewish citizen sued Ali, the fourth caliph and the son-in-law of the Prophet, because Ali accused him of stealing his shield. Ali lost the case, since he was unable to prove that the shield belonged to him. When the judge asked Ali if he was upset, Ali gave a remarkable answer that shows the sense of justice achieved at a time when the rest of the world had no proper legal codes. He said, *"I am upset because when you called each of us to stand, you called the plaintiff 'O you Jewish person' and me 'O the caliph of Muslims'. This is injustice towards the plaintiff."* Similarly, the Ottoman Sultan Mehmet II, the Conqueror, was found guilty of unjustly punishing one of his non-Muslim engineers for making a mistake in the construction of Topkapi Palace. He had to pay heavy compensation from his personal wealth. These are but a few of many examples in Islamic history, which shows that a leading statesman is equal in the court of law to a pauper, a Muslim has no extra favouritism over a non-Muslim and that justice will prevail irrespective of the plaintiff or the matter.

Some Muslims, in their call for the implementation of *Shariah*, want a return to a system inspired by Islam. What they are really after is freedom, justice and an end to laws in the service of a military dictator or an oppressive secular regime that seem to hold back a rapidly changing society. Since Muslims were very successful and happy when they had a God-oriented society, they believe that their problems will end by returning to a social order informed by Islam.

Can laws of Islam be changed and to what degree?

Islamic law has been a dynamic legal system for many centuries. Over the last few centuries it did not get a chance to develop due to various internal and external factors. While the sources of Islam cannot be changed, there is a possibility for change in their organisation, interpretation and the deductions obtained using these sources. Since change in religious understanding cannot be imposed on Muslims (due to freedom of speech), change usually occurs over time through a process of natural selection and education.

Some Muslims assume that since Islamic law was based on the Qur'an and the Sunnah of the Prophet, it is also to be considered sacred and divine. Strictly speaking, though, the *Shariah* in its totality is not divine. It is a human attempt to understand the divine will in a particular context using the divine sources of the Qur'an and the confirmed Sunnah. Since the social settings of societies and their associated needs and relationships change, the *Shariah* should respond to the changing circumstances of the times to find solutions to new needs and problems. For example, organ transplant was a contemporary issue that required a new solution in modern times. The human endeavour to come up with a solution to a new need using the sources of Islam is called *ijtihad*. Given that *ijtihad* is a human activity, other qualified people can theoretically change a previous legal ruling if room for change exists. So how did Islamic law change over time?

Islam came to a society where tribal customs were the only law that existed. When the fledging Muslim community established itself in Medina, Qur'anic revelation and the Prophet's own practice became the sources of social and legal guidelines for Muslims. For as long as the Prophet was alive there was no need for systematic law or jurisprudence. Whenever someone had a question in religious matters, he or she would ask the Prophet directly. In return, he would receive a new revelation of the Qur'an or human advice from Muhammad himself. The Prophet had a school next to the mosque where he personally taught Islam and the Qur'an to hundreds of his companions. He also stipulated that his governors were to make decisions based on the Qur'an and his example.

After the Prophet, his companions spread out in the rapidly expanding Muslim world. Each scholarly companion of the Prophet became a centre of learning. They taught Islamic practice and gave legal rulings according to the Qur'an and what they knew from the *Sunnah* of the Prophet. When they were faced with new situations they tried to find an answer in the Qur'an and the *Sunnah*. If they could not find an answer they used their own judgment to find a solution. In doing so, they took into account the principles of equity and public interest as well as the circumstances of the times, customs and culture of the people they were living amongst, just as the Prophet Muhammad stipulated when he appointed governors.

After the generations of the companions, the Islamic law started to develop in streams independent of each other due to differences in methodology, geographic separation, variance in the availability of the *hadith* (sayings of the Prophet) and cultural influences. Astute scholars of this time realised the need to standardise religious legal methodology into disciplines based on the primary sources of religion. They started to develop large volumes of deductions from the Qur'an and the *Sunnah* of the Prophet covering worship, commercial, criminal and civil law in an attempt to identify clearly the rules and regulations of religion in a comprehensive legal code covering all aspects of life. Consensus was reached in the Muslim world that essentially there were four recognised sources of law:

1. The Qur'an: As the primary source of God's revelation, the Qur'an is the sourcebook of Islamic principles and values. About

600 out of 6238 verses are related to law and only about 80 can be considered legal verses in the strictest sense of the word.

2. Sunnah of the Prophet: Qur'anic principles and values are interpreted by the second and complementary source of law, the Sunnah of the Prophet. The importance of the Sunnah is well rooted in the Qur'an: *"If you should quarrel over anything refer it to God and the Messenger"* [QUR'AN, 4:59] and *"In God's Messenger you have a fine model for anyone whose hope is in God and the last Day"* [QUR'AN, 33:21]. Hadith scholars evaluated the vast volume of narrations from Muhammad focusing on the chain of narrators and the content. Tough and objective criteria were applied to the chain of narrators, link by link, for every *hadith*. The content of the *hadith* was examined to see if it contradicted the Qur'an, an already verified *hadith* or human reason. Thus, a set of authoritative collections was compiled.

3. Consensus of the Community (*ijma*): Based on the saying (*hadith*) of the Prophet, *"My community will not agree on an error"*, consensus of the community is the third source of the law. Being educated by Muhammad himself, the consensus of his companions became another powerful source of law. Where the Qur'an and Sunnah are silent, legal jurists use their reason based on *custom (orf)*, *public interest (maslaha) and equity (istihsan)* to come up with a legal deduction. When a certain ruling lasts the test of time, more and more jurists as well as people accept the ruling, thus forming a consensus.

4. Analogical Reasoning (*Qiyas*): When faced with a new situation and problem, legal scholars sought a parallel in the Qur'an and the Sunnah. The key is the discovery of the effective cause or the reason behind the existing ruling. If a similar cause is identified in the new situation, the ruling was extended to resolve the matter. For example, based on the prohibition of wine, a broad prohibition for alcohol is deduced. The root cause here is the mind-altering nature of both.

What happens when there is more than one possible interpretation? This is perfectly normal and acceptable in Islamic Law. For example, there is a difference of opinion among scholars with respect to smoking. Some jurists say that since the Qur'an prohibits damaging one's body, smoking should be prohibited as it causes cancer and clearly damages the body. By contrast, others say that smoking can at most be classified as not recommended as there is no direct prohibition in the Qur'an against it. The Prophet Muhammad recommended people to follow their conscience in matters that fall in the grey area and to choose the safer or easier option in order to protect themselves and make religion easier to practice.

The issue of tobacco consumption can also be given as an example of a ruling changing over time. When tobacco first appeared in Muslim countries, jurists looked at it and deemed it to be "allowable" (*mubah*) as there was no apparent harm or benefit in its consumption. Some scholars considered it "disliked" (*makrooh*) as it was a waste of money. However, over time medicine proved the lethal nature of tobacco. Using the principle of protecting human life, more and more jurists are now tending to classify smoking in the category of prohibited (*haram*) activities. However, as yet a consensus has not been reached.

It is important to note that all rulings and interpretations together form Islamic jurisprudence, since all of these interpretations are possible within the context of the sources of Islam. Different rulings usually occur on peripheral issues, while the core theology and practices do not change over time. No Muslim, for example, would come out and say that Muslims will no longer believe in life after death or that Muslims are no longer required to fast. Having more than one interpretation in practical Islam builds immense flexibility in the practice of Islam. This situation is a testimony not only to the freedom of speech enjoyed by millions of scholars since the birth of Islam but also to the non-existence of the imposition of a single view on the whole Muslim community.

There is a perception in non-Muslim circles that Islamic law is outdated and that Muslims are very static in their approach to law and religion. They say it is Islam that needs reform but Muslims are not prepared to change. While it is true to say the manifestations of Islam in the political and social spheres need a fresh outlook to meet the contemporary needs of Muslims around the world, nevertheless, the slowness of change does not stem from Islam itself but from the inertia caused by three important internal and external factors.

The first is the freezing of interpretation. The closure of the gates of *ijtihad* has caused Islamic legislation to freeze in time. Initially, this appeared to make sense. The creed of Islam was clearly set out in the Qur'an and all Muslims understood it. Islamic practice was firmly established and based on the Sunnah of the Prophet, which was collected in volumes of *hadith* books, sorted, filtered and ordered in every imaginable way. Every verse of the Qur'an and every narrative from the Prophet were examined for legal deductions. It seemed all that is humanly possible was done in the development of the *Sharia*. People came to believe there was nothing else that could be done. An error of judgment, the mistaken assumption that the social aspects of life stay constant, extended the legal freeze to the social sphere. This freeze was not imposed on people but scholars and people saw it as the natural end of a long process. In spite of this view, the development of legislation continued, especially in the Ottoman Empire. Towards the end of 19th century, a major project was initiated to codify the *Shariah* in the format of contemporary legislation, and then to develop it to meet the needs of the time. As a result, a number of volumes of what came to be called *Mecelle* started to emerge. Unfortunately, this project came to a grinding halt with the second major devastation to face the Muslim world since the Mongol invasion.

The second major factor that stopped the development of Islamic Law was the destructive impact of European colonisation of the Muslim world. With all their political, civil, cultural and religious institutions destroyed, Muslims had to struggle for their very survival and the survival of their religion, let alone develop Islamic law to meet the needs of contemporary Muslim society. This created a historic gap of at least a century between the past and the present. This gap still exists today.

The third reason is that modernity ushered in rapid changes in the political, economic and social spheres all around the world, including the Muslim nations. Globalisation, mass media and ease of travel accelerated the wave of exposure of Muslims to overwhelming alternative systems, cultures and norms. Although Muslims are not against change, the speed of change is daunting, especially when they feel they have very little influence over it.

For the above reasons, wherever the *Sharia*, that is, the legislation of the past, is implemented in a Muslim country, Muslim societies take on a medieval appearance. There is a consensus in the Muslim world that the *Sharia* needs to be reviewed and codified in the modern context to meet the needs of a changed world while at the same time staying true to the spirit of Islam and the principles of the Qur'an and the Sunnah. Speed of change coupled with adverse political circumstances do not give Muslims a chance to develop a contemporary context for Islamic Law.

There are many attempts to carry out this revision. Given that an interpretation cannot be imposed on Muslims from above, change will take time. There needs to be a long enough application in a Muslim country for it to mature in the modern world. Furthermore, there are deeper problems that exist in the Muslim world before this task can be undertaken. See my answer to QUESTION 101 to have a preview of a possible future for the Muslim world.

In other religions scholars or clergy have made fundamental changes in their religion. Did this occur in Islam?

In Islam and for the majority of Muslims, fundamental changes taking it in new directions against the spirit of religion did not occur. In the long history of Islam there have been some religious or political leaders who introduced new doctrines or radical interpretations to Islam. Kharijites of old and Osama bin Laden of today are examples of people who have interpreted Islam as a way of violence. Such extreme interpretations never found a mass following within the worldwide Muslim community. The self-preserving nature of Islam and the protective instincts of Muslim scholars were instrumental in keeping Islam preserved intact until today.

When a genuine change or a new perspective is necessary, how does this occur in the Muslim world? Naturally, individuals with little or no influence will not cause a lasting change. State initiated changes also do not work, as shown by the failure of the Taliban and the theocracy of Iran. The only way to effect lasting change is by way of a highly trusted and respected spiritual leader with a mass following. It is for this reason that the Prophet Muhammad said that the learned scholars (both men and women) are heirs to the religion of Islam.

Muslim scholars have always understood their role to be to investigate, understand, codify, simplify and explain the details of Islam to common Muslims who do not have the time to do this for themselves. They did not see their role as making fundamental changes in religion. On the contrary, they felt a sense of responsibility to preserve the message of Islam. The rationale is this: since Islam is the last and perfected message of God, it should be preserved in its pristine form. The duty of learned scholars is to preserve Islam by removing any interpretations that might cloud the unspoiled message of Islam over time.

Islam is like a rose whose petals unfold with time as humanity develops. The Prophet Muhammad said that since there will not be any prophet succeeding him, God will inspire a *mujaddid* (renewer) every one hundred years to renew the message of Islam.[15] The role of the *mujaddid* is to express the pristine message of Islam in a way comprehensible to the contemporary world and solve the major challenges facing the Muslims at the time.

Imam Shafii, for example, is considered to be the *mujaddid* of the 9th century (CE). He was able to facilitate consensus between Muslim jurists under a single methodology, thus solving the dilemma of how human reason should merge with the Sunnah in establishing legal rulings. Another commonly recognised *mujaddid* is Al-Ghazali, the 11th century scholar, who was able to give a unique synthesis of law and spirituality by way of the example of the Prophet, and thus ending the divide between philosophy and Sufism. Said Nursi (1876–1960) is a contemporary scholar who is also considered to be the *mujaddid* of the last century by a considerable number of Muslims. Relying solely on the Qur'an, he was able to explain the essentials of Islamic faith and reconciling the apparently conflicting spheres of science, philosophy and spirituality.

The impact of Said Nursi in the last century on Muslim consciousness and religious thought has been significant, particularly in Turkey. For Nursi, the problem facing the Muslim world lay deep beneath current events. The root cause was the collective attack of materialistic philosophy and its atheistic assertions, which were causing people to have doubts and leave religion altogether. Lack of faith, in turn, was causing people to take up vices that were threat-

---

15 Abu Dawood, *Malahim*, 1.

ening the very fabric of society. According to Nursi, the remedy had to be a reconciliation of material science and religion, thereby protecting and strengthening people's faith. Nursi said that it was futile to have a political struggle since it was neither the root cause nor was it effective. All efforts had to be exerted in support of an intellectual struggle. He powerfully showed not only that reason and faith were compatible with Islam's tenets, but that the Qur'an encouraged the use of human reason to attain certainty in faith based on strong convictions. He proposed that the solution to the problems of the Muslim world would have to start with an education that combined the religious and material sciences, so that wisdom can prevail rather than either religious bigotry or atheism.

Perhaps the next *mujaddid* will be the one who comes up with a realistic model for society and politics in the Muslim world based on the principles of Islam and acceptable to the majority of Muslims which would also appeal to the non-Muslim world at the same time.

Why does Islamic law appear to be so restrictive? For example, the fact that drinking alcohol is totally forbidden. Why does Islam prohibit the consumption of alcohol?

Alcohol and other intoxicants are prohibited in Islam because of their mind-altering effect, the loss of control of one's actions, the damage it does to the consumer's body, and its repercussions on the safety and social fabric of a society.

The word "alcohol" entered English from the Arabic word *al-cohol*. Muslim chemists who isolated alcohol did extensive research into the substance in medieval times. Alcohol is an essential substance for life in the way it is involved in organic reactions. It appears in trace amounts in natural form in breads, yogurt and many other foods. What was created as a useful substance for life becomes harmful when taken in excessive amounts in the form of alcoholic beverages. The Qur'an actually alludes to this nature of alcohol when it says, *"They ask you concerning alcoholic drink and gambling. Say! There is great harm and (some) benefit for men, but the harm in them is greater than their benefit…"* [QUR'AN, 2:219].

Islam's commandments and prohibitions centre on the protection of five essential human rights and principles: freedom of the mind (speech and belief), the right to live, the right to own personal property, the right to reproduce, and the right to lead a healthy life (both mentally and physically). Along with other intoxicants alcohol violates two of these principles, freedom of the mind and health. It is common knowledge that alcohol damages the liver and the brain and many other organs. Australian national health guidelines recommend consumption of "no alcohol" at all.

If the damage alcohol has done was confined only to the individual, perhaps it would not have been prohibited outright. However, once a person loses the control of his or her mind, the

QUESTION 70

subsequent uncontrolled behaviour becomes a time bomb for the whole society. There is a direct relationship between alcohol and the increased crime rates, car accidents, family break-ups and decreased productivity. It is inconceivable for a merciful God to allow the consumption of such a harmful substance.

Some Muslims may prefer not to go to places or sit at tables where alcohol is freely served. This is because Muslims feel they cannot engage in intelligent conversation when people's behaviour starts to shift due to the effect of alcohol. It also sends a quiet message that Muslims do not condone the consumption of alcohol.

I should point out that the prohibitions of Islam are the exception rather than the rule. About 95% of everything that it is possible to do or consume is allowed, giving a very large zone of freedom that is enough to satisfy normal human desires. Of all the drinks and juices available, for example, all are allowed except blood and alcohol.

In the case of alcohol a total prohibition is required because usually people who acquire an addiction do so by starting with small amounts. When lawmakers legislate a law for theft, for example, they do not differentiate between stealing a battery from a shop and robbing millions of dollars from a bank. Although the penalty is different for the two offences, essentially both are crimes and prohibited. Also small offences may lead to more serious crimes.

Furthermore, when bush fires took place in December 2001 in Sydney, there was a complete fire ban all over NSW, including fires lit for barbecues at home, although they were small fires and under control with an extremely small probability of fire spreading from them. The ban was imposed because of the serious consequences for the environment and people if the remote possibility became a reality.

In a similar way, in cases such as gambling, consumption of intoxicants and adultery Islam lays down a total ban because of the serious negative consequences not only for the individual, but also for the immediate family and society as a whole. Recent research shows that about 20% of people are genetically susceptible to addiction. When this 20% get addicted to a substance not only do they make life unsafe for themselves but also for the whole society.

Since it is not possible to know who will end up as an addict, Islam puts a total ban on intoxicants, placing the boundary at a safe distance for everyone. This is like setting up the fence at a distance from the site of a nuclear testing rather than in the immediate area of the explosion. Therefore, potential addicts-to-be and those of us who would be negatively affected by the consequences, that is, the whole society, are protected. The Prophet Muhammad also advised Muslims to stay at a safe distance from what is prohibited so as to be completely safe.

Q71

Why are the punishments for crimes such as adultery and theft so harsh in Islamic law? They even look barbaric when judged by today's standards.

In any legal system there are heavy penalties for what are considered to be serious crimes. Some countires, for example, have capital punishment for drug smuggling because it is seen as a serious problem that has to be stopped at all costs. The general purpose of setting penalties for crimes is their prevention. As far as the majority of people is concerned, the severity of the penalty is irrelevant since they would not commit the crimes in any case. Therefore, criminal penalties serve to deter those individuals who would be inclined to commit the outlawed crimes.

Once a law is established, an authority is needed to apply the law for it to have a preventative effect on those individuals who overstep the law. Without such an authority, the safety of the whole community would be at risk. The widespread looting that went on in Iraq after the fall of Saddam Hussein's regime shows that without an authority lawlessness prevails, rendering life dangerous for all because of the actions of the few.

There is a dilemma that faces law-makers. What is the right level of penalty that would stop the majority of criminals without being too cruel to the criminal? Today people are divided between two contested views. One view is that very tough penalties should be set in order to make sure there is effective prevention. The second view is that the punishment should not be too excessive and a criminal should be given a chance to rehabilitate into the mainstream community. Usually Western countries have adopted the second view even though many people in those countries might favour tougher punishments.

The increased crime statistics in the West would show that the light prison sentences are not working. People are still committing crimes in epidemic proportions if they think that they can get away with it. Criminals are usually repeat offenders, and in many cases come from an educated background. Rather than correcting behaviour, the prisons become a place where people gain new criminal tendencies. Funds spent on the prison system are soaring. Insurance policies and security costs are wasted on an unsafe society. Yet we still put double locks on our doors, iron bars on our windows and install security alarms to secure our property and make ourselves feel safe.

In dealing with the fundamental dilemma of law-making, Islam takes the view that penalties should be very tough in cases where the very fabric of the society and the safety of all people are seriously at risk, so that there is effective crime prevention. Murder, theft and adultery fall into such a category of crimes, crimes in which the damage done to victims and society are extensive and irreversible. If these three crimes are reduced to considerably low levels, then other peripheral crimes would also disappear. Adultery, for instance, causes family tragedies that not only affect many individuals for life but also the community in which it happens. Both theft and adultery also cause murders to be committed as a by-product. Therefore, they need to be stopped before they happen.

In Islamic law, the penalty for adultery is capital punishment and the one for theft is amputation of the left hand. Since these penalties are very tough, Islam lays down very heavy conditions that must be fulfilled before they can be applied. In the case of adultery, four reliable witnesses are required for adultery charges rather than the usual two in other crimes. No indirect inference of adultery is acceptable. The witnesses have to see the act taking place. Islam also does not accept the testimony of any witness at random. Witnesses must be balanced, decent individuals who are not known to lie. People could be banned from witnessing if they are caught giving false testimony. In the case of theft, the stolen amount must be above a certain threshold before the law applies. Also if the theft occurs out of necessity to survive, the law does not apply. Therefore, the law is applicable only to a professional thief who has made a career out of stealing. During a drought, the second caliph Omar reportedly suspended the law of theft since the circumstances made it difficult for people to survive.

With such tough conditions, these punishments are so rarely applied as to become symbolic. For example, during the six hundred years of Ottoman reign, less than a dozen cases of amputation for theft occurred. This shows the low crime rate as well as the difficulty placed in the application of these tough laws. Nevertheless, since there is always the possibility of the laws being applied, they become a strong deterrent.

The laws of Islam ensured that Muslim societies were the safest societies in human history. The great majority of people had no problem with the laws of Islam since they were decent people. Only the criminally inclined had to worry about these laws. The almost too-good-to-be-true society established by the Prophet Muhammad was almost a crime-free society with no police force to maintain safety. This trend continued for most of Muslim history. Even though in many ways Saudi Arabia is not a perfect example of an Islamic state, due to the application of these laws the society is very safe to live in. People do not lock their shops and houses when unattended and the crime rate is very low. Nevertheless, in countries where Islamic laws are practised, the way these penalties are implemented needs to be revised taking into account the sensitivities of modern civil societies.

Q72

**What does *halal* mean? What makes food *halal*?
Why can't Muslims eat just any meat?
Why aren't Muslims allowed to eat pork?**

The word *halal* simply means "lawful" or "religiously appropriate". In Islam, rightfully earned income, for example, is considered to be *halal*, while stolen property, money or foods are labelled as *haram* (unlawful). Just as a practising Muslim would not buy a cheap but stolen stereo, he or she would not consume food or meat that is *haram*.

For meat to be *halal*, it needs to satisfy two simple criteria. Firstly, the meat of all animals may be eaten with the exception of "*...dead meat, and blood, and the flesh of swine, and that on which any other name has been invoked besides that of God. But if one is forced by necessity, without wilful disobedience, nor transgressing due limits, then he is guiltless. For God is Oft-forgiving Most Merciful.*" [QUR'AN, 2:173] Notice the remark at the end of this verse that in times of necessity or when there is nothing else to eat to survive, the forbidden meat mentioned in the verse can be consumed. This is called the "principle of necessity" in Islamic Law and extends to all prohibitions. A prohibition is temporarily lifted at times of crisis and absolute necessity.

The second criterion is the way in which an animal's life ends, which has to be in accordance with Islamic regulations. Life is a sacred blessing of God to creation, animals as well as humans. If the life of an animal has to be ended in order to survive, then its life should only be taken in the name of God. Hence, the phrase *bismillah* (in the name of God) must be uttered just before slaughtering an animal. Only a Muslim or a monotheistic person such as a Christian or a Jew can fulfil this criterion. Muslims, therefore, can eat the meat slaughtered according to Christian and Jewish religious guidelines. Muslims cannot consume the meat of animals that are sacrificed in the name of any deity or idol.

When animals are slaughtered for the purpose of food, all blood has to come out of the body. This is achieved by an incision to the jugular vein of the animal. The Prophet Muhammad also advised that the task is to be completed with one incision while the eyes of the animal are covered so that it does not see the instrument. An animal should not be slaughtered in front of another so as to cause unnecessary stress. Some people allege this is inhumane and causes a lot of pain to the animal. They give as evidence the body of the animal convulsing vigorously after the cut. In reality though, as proved by Professor Schultz of Hanover University in Germany, the Islamic way of slaughtering an animal gives no pain while the alternative method of Captive Bolt Stunning (CBS) is quite painful. He did this in an experiment, where the sensations of the brain activity of animals were measured and compared by EEG.

The first three seconds from the time of Islamic slaughter as recorded on the EEG did not show any change from the graph before the slaughter, thus indicating the animal did not feel any pain during or immediately after the incision. The EEG recorded a condition of deep sleep or unconsciousness caused by large quantity of blood gushing out from the body. After 6 seconds, the EEG recorded zero, showing no feeling of pain at all, even though the heart was still beating and the body convulsing vigorously (a reflex action of the spinal cord), driving maximum blood from the body, resulting in hygienic meat for the consumer. Whereas with CBS the animals were apparently unconscious soon after stunning, the EEG showed severe pain immediately after stunning. The heart of the stunned animal stopped beating, resulting in the retention of more blood in the meat, rendering it unhygienic for the consumer. It is for these reasons that Muslims establish *halal* labelled butcher shops in order to make hygienic and religiously pure meat available to Muslims.

Some Muslims also pay attention to additives in processed foods and check for *haram* or suspicious ingredients. Foods with animal additives (fats, gelatine, etc.) are usually rejected out of concern that they might come from non-*halal* animals.

Consumption of pork is prohibited as it is considered "impure" [QUR'AN 6:145]. Many health risks are associated with the consumption of pork as it may contain dangerous worms (trichinosis) and germs. Since it is not possible at all times and places to get "healthier" pork, its consumption is prohibited. Because of the direct relationship between our behaviour and what we consume, consumption of pork is also thought to adversely effect human behaviour. Since pigs have certain instincts that are necessary for their role in their ecosystem but undesirable if humans were to display them, Muslims do not eat pork. Having said that, pigs play an important role in cleaning the environment and becoming a food source for other animals in the ecosystem in which they live.

What is the Islamic community's involvement in schools, hospitals and charities?

In my answer to QUESTION 42 I have outlined the major charities in Islam. I have also shown that when the Muslim world was prosperous it produced a culture of charity that lasted many centuries. The institution of *zakat* has been so successful that even from the time of the Prophet Muhammad, poverty was rapidly eradicated from the Muslim world. Merely one hundred years after the Prophet, during the caliphate of Omar Bin Abdulaziz, there were excess *zakat* funds, which were distributed to Christian counties in Africa. This kind of international help was unheard of in the 8th century CE. During the Ottoman reign, people would go from door to door trying to find poor to whom they could give alms, irrespective of their religious background.

In Islamic charity, it is important not to taunt people who are receiving help. Not even a word of thanks should be expected, *"and feed with food the needy wretch, the orphan and the captive, for love of Him (saying): we feed you, for the sake of God only. We wish for no reward nor thanks from you."* [QUR'AN, 76:8–9] Apart from those in mosques, there were alms-boxes placed in public places so that the poor could take money freely without feeling the humiliation of receiving money from someone else. The poor were also mindful they were not the only needy around, thus they would only take sufficient amount of money to meet their immediate needs. They would be careful to not take the share of their fellow brethren. This idea led to the establishment of endowments called *vaqfs*, which acted as a third party for charity distribution.

Another important reason for the development of *vaqfs* was the Prophet's saying that, *"When a person dies, his or her book of deeds is closed except in three cases;* **public charity***, useful knowledge left behind and a* *child that prays after the parents"* [MUSLIM 1631]. Muslims hoped to gain the rewards of good deeds by leaving a lasting charitable legacy after their death. In doing so, they competed with each other in the establishment of charities [QUR'AN, 2:148, 3:144].

As a result, Muslim society was an extremely civil society where all civil services from education to health were provided by endowments and foundations established by the rich. The culture of charity was elevated to a culture of civil servanthood not only to humans but also to the environment. In Istanbul, for example, an endowment was established that only looked after storks, which were injured on their annual journey of migration. The staff of the endowment treated the birds and set them free at a suitable time.

The spirit of charity is still strong in the Muslim world, even though poverty has afflicted many of the Muslim nations around the world. This is because of the attitude of helping the other even if one is in need themselves. Ali, the son-in-law of the Prophet, did not eat his meals for three days when a beggar knocked on the door of his home just before the family was about to sit for dinner. Another companion of the Prophet pretended to eat in the dark so that his hungry friend would not know that there was only enough food for one. Such was the sense of charity and sacrifice among the followers of the Prophet.

Muslims still sponsor schools, hospitals and many other forms of charitable services all around the world. The local governments in Istanbul and Cairo, for example, set up huge tents during Ramadan offering food to poor Muslims. Anonymous Muslims sponsor these tents. All Muslim movements and organisations engage in some form of charity. For example, one of the most significant spiritual movements, inspired by M. Fethullah Gulen, has established hundreds of schools in Muslim and non-Muslim countries as remote as Burma, Tanzania and Ghana.

QUESTION 73

In countries where Muslims are a minority, such as Australia, the charity efforts mainly focus on educational activities. Muslim communities established schools in Australia to ensure their children are educated and become contributing members of society.

Muslims in Australia also established organisations such as Muslim-Aid Australia that organises clothes appeals, food assistance to the poor and needy all over the world, especially third world countries.

PART III

ISLAM IN THE MODERN WORLD

Chapter 7

Saved by the Veil – Women in Islam

Women have always had a tough ride in human history. The emancipation of women in the West was a long and painful experience. Even though there are many rights given to women (ironically, by men), the practice leaves a lot to be desired. Islam has been heavily criticised for the perceived poor status of women in some Muslim countries.

In this chapter, I will explain the rights and roles of women in Islam; how Islam transformed the status of women back in the 7th century; why Muslim women cover their hair; and the rights and involvement of women in marriage. You'll be surprised to know that Islam not only gives many rights to women but it also has many injunctions to protect women in any patriarchal society.

Q74

Are there gender differences in rituals and expectations within the "church"? Why do men and women pray separately in congregation? When I see Muslims praying in a mosque on TV, I always see men. Are women allowed in a mosque?

I should firstly point out that in Islam a mosque does not belong to a "church establishment". It belongs to the community of Muslims and is managed by a committee representing the community [SEE ALSO THE ANSWER TO QUESTION 69].

Islam does not differentiate between males and females in religious obligations and expectations. The Qur'an clearly gives equal responsibility to men and women in the five pillars of Islam and moral behaviour: *"For believing men and women, for devout men and women, for truthful men and women, for patient men and women, for humble men and women, for charitable men and women…"* [QUR'AN, 33:35] The verse continues to list desirable actions and virtues expected of both genders and concludes by saying, *"…for them has God prepared forgiveness and a great reward."* It is interesting that the phrase "men and women" is repeated after each attribute to send home the strong message that both men and women are equally responsible for good conduct and therefore both will be rewarded, not just men.

Furthermore, according to Islam, God does not look at one's gender or colour but rather the heart and the level of spiritual development and righteousness [QUR'AN, 49:13]. Islam goes a step further and transcends gender differences by regarding both men and women as human beings completing each other in their natural dispositions, just as God has intended: *"The Believers, men and women, are protectors one of another: they enjoin what is just, and forbid what is evil: they observe regular prayers, practice regular charity, and obey God and His Messenger. On them will God pour His mercy: for God is Exalted in power,*

Wise." [QUR'AN, 9:71] In this view, neither has an important disadvantage or advantage. Each gender has strengths and weaknesses. Only the communion of the two produces a complete humanity. Considering this was the final verse revealed on the relationship between men and women, we could say that it is the ideal which the Qur'an endorses. Since the Qur'an was revealed over a twenty-three year period, it often sought to improve society progressively educating people in all matters, including the relationship between men and women.

Nevertheless, some differences in certain practices exist, mainly due to some unique characteristics of the two genders or because differentiation becomes necessary in practical terms. The most visible aspect is in the way men and women are required to cover portions of their bodies. While both men and women need to cover certain portion of their bodies, women also cover their hair [SEE QUESTION 81 ON WHY THIS IS THE CASE]. It is also not compulsory for women to attend the Friday prayer; they can defer fasting during the time of breast-feeding; and they are not required to perform the daily prayers when menstruating. These exceptions for women are laid down so that they are not pressured into compromising situations at times of difficulty.

Women are free to go to a mosque anytime they wish. The Prophet Muhammad said, *"do not prevent your women to enter the mosque"*. Women can also join the congregational prayer sessions when they are in the mosque. Because of the physical nature of the prayers, where Muslims are required to line up in tight rows with shoulders touching and involves the movements of bowing down and prostration, women line up in separate rows behind men for greater concentration and spiritual benefit. Some mosques have a gallery level reserved for women or a separating barrier between men and women. None of these practices existed at the time of the

Prophet Muhammad. In the mosque where he led prayers there was only one internal area where both men and women prayed.

It is because of the way Muslims line up in prayer that when pictures are taken of a segment of the congregation, it is usually the men's lines that are filmed or photographed. Also Muslim women do not usually choose to go to a mosque to pray as prayers in Islam can be performed in any clean location. Women with children also have the difficulty of finding child-care five times a day to go to the mosque. Because of the fact that media photographers and cameramen are usually male, Muslim women are not comfortable to allow them to take their pictures when they are praying in private or congregation. All of these factors combine to create images of mosques where more men than women are shown.

The interaction between men and women in a Muslim society in modern times varies from one country and culture to other. In many Muslim countries women work and interact freely with men, while in others, such as Iran and the Indian subcontinent, women are encouraged to stay out of public space. Again, this practice is restricted to those regions only and is a remnant of pre-Islamic culture. Nevertheless, Iran has more elected women in the parliament and more women professors in universities than in many Western countries. Women also have held the position of Prime Minister or President in Pakistan, Turkey, Bangladesh and Indonesia. [ALSO SEE THE ANSWER TO QUESTION 64 RELATING TO CULTURAL INFLUENCES ON RELIGIOUS PRACTICES.]

In Australia, the only point of demarcation between men and women is in the modesty of women's clothing and the mutual respect shown in their interactions. Women are actively involved in charitable and educational work in mosques and community organisations. They are involved as office holders and in management.

Islam appears to restrict the rights of women. They do not have the same freedom as men. You have to convince me that Islam does not disadvantage women. What has Islam brought to women?

In the media we often see women in Islamic countries portrayed as subservient to their male counterparts and lacking any semblance of basic human rights. What we are really witnessing, however, are problems of the Third World that are commonly and incorrectly associated with the doctrine and practices of Islam.

In 7th Century Arabia, when the Qur'an was revealed to the Prophet Muhammad, rights for the women were non-existent under the deeply entrenched system of patriarchy. Infanticide of the first-born female child was a common practice. The status of women in the rest of the world was no different. Europe was discussing whether women had souls, or even if they went to heaven. Women had no say in marriage in India, while, in China, women could not get an education and were often killed at birth.

In stark contrast to the global norms of the 7th Century and the current imagery, the Qur'an provides women with explicit rights of inheritance, independent property, divorce and the right to testify in a court of law. In one of the first revelations of the Qur'an, women are enjoined to seek knowledge in the same manner as men. Men and women are equally expected to fulfil all religious duties and women are included in the final, ultimate reward: *"...Whoever does an atom's weight of good, whether male or female, and is a believer, all such shall enter into paradise..."* [QUR'AN, 40:40]

In the time of the Prophet Muhammad and ever since, women have been active participants at all levels of community affairs – social, political, religious, educational and intellectual. This is still visible today at various levels of society in different communities. The Prophet's wife, Aisha, was one of the foremost scholars at the time and second only to the Prophet. She was an authority in Qur'anic commentary, jurisprudence and the narratives of traditions from the Prophet. She is among the top reporters of *hadith* (narratives from the Prophet) with 2210 narrations. At the time of the second Caliph, Omar, who ruled the Muslim world for twelve years, we witness a woman entering into a debate with the Caliph over a governmental policy in front of a crowded congregation and Omar conceding defeat. This was unprecedented at the time elsewhere in the world and even today in many countries and cultures.

The Qur'an clearly states that women are not to have a place lower than men in society, within the confines of the home, and in particular, within marriage: *"And for women are rights over men, similar to those of men over women"*. [QUR'AN, 2:26]

Islam has elevated the status of women to such a level and gave them so many rights that it has set new standards. Prolific author Karen Armstrong said in an interview, *"in the middle-ages, Islam was criticised by the Christian world for giving too many rights to women."*

"Islamic law embodies a number of Qur'anic reforms that significantly enhanced the status of women. Contrary to pre-Islamic Arab customs, the Qur'an recognised a women's right to contract her own marriage. In addition she, not her father or other male relatives as had been the custom, was to receive the dower from the husband [4:4]. *She became a party to the contract rather than simply an object for sale. The right to keep and maintain her own dowry was a source of self-esteem and wealth in an otherwise male-dominant society. Women's right to own and manage their own property was further enhanced and acknowledged by the Qur'anic verses of inheritance* [4:7, 11-12, 176], *which granted inheritance rights to wives, daughters, sisters and grandmothers of the deceased in a patriarchal society where all rights were traditionally vested solely in the male heirs. Similar legal rights would not occur in the West until*

QUESTION 75

the nineteenth century."[16] In addition to these, women had no financial responsibilities in a family. She could keep and invest all her assets.

When it arrived on the world stage Islam transformed the status of women. All that Muslims need to do is to reinstate these rights in societies where poor economic and social conditions, culture and patriarchy usurped them.

---

16 Esposito, John, *Islam. The Straight Path*, Oxford University Press, (1998), p. 95.

What is the role of women in Islam and Islamic society?

I have thought about this question a lot. In my readings of the sources of Islam and the views of past and contemporary Muslim scholars, I could not find a definite set of roles for women and for that matter definite roles for men. I came to appreciate this because Islam does not focus on confining people by titles or roles but is concerned about how people, men and women, behave when they assume a particular role in the family or in society. Even the question really goes against the spirit of Islam, for Islam does not divide a society into competing camps of men and women. In spite of this insight, there are some principles Islam considers important.

- The physiological and emotional make-up of men and women complement one another.
- There are natural or default roles that men and women assume in a family or society.
- Women have no inherent religious or social limitations to prevent them assuming any role.

It is very clear from the physical differences between men and women that they are designed differently. Just as it is wrong for men to claim superiority over women because of their physical strength, it is equally wrong for women to go out of their way to drive trucks or work on contruction sites to prove that they can do what men can. In his book, "The Unknown Human Being", Nobel Prize winning French biologist and sociologist Alexis Carrel examines the physiology of men and women and talks about the sorts of duties that are suitable for each. However, in the information age that we live in where intellectual property and emotional intelligence are the currency, physical strength becomes less of a differentiator.

In Islam, physical attributes are not a source of superiority [QUR'AN, 49:13]. Since Islam claims humans were designed by God,

QUESTION 76

the design of men and women gives them implicit inclinations as to the roles they might choose to take in real life. This is further augmented by our natural career choices in fields where we need the least amount of training to make it easier for us to adapt to the working conditions.

The general spirit of the Qur'an is that men and women should not compete for supremacy, but work to compensate for each other's limitations and weaknesses, because, *"they are your garments and you are their garments"* [QUR'AN, 2:187]. The choice of the word 'garment' in this verse is very appropriate and significant. The Qur'an in verse 9:71 says that, *"the believers, men and women, are protectors one of another."* While the nature of protection may be different, the role of being a protector is reciprocal. Men and women also fulfil each other's need for compassion and love [QUR'AN, 30:21]. Therefore, neither sex has an important disadvantage or advantage over the other. Each gender has strengths and weaknesses. Only the communion of the two produces integrated human experience.

Just as do men, women have natural roles to play in a family. The roles of a woman are those of a wife, mother, daughter or a sister. The subjective importance of a role given in a society determines the feeling of satisfaction a person gets in that role. Islam gives great importance to the role of motherhood for example. It does so to give self-assurance that motherhood is not a punishment or disadvantage but a highly regarded role in the sight of God. Of the women mentioned in the Qur'an, the mother of Moses and Mary, the mother of Jesus, are particularly highlighted. The Prophet Muhammad said, *"Heaven is under the feet of mothers."* When a person asked whom should he serve first, three times the Prophet told him to serve his mother. Only on the fourth occasion did he mention serving his father. The winner of the 1973 Pulitzer award, the child psychiatrist Robert Coles says, *"Many working class women kept telling* me that they work because they must – to stay afloat financially – but that they would very much prefer to stay at home and be with their children."[17] By highlighting the importance and the high status of motherhood as well as giving financial responsibility for the family to men, Islam prevents the current unsatisfactory situation that women find themselves in contemporary society.

There are three areas where women have been denied rights in many cultures and religions. These are education, and religious and political leadership.

Islam gave women the right to education and actually encouraged them to get involved in scholarship. The Prophet Muhammad's wife Aisha was an important scholarly figure in the early history of Islam. There are many women in the chain of narrators in the references of the reported sayings of the Prophet Muhammad. Even today women are in the top academic elite even in countries such as Iran, where this would not be expected.

Islam also does not set any limitation to women in religious leadership and teaching. Rabi'a al Adawiya (d. 796), a famous Muslim woman mystic, had many male students. Women can also lead other women in prayer. Men lead combined congregations due to the practical difficulties in forming tight rows when praying. Since there are no clergy in Islam, the issue of the ordination of women does not arise. Women usually skip the lesser role of leading prayers and go on to the more esteemed role of religious scholarship.

The Qur'an clearly states that women are not to have a place lower than men in a society or within the confines of the home or in marriage: "...*And for women are rights over men, similar to those of men*

---

17 Coles, Robert, *The Inner Life of Executive Kids*, Harvard Business Review, November 2001.

over women…" [QUR'AN, 2:26] At the time of the Prophet and thereafter, women were active participants at all levels of community affairs – social, political, religious, educational and intellectual. This can still be seen replicated at various levels of society in different Muslim societies today. The second caliph, Omar, appointed women to top state leadership positions.

The only contentious issue is whether a woman can be a head of state. Does Islam allow this? The Qur'an does not set any limits in this regard. On the contrary, the Queen of Sheba is depicted in the Qur'an as a wise woman skilled in leadership and the art of diplomacy in matters of international relations [QUR'AN, 27:23–34]. Some Muslim jurists cite the saying of the Prophet, *"A people who select a woman as a leader will not be successful"*, when they argue that the head of state should not be a woman. This saying of the Prophet was uttered in response to being asked to state his view when the daughter of the Persian Khusrau became the queen. It is highly likely that he said it to emphasise the Qur'anic prediction of the downfall of the Persian Empire. Or he might have alluded to the stark reality that (even today) some men find it hard to accept the political leadership of women, which leads to political factions and conspiracies that eventually bring a country down. Moreover, in this saying there is no clear prohibition but at best a recommendation. The Prophet's wife led an army of men. Women have also been elected as Prime Minister or the President in some Muslim countries.

Why do women have to cover their bodies including their hair and men do not? Do women always wear head coverings? I see some Muslim women, for example in Iran, covered from head-to-toe. Do all Muslim women have to dress like that? Is covering the hair a religious requirement or a cultural practice?

Muslims cover their bodies because they believe that it is a requirement of their religion, an instruction given by God in the Qur'an. Islam's perspective is that God created the whole universe including human beings and God is the true owner of all creation. God has entrusted us with our bodies and the environment in which we live. We are enjoined to protect them from any physical and spiritual harm. Since God knows us better than we ever can, it is only natural that He provides guidelines for humans to follow to ensure happiness for all in a society. These instructions include the principles of human attire.

Muslims, men and women alike, are enjoined to cover certain portions of their bodies, as is also the case in Judaism and Christianity. The Qur'an says, "*Say to the believing men that they should lower their gaze and guard their modesty:* **that will make for greater purity for them**: *And God is well acquainted with all that they do. And say to the believing women that they should lower their gaze and guard their modesty; that they should not display their beauty and ornaments except what (must ordinarily) appear thereof; that they should draw their veils over their bosoms and not display their beauty…*" [QUR'AN, 24:30–31]

The primary goal of Islam for individuals is to facilitate spiritual and social development in a balanced manner. This goal and the spirit of the above verses inspire us to argue that the fundamental purpose of both men and women in covering parts of the body is to facilitate spiritual development by shifting one's sexuality to the background. According to Islam, the human being is God's highest creation [QUR'AN, 17:70], and as such has the choice and potential to either personally evolve to the greatest heights or slide downwards to the lowest depths [QUR'AN, 95:4–5]. Higher levels of spiritual states cannot be attained when one is attached to physical desires and in particular if the mind is preoccupied with one's physical appearance. Modesty in dress frees a person from judging others or oneself by their physical looks or sexuality. This is a liberating experience as people find that they no longer need to draw their sense of security or self-esteem from looking attractive. Instead, a sense of personal esteem and security comes from one's identity, character and innate self-worth. There is a tendency for men to be attached to wealth, status etc. while women tend to focus on their looks. The number of stores in shopping centres that target women rather than men is enough evidence to illustrate this argument. Therefore, Islam also requires women to cover their hair.

Islam wants women to be treated as having equal status with men without placing their sexuality in the foreground. Emphasis of sexuality in popular culture causes women to be treated like sex objects. Magazine covers are a testimony to the fact that society has an inclination to exploit women. Islam enjoins women to cover their bodies and their hair so that they are not sexually harassed by the stares of strangers. Contemporary Western law-makers are considering the inclusion of "staring at women" in sexual harassment legislation. Some cities in United States are contemplating having women-only sections in train carriages in order to stop sexual harassment. In the end, it is in the interest of women to cover themselves for protection from all possible harm.

The issue of covering the body is closely related to the issue of nudity. The increase in rates of rape since the sexual revolution show the close relationship between sexual promiscuity, nudity and sex-related crimes such as sexual assault. It seems that even good education is not able to impede the criminal inclinations of some men. A survey of college students in Canada revealed that a scary 60% of male students confided that they would rape women if they thought they could get away with it. Islam's dress code aims to stop this in favour of women and directs the expression of sexuality to the private lives of lawful partners.

If and when a Muslim female reaches the age of puberty, covering the hair becomes an obligation. Some parents ask their daughters to cover their hair earlier than this age so that they can get used to it. For women, the whole body is to be covered, excluding the face, hands and the feet. Men are also required to cover their bodies from the top of the belly to below the knees. As long as this obligation is fulfilled, the type or colour of dress is optional and left to the individual. The types of dress that are often shown in the media are cultural rather than Islamic. More elegant ways of dressing are also seen in many parts of the Muslim world.

In daily life, most women, whether they are Muslim or not, cover most parts of their bodies anyway. Even without covering the hair, 95% of this requirement is achieved most of the time. Covering the face is not a requirement of Islam. Some women might choose to do so as an outward expression of piety. Cultural customs are also the cause of such a practice in some countries, for example Iran or Afghanistan, where this is more prevalent.

It is important to note that the requirement to cover the hair has a lower level of importance in comparison to faith and the practice of the five pillars of Islam, such as the prescribed prayers and fasting. Not covering the hair or not feeling ready to practice this requirement should and does not prevent a woman from having faith in God and choosing Islam as a religion. It certainly does not prevent a woman from practising other more important aspects of Islam.

QUESTION 77

Usually, Muslim women feel the need to cover their hair when they reach the spiritual maturity to do so.

This is what some new Muslim women had to say about their experiences with practising the covering of the hair and rest of the body:

"I've been wearing the hijab (veil) three years now. For me, it's been very liberating. To tell you the truth, it allows you to be a person, and not just a woman/thing to be looked at. People listen to you. I used to be very heavy... When I lost the weight again, I noticed those looks and things, where... someone is talking to you, but they're looking at your chest. With the hijab, I notice it's gone away."

"Wearing it makes me feel like when people look at me, they're looking at me not for what my body looks like, but more for what I do and what I contribute."

"I do it because that's what God has ordained. ...I also wear it as a form of modesty... And it protects us from sexual harassment. I saw a woman wearing a short skirt, and I saw these men just looking at her, talking and smiling, and I'm like, 'They don't even respect women.' I'm thankful that in my religion, women are respected."

As these testimonies show, Muslim women who wear the veil feel freer, contrary to the common belief that the veil oppresses them. Also, wearing the veil is not a practice that is forced upon women. Women choose to wear the scarf as they go through their spiritual development. They also feel offended when people judge them as uneducated and unskilled just because they are covered. This, they say, is the real oppression for Muslim women.

Q78

In the media we see very bad treatment of women in Islamic countries. Does Islam really condone this treatment? I watched a few movies about women being oppressed in Muslim countries. Is this part of Islam?

Oppression of women is not taught or encouraged by Islam. Rather, in both Muslim and non-Muslim communities, the roots of the poor treatment of women lie in the lack of education and maturity of men responsible for such treatment. In fact, Islam forbids any ill treatment of women. Some of the images you may see in the media are somewhat biased and hence paint a distorted picture. This type of media coverage only shows the cultural practices of some Muslims, and these cultural practices are mistakenly confused with Islam as a whole.

Oppression and injustice of any sort is totally against the spirit of Islam. When Islam arrived on the scene, it liberated women. It was the only religion at the time, which gave meaningful rights to women. Karen Armstrong, author of "History of God", says that, *"Historically, Islam was criticised by Christians for giving too many rights to women."* [18]

Islam considered and treated women as religiously, socially and legally equal to men. Just as there are examples of the poor treatment of women in the Muslim world, there are also many examples of superior treatment, especially from men who have a good knowledge of Islam, and understanding and spiritual growth endowed to them by Islam. In the Muslim world experienced women actually look for men who practise Islam properly, for they know that they will find happiness in partnership with such men.

---

18 This quotation is taken from www.amazon.com, interview with Karen Armstrong.

QUESTION 78

Women are treated badly by men who have little or no knowledge of Islam or are not following the teachings of their religion.

Unfortunately, movies and the media mostly zoom in on a particular issue, usually from a limited angle. Viewers mistakenly generalise these examples as though they were true for the whole Muslim world. What's worse is that they wrongly conclude that poor treatment is because of Islam. An example is the *burqa* that we got so used to seeing in the Taliban's Afghanistan. In reality, this type of clothing is confined solely to Afghanistan and before the Taliban Afghan women willingly wore it as a status symbol. Most women did not stop wearing it even after Taliban was no longer in power.

Islam allows men to marry up to four women at the same time. Why does it allow this?

When Islam first appeared in the 7th century (610 CE), it effected improvements and changes in individual and social life by bringing in new laws and prohibiting or regulating the existing ones. The practice of regulated polygamy falls into the regulation category. Islam did not invent polygamy, but rather has regulated it. Before Islam, a man could marry as many women as he wanted or could afford. Islam put a limit on the number of women that a man could marry, along with some tough conditions.

The verse that allows Muslim men to marry more than one woman is as follows: *"Marry women of your choice, two, or three, or four; but if you fear that ye shall not be able to deal justly (with them), then only one."* [QUR'AN, 4:3] While allowing marriage with up to four wives, this verse discourages its practice by imposing some tough conditions such as achieving justice between wives, and encourages marrying only one. Being just between wives means providing them with equal food, accommodation, clothing and time spent with each of them. The consequence is that a man with four wives must provide four houses and must sleep in a different house every night, only returning to the same house less than twice a week. He must provide food and clothing equally between each of his wives and enjoy their company equally, even though one may be twenty and one forty. This is a very tough lifestyle for any man. As a result, the great majority (about 99%) of Muslim men have only one wife. This fact is true for all Muslim countries with slight differences in the marginal rate. This large percentage of monogamy was more or less maintained throughout the history of Islam. According to a survey conducted of the Ottoman archives, the percentage of men married to only one wife never fell below 92%. That is, only 8% of the total male population were married to more than one wife at any one time.[19]

According to Islamic law, if a man were known for his unjust behaviour, he would not be allowed by the State to marry more than one woman at any time. A woman can stipulate in her marriage contract that her husband-to-be cannot marry a second woman during the lifetime of their marriage. Furthermore, if the licence to marry more than one woman is abused or becomes widespread in society, the State can impose tight regulations to prevent the abuse for the benefit of the greater society. The shortcomings of individuals should not be used to blame Islam.

Sometimes polygamy becomes a practical solution to serious social problems. Throughout history, and still in developing and third-world countries, women depended on men's economic support. Some women may not be able to bear children. In such cases, if the husband wants to have children, he may marry again instead of divorcing his first wife. A "barren" woman may find it hard to marry again if this weren't permissible. Moreover, after wars, there is usually a shortage of young men. This was evident in Australia after World War I, as it was difficult for many widowed women or even young ladies to marry as there was a limited amount of available men. To maintain the stability of society in such instances, some men should be allowed to marry more than once. More importantly, their second wife should be a widow. For example, after World War I, the famous writer Victor Marguerite, after the decrease in the male population of France, said the following: "*18 million European women have been the victim of the system of living as a widow because of the death of their partners. As a result, they are condemned to*

---

19 Akgunduz, Ahmet, *Bilinmeyen Osmanli (Unknown Ottomans)*, Istanbul (1999), p. 418.

misery, economically and morally". Bearing in mind that only in the last few decades did women gain economic independence and only in Western countries. Ultimately, regulated polygamy ensures the economic security of marginalised women.

In summary, Islam regulated the uncontrolled practice of polygamy and laid down some tough conditions for people who choose to enter such a practice. This has greatly reduced its occurrence and polygamy became the exception rather than the rule. Islam has not abolished the practice, as this could lead to the social evils of adultery, prostitution and the economic alienation of women. It should be stressed this is an allowance, not a regular practice. This practice is designed to allow women, generally those that are barren, widowed, or where there are not enough unmarried men, to enjoy a married life being loved and wanted where it would not be possible if monogamy was the rule.

How does marriage and divorce take place in Islam? What are the ceremonies? Can a woman divorce her husband? How does divorce occur according to Islamic law? What rights do women have during or after the divorce?

The way a marriage is carried out has many cultural variants in the vast Muslim world that extends from Indonesia to North America. Essentially, however, a marriage must satisfy the following Islamic requirements:

- The couple must be willing to take part in marriage out of the exercise of their free choice.
- A marriage contract comprising of certain conditions and *mahr* (dowry, usually in the form of money or another asset) is formulated in front of at least two witnesses.
- The marriage is announced to the community.

Since Islam does not sanction the Western customs of dating or courtship, it is common for future spouses to be introduced by parents or by friends. This introduction may occur in a myriad of ways. It is more common today for a couple to meet at a particular social occasion and seek to get to know one another through friends and relatives. Although the practice may vary from culture to culture and according to the level of Westernisation of a Muslim country, there are a number of important elements in relation to how marriage occurs in a Muslim society.

The first step is for the prospective couple to see one another and discuss marriage with the supervision of a trusted person. At no time should the couple be alone, either in private or in public. The third person is usually a guardian from the woman's side, with the power to end the talks if she decides to have no more contact with the man. This phase can last for as long as the couple wishes to get to know one another. There is no obligation to continue meeting if either of them decides to end the relationship.

If the couple decides to get married, the family of the man makes a proposal to the guardian of the woman. This step can also vary from culture to culture. The key factor here is that families are involved at this point to ensure the protection of the woman. The freely-given consent of both the future husband and wife is essential.

If both the man and the woman give their consent, the engagement period commences. The period of engagement is flexible and can be a few weeks to a few years. During this period, the future couple gets to know one another better and makes the arrangements for the marriage ceremony. Love usually develops in this period and after the consummation of marriage when the couple gets to know one another intimately. Islam does not condone the idea of "trying out the person" before marriage. Break-ups could also occur if the couple notices serious incompatibility during the engagement period.

The final step is the wedding ceremony where the couple is married, usually by an imam or official. At this ceremony the two people profess their commitment to marriage in front of at least two witnesses. The wedding ceremony does not have to be performed in a mosque. A marriage contract is also signed where the bride sets the *mahr*, which acts as an insurance policy for the bride if the marriage ends after a short time. The wedding includes a reception where the marriage is announced to the community and celebrated by family and friends. The reception may be immediately after taking the wedding vows or some weeks later depending on individual circumstances. The marriage does not proceed unless both sides agree to the terms of the contract.

The most colourful aspect of the marriage is the reception or the public announcement. This is where most of the cultural elements step in, as Islam does not stipulate a fixed way of holding the reception. It usually involves a feast sponsored by the families and entertainment for men and woman in separate quarters.

Centuries of this practice have been very successful, as the divorce rates have been very low in Muslim societies. Even today, divorce rates in Muslim countries are much lower than those of many Western countries.

While Islam encourages men and women to get married to form families, it also recognises that over time people may no longer be compatible or may have irreconcilable differences. The Qur'an persuades men and women to think twice about divorce and even use third party mediators to reconcile differences. Although divorce is said in Islam to be *"the least liked of all lawful things by God"*, Islamic law (*Shariah*) allows it to proceed regardless of who instigates it. Just like marriage, divorce also occurs by making a certain affirmation of separation and making a public announcement that the couple is no longer married. Contrary to popular myth, divorce in Islam is not of the prerogative of men. Either party can initiate divorce. The divorce process is simple. Why should it be bitter and involve expensive proceedings that take their toll on everybody?

Divorce at the instigation of the men is called *talaq*. In this case, the man pronounces to his wife a statement such as *"I divorce you"* three times. This pronouncement initiates the first phase of the divorce process. At this point, all sexual activity stops between the couple for a period of three menstruation cycles, known as *iddah*. The Qur'an states, *"...The divorced woman shall wait concerning themselves for three monthly periods."* During this period, the man must pay the bills for the woman and not abuse her emotionally. If the woman is found to be pregnant, then there is a very good reason to re-think the divorce. Also in case of divorce being final, the parentage of the child will be known. If the couple has sexual relations during the *iddah* period, the divorce process stops and marriage continues as before. If the *iddah* period expires and they want to stay married, the man must propose and another wedding must take place. In order to give a strong message to the man to think twice before initiating a divorce, this process of *talaq* can only be repeated three times. After the third time, he cannot remarry her unless she is legitimately married to someone else and then divorced. Since this is unacceptable to any man, it serves as a real deterrent.

Divorce at the instigation of the woman is called *khul*, derived from *khul al-thaub* which translates as "removing the dress" – from the Qur'anic verse [2:187], which states, *"…the women are your garment and you are their garment"*, indicating the complementary and equal status of man and woman in marriage. A woman may ask for a divorce if there is sufficient reason. There are six reasons why divorce initiated by the wife is acceptable. They are:

1. In instances of continued domestic violence and cruelty.
2. Non-fulfilment of the terms of the marriage contract.
3. Insanity on the part of the husband.
4. Incompetence or impotence.
5. The abandonment of the wife and any children by the husband.
6. Any other reasons deemed consistent with the law.

The Qur'an states, *"…If a wife fears cruelty or desertion on her husband's part, there is no blame on them if they arrange an amicable settlement between themselves; and such settlement is best…"* If a woman divorces her husband, she is required to return all or part of the *mahr* or dowry given to her as a gift on the occasion of her marriage. This is not required if the husband initiates the divorce. The Qur'an encourages men to donate this in any case.

Maintenance (*nafaqah*) is another right of the wife, given to her in marriage and extended in the event of divorce. This includes the right to food, clothing and residence, essential services and medicine, even in the event the wife is a wealthy woman in her own right. The Qur'an outlines the responsibility of the man in providing maintenance in the case of divorce: "...*Let the woman live in 'iddah in the same style as you live, according to your means: Trouble them not so that you make things difficult for them.*"

The mother automatically gets the custody of children, as Islam recognises the greater emotional need of the small children for their mother. After the age of seven for boys and the age of puberty for girls, the father can file for the custody of his children. The court decides who is the most suitable guardian for the children at this point.

Is arranged marriage part of Islam?

There is a perception that in Muslim countries women have no rights in marriage, that they are forced into a marriage with an unwanted man, and the cause of this is Islam's segregation of women. The truth of the matter is that in Islam, a woman has the right to choose her partner or decline a proposal for marriage. This right was given to Muslim woman fourteen centuries ago at a time when women generally had no marriage rights in the most of the world.

The reader must make the distinction between forced marriages and arranged marriages. The freely given consent of both, the future husband and wife, is essential in Islam. The Prophet Muhammad stated, "...*The woman shall not be married until her consent is obtained.*" Another statement attributed to the Prophet is, "...*When a man gives his daughter in marriage and she dislikes it, the marriage shall be renounced...*" He also declared a marriage as invalid when the bride complained to him that her father forced her into marriage. Clearly, forced marriages are outlawed in Islam.

Nevertheless, in some Muslim countries, as in some non-Muslim countries, the father or a male relative of a woman may force her to get married to a man that she does not want. The parties that force a woman into marriage obviously are not following the teachings of Islam. This might be simply because of their lack of religious practice and knowledge. Surely, the failure of some Muslims to follow their religion's injunctions cannot be attributed to Islam.

Arranged marriages are not part of Islam nor does Islam strictly require it. There is no reference in the Qur'an or in the practice of the Prophet Muhammad that instructs Muslims to arrange a marriage. Just as in many other cultures, arranged marriages arise out of the practical need to facilitate the meeting of a couple for the purpose of marriage. Since Islam does not sanction the Western custom of dating and courtship, it is common for future spouses to be introduced by parents or friends. This introduction may occur in a myriad of ways and is by no means binding on the couple. They can break up at anytime in the process of getting to know one another. The only requirements of Islam are that the couple should not be alone either in private or any public place and the purpose of the meetings should be for the intention of marriage.

Dating did not exist in the Western world a hundred years ago. Matchmaking and dating services in the contemporary Western culture are a way of returning to the old arranged culture with a modern twist. Although it is not endorsed in Islam, some people are comfortable with arranged marriages and latest studies show that arranged marriages are more successful than other methods. The divorce rates as high as 50% in the United States show that dating does not guarantee success in a marriage. Divorce rates in Western countries have actually been on the increase since the sexual revolution of the sixties. It is increasingly alarming that people who decide to co-habitate before marriage seem to be more susceptible to divorce after marriage. Therefore the notion that through dating one will find the most suitable partner in life is not entirely supported by available social evidence.

Q82

Can a Muslim marry someone from a different religious background? What happens to the children if one of the couple is not Muslim?

In Islam, a Muslim man can get married to a Christian or Jewish woman (people of Scripture) but not to a person who does not believe in God. A Muslim woman can only marry a Muslim man. What appears to be a somewhat discriminating injunction is really designed to ensure freedom of belief and the protection of women in marriage.

Not only Islam but many other religions and cultures value a long and healthy relationship of a male and a female in marriage. Marriage has become a universal way of expressing one's commitment to a partner where the union produces a family, which is the fundamental component of a society and a nation.

The most important aspects of a family are its health, longevity and ability to raise mentally and spiritually healthy children so that children can become contributing members of a society. Since religion plays a large part in one's way of life, behaviour and motives, Islam recommends that Muslims get married to other members of the Muslim community. If a non-Muslim wishes to marry a Muslim man or woman, it is expected from that person, whether male or female, to consider converting to Islam if they are convinced of its teachings.

Inter-religious marriages could work well between individuals for whom religion is not an important part of life. In this case, their way of life is the common culture of the society rather than either person's religion. The marriage may be doomed to failure from the start if either person or both are committed to religion. It is almost unavoidable not to have any conflict in an intimate relationship such as marriage. Therefore, the couple should seriously consider the future of their marriage and only take the step if they are convinced that it will work.

So why does Islam allow men to marry women from another faith, but not the other way around? Even though there are exceptions to the rule, the general observation is that men have a tendency to be more prominent in the family than a woman as he bears the prime responsibility for the welfare of the family. Since Islam commands a man to deal in a fair manner with his wife, a Christian or a Jewish woman has the legal and moral guarantee that she will be looked after well and allowed to practice her religion without fear or oppression from her husband. The Prophet Muhammad said, *"the best among you is the one who has the best character and the best of those are the ones who treat their wives the best"*. Provided that a Muslim man is a good practising Muslim, the woman in marriage should be guaranteed a very good life. This is the reason why most Muslim women look for practising Muslim men to marry.

Islam requires a Muslim to believe that Moses and Jesus were appointed by God to guide humanity during the time when they lived and that the Scriptures that they brought were revelations from God. Naturally, a Muslim man will have natural affinity to a Christian or a Jewish woman in marriage. However, such an affinity does not exist between a Muslim woman and a man of other faiths and traditions, including atheism. Therefore, the marriage of a Muslim man to a Christian or a Jewish woman can work well. In this situation, the couple should agree before marriage that the children in the marriage should be educated as Muslims. Again children who are Muslim accept Moses and Jesus and their Scriptures as well as Muhammad, therefore the expectations of both partners are satisfied.

In the reverse scenario, where a Muslim woman is married to a non-Muslim man, the marriage does not ensure the religious freedom of the woman. Since a Christian or a Jewish man does not recognise Islam and its Prophet, there is no guarantee he will not use his economic and physical dominance (in most cases) against the Muslim woman to limit her freedoms and in some cases force her to convert. She can never be sure that she will have the freedom to practice if she is married to a non-Muslim man. At the very least, there may be a lot of conflicts in everyday life situations and the raising of the children. What will the Muslim woman do if her husband asks her to cook pork for dinner? The whole marriage will mean that each person will have to continuously compromise so as not to offend the other. This may lead to frustration, arguments and eventually to divorce. Therefore, Islam does not allow Muslim women to marry non-Muslim men.

Chapter 8

Muslims' Perspectives on Life

Our lives have many influences in the modern world. As human beings are conditioned beings, we cannot prevent the inevitable influence of the dominant culture. A culture determines the way we think, the way we act and the life assumptions that determine our behaviour.

The life of a Muslim has been an enigma for many curious minds. For Muslims, Islam is a chosen way of life. They have the comfort of knowing that Islam is a source of reference and inspiration. Islam bears its positive influence from birth to death and throughout life by way of its values and principles.

What are the fundamental Muslim values?

In recent times, especially after the Taliban experience in Afghanistan and September 11, 2001, there have been many statements in the media and by world leaders and analysts that Islam's values lag far behind the values of current world civilisation. Islam is depicted to be a system with values incompatible with modern life and with human needs in the 21st century and beyond. Yet when we examine the values of the materialist philosophy on which the current popular wisdom is based, and the fundamental principles of Islam according to the Qur'an, not according to what some Muslims might do today, a different picture unfolds.

In the popular wisdom of materialist philosophy, social life depends on the notion of *power*. The powerful rule and might is right. A rationale is provided to justify whatever the powerful do. The outcome of brute power is the transgression of the rights of weaker individuals and nations. This especially becomes manifest when one is in a position of power. The purpose of existence centres on the idea of personal and national *benefit*. The "What's in it for me?" mentality becomes the guiding principle of decision making. If there is no benefit, the plight of people is ignored. This attitude results in fighting and competition when two or more parties target the same finite *benefit*. The unifying agent in the popular wisdom of materialist philosophy is either *race* or *negative nationalism*, which leads the person or the group of people to see themselves as superior to other races and nations. This attitude justifies the exploitation and the occupation of the other "inferior" people or races. The principal notion of life is that *"life is a struggle"*. *"Others are out there to get me"* is the general attitude, resulting in personal and social conflict. The purpose of life is to *satisfy the self*. The masses are typified as "consumers". Mass advertising targets insatiable human desires to convince "consumers" to consume products that they don't really need. The result is a cycle of never-ending dissatisfaction and ever-increasing dependence on products that one does not really need to survive.

The general outcome of this popular wisdom has been the material happiness and comfort to a small percentage of the national and world population, while great masses work and live in undesirable conditions to perpetuate the comfort of the minority elite. After two world wars, the perils of this materialistic worldview have become apparent. In the last few decades some changes in attitude and the slogans have occurred, but the evidence suggests that this mindset is still widespread and the dominant norm.

By contrast, Qur'anic wisdom is quite different. Social life in Islam depends on *truth* and *justice*, which leads to trust between individuals in society and its legal system. Trust leads to social unity and cohesion. The purpose of existence is to *recognise and worship God*, to reach a level of personal integrity built on virtue and to express these in good works performed to attain the acceptance and approval of God. This attitude leads to interdependence within a society made up of independent individuals respecting each other's rights. The unifying agent is not race or nationality, but *humanity* and *faith* as more universal centres of social gravity leading to a sense of egalitarian brotherhood. The principle motivation in life is to *help one another* rather than to engage in a struggle, thus resulting in peace and harmony in the interpersonal and social spheres. The purpose of life is to reach *spiritual contentment* while restraining the desires of the self to those of a lawful satisfaction. For the majority of people the outcome of restraining the self and developing spirituality is happiness in both this world and the next.

The history of Islam bears testimony to the successful application of these principles that has brought material and spiritual contentment to all of society. It is a great society that was the outcome of implementing these fundamental principles of Islam that led H.G. Wells to say in his book, *The Outline of History*, that, *"Islam has created a society more free from widespread cruelty and social oppression than any other society had ever been in the world before."*

Muslims today are well aware that present-day Muslim societies are distant from some of these principles, at least at the state level. They also know that it is practically possible to implement them as was the case in the early society established by the Prophet and thereafter by the Rightly-Guided Caliphs and many other rulers since the early period of Islam. Therefore, contemporary Muslim populations feel they have what is needed to resolve their problems. Muslims say the solution lies in the implementation of the fundamental social principles of Islam.

The challenge for Muslims is to be clear that it is these fundamental principles that need to be implemented and not some of the human practices that worked in the past under the unique circumstances of the day but may no longer be effective. Therefore, the key challenge for Muslims is how to package the fundamental principles of Islam in today's world. Muslims need to find a workable social model that not only meets the needs of today, but also launches Muslim societies into a bright future.

QUESTION 83

Fundamental Areas	Materialistic Philosophy		Wisdom of the Qur'an	
	Principle	Outcome	Principle	Outcome
Social Life Dependence	Power	Transgression	Truth, justice	Social unity
Purpose of Existence	Benefit	Competition, Fighting	Integrity, worship and acceptance (*ridha*) of God	Inter-dependence
Unifying Agent	Race, negative nationalism	Exploiting the other, Occupation	Humanity, Religion	Brotherhood
Principle Motivation of Life	Struggle	Conflict	Helping one another	Peace, Harmony
Purpose of Worldly Life	Satisfying the self	Dissatisfaction, Increase in personal needs	Spiritual contentment and lawful pleasures	Happiness in the world and the hereafter
	Result: Material comfort to about 20% of people at the expense of the remaining 80%.		**Result:** If practiced, happiness to the whole (100%) of people in this world and the hereafter.	

Is the Islamic religion "a way of life"?

Islam as a religion is indeed a "way of life" in that it offers a complete set of guidelines for both the practical and spiritual dimensions of everyday life. The Arabic word for "religion" as it appears in the Qur'an is "deen", which also means a "way of life". All essential life experiences are covered by the Qur'an and the sayings of the Prophet Muhammad, known as the *hadith*: from the social, the mental, the physical, the legal (by the system of Islamic law known as the *Shariah*) to of course the spiritual. This coverage, though, does not impose a static model on people, but rather provides solutions to choose from in all life scenarios to ensure our individual and communal happiness.

I should also note that not all of Islam's guidelines are absolutely compulsory. In fact, its compulsory prohibitions and commandments are very few in number. The great majority of the sayings of the Prophet are recommendations to Muslims, who are free to choose to follow them or not. On the other hand, the Qur'an tells us that the Prophet is an excellent example of Islam's ideals and encourages Muslims to voluntarily follow his example if they want direction in personal development [SEE ANSWER TO QUESTION 15 FOR MORE ON THE ROLE OF THE PROPHET IN ISLAM].

Faith in God provides a firm foundation for all elements of daily toil for a Muslim. As the Qur'an states, "...*The faithful are only those who believe in God and His Messenger, then they doubt not and struggle hard with their wealth and their lives in the way of God...*" [QUR'AN, 49:15] and also, "...*Whoever submits himself entirely to God while doing good (to others) – he has his reward from his Lord...*" [QUR'AN, 2:112] This willing submission is the essence of being a Muslim. He or she begins each new undertaking with God in their mind. Thinking about God at the moment of choice connects the daily life to the Divine, rendering every act an act of worship. This is why Muslims are encouraged to say "*Bismillah-ir Rahman-ir Rahim*" (in the name of God the Most Gracious, the most Merciful) before they begin to eat, read a book or enter a house.

Many sayings of the Prophet relate to the fact that Islam is not a religion concerned with hard theological exercises, but rather it is focussed upon leading believers towards a life filled not only with devotion for God, but also a life of learning, acceptance of responsibility for one's actions and selfless acts of good deeds towards other fellow human beings.

Excess in religion is discouraged. According to the Prophet Muhammad, consistent but less religious practice is preferable to sudden bursts and deflation of religious fervour. Islam emphasises that human life has many spheres of experience as well as responsibility. Abdullah ibn 'Amr reported a conversation between himself and the Prophet Muhammad, "...*The Messenger of God (Peace and Blessings of God Be Upon Him) said to me 'O Abdullah! I am told that you are fasting during the day and standing up in devotion (prayer) during the night?' I said, 'Yes, O Messenger of God'. He said: 'Do not do so; keep the fast and break it and stand up in devotion (in the night) and have sleep, for your body has a right over you, and your eye has a right over you, and your wife has a right over you, and the person who pays you a visit has a right over you...'*"

From this and many other similar narratives from the Prophet we learn that the fundamental spirit of religious practice in Islam is to strive to find balance and equilibrium in one's beliefs, emotions, actions and personal development.

What is the significance of ceremonies performed at the time of birth and death?

The events of birth and death in the life of a human being are seen as significant milestones, as Muslims say, "...*we belong to God and to Him we shall return*" [QUR'AN, 2:155].

Muslim parents joyfully thank God for the birth of a new child. In Islam, all children, male or female, are viewed as gifts, an entrustment from God and a great blessing. A new child is welcomed into the Muslim community (*ummah*) as soon as it is born. The birth ceremony *aqiqah* is divided into several parts. Whether all of these customs are adhered to or not depends on the family's cultural background as well as religious knowledge.

The head of the family or a religious leader takes the baby into his arms and whispers the call to prayer (*azan*) into the baby's right ear so that the very first words the child hears is *"there is only one God"*. The *iqamah* (a slightly modified version of the *azan*, called just before the start of the congregational prayer) is whispered into the left ear of the baby. The short period between the *azan* and *iqamah* (5–10 minutes) symbolises the shortness of life.

A small piece of mashed date, sugar or honey is placed in the baby's mouth by the oldest or most respected relative, symbolising the wishes and prayers of the family for the baby to have a sweet and pleasant life free from troubles and full of goodness.

The baby will then be named after an elderly family member such as a grandfather or grandmother or after one of the prophets mentioned in the Qur'an or the companions of the Prophet Muhammad. There are many Muslims with the names Maryam (Mary), Isa (Jesus), Musa (Moses), Ibrahim (Abraham), and so on. Names can have overtly religious connotations such as *Abdullah* (the servant of God) or more ordinary such as *Alif* (the first letter in the

Arabic alphabet). Receiving a good name is considered to be a fundamental right due to the baby from its parents.

Seven days after the birth, a sheep or a goat (*aqiqah*) is prepared as a meal for the family, friends and the poor in the neighbourhood. The baby's hair is shaved and traditionally the shaved hair's weight in silver or gold is given to the poor as charity. This immediately connects the child with the community as well as being a symbol of the child's lifelong commitment to the poor.

Circumcision of male babies can take place in a long period starting after the *Aqiqah* ceremony to about five years old and before starting school. Depending on the culture, a circumcision celebration may be organised by the family. Although circumcision is not a religious sacrament, all male children are circumcised for cleanliness and hygiene. Contrary to some media coverage, female circumcision is neither a requirement nor is it considered beneficial from a religious perspective. It is only practised in some parts of Africa as a remnant of pre-Islamic tribal custom and is equally practised by Christians living in the same regions.

The practice of these religious customs around birth depend largely on the commitment of the parents to Islam, their knowledge of the religion, the economic status of the society and the level of Westernisation of the country in which they live.

Given all babies are considered to be born as a Muslim, that is, born with the natural disposition (*fitrah*) to believe in God, to be truthful and so on, there is no equivalent of "baptism" in Islam. For the same reason, people who accept Islam are called "reverts" rather than "converts".

When the news of the death of a family member or friend reaches Muslims, they repeat the recommendation of the Qur'an: "...*Say: we belong to God and to Him we shall return*" [QUR'AN, 2:155]. According to the Muslim tradition, a dead person should be buried (not cremated) as soon as possible. The funeral process consists of three stages:

1. Firstly, the body is prepared for burial. The body of a male Muslim is ritually washed for the final time, usually by a male relative or male *imam,* and the body of a dead Muslim woman will be washed by a female relative or midwife or a female spiritual leader. The body is laid out with the arms alongside the body and shrouded in white linen.

2. The prepared body is then transported to the mosque for a short funeral prayer. The funeral prayer is conducted in congregation where Muslims line up behind the coffin. The standard parts of Muslim prayer (*salat*) such as bowing down and prostration are not required for the funeral prayer. The prayer is followed by a round of acknowledgements of the good deeds of the person and people are invited to forgive whatever rights they had over the dead person.

3. The coffin is then transported to the cemetery in a funeral procession. The body is preferably buried without the coffin. It is laid on its right side with the face turned towards the *Ka'bah.* Usually all participants in this ceremony will cast three handfuls of earth in the grave while reciting passages from the Qur'an and asking forgiveness from God for the deceased person. Extravagant grave structures and covered graves are frowned upon. The expense is better spent as charity for the living.

During this funeral process and thereafter, friends, neighbours and relatives visit the family of the deceased expressing their condolences saying, "*may God bless her (or his) soul with His Grace*". They also bring food with them knowing that the family would be too grieved to be concerned with food preparation. Recitation of the Qur'an for the spiritual benefit of the deceased is also a common practice.

Q86

What is the place of the Qur'an in the life of a Muslim from birth to death?

The Qur'an is the source of guidance and spiritual nourishment for Muslims from birth to death. Muslims believe that the Qur'an is the literal word of God and is the most important message [QUR'AN, 38:67] sent to humanity, summarising the wisdom of previous revelations. Naturally, humanity is the audience for this message.

The recitation of the Qur'an in its original Arabic form has a truly profound effect on the human soul even if one does not understand the language. Reciting or listening to the Qur'an is a means of getting spiritual uplift and reward. Thousands of Muslims fill halls just to listen to a renowned reciter, in the same way that people flock to a concert.

It is for this reason that some pregnant mothers make their babies listen to the Qur'an even before they are born. The Qur'an can also take on the role of a lullaby in early childhood. Along with learning to read and write in their native language, most Muslim children are sent to Qur'an classes to learn how to read the Qur'an and memorise certain passages for future use in their prayers. For some select children, memorisation of the Qur'an extends to cover the complete book over two years usually between the ages of 8–10. The tradition of memorising the whole Qur'an has continued from the time of the Prophet till today.

In later years of adolescence and adult life, understanding the Qur'an and applying it as a source of guidance in one's daily life takes priority. The Prophet Muhammad has urged his followers to read the Qur'an repeatedly and practise its teachings at such a level that the Qur'an and the person should be in perfect concord. As mentioned previously, after the demise of the Prophet Muhammad, a group of men came to his wife Aisha and asked about the character of the Prophet. She replied, *"Don't you read the Qur'an? He was the living Qur'an"*. Muslims should strive to match their prophet in fulfilling this ideal.

The Qur'an is considered to be the manual for the conduct of life for both men and women. When you read it, you get the strange feeling that it is talking directly to you. You get the impression that it immediately knows your feelings. What's amazing is that it responds to your feelings in real-time. Reading and trying to understand the Qur'an is a lifelong process for Muslims. Every reading unravels new meanings and insights. I am personally amazed on how I could have missed such obvious meanings when I last read a passage. The reality is that as we develop intellectually and spiritually the codes of the Qur'an are naturally exposed to the reader, perpetuating development until the last breath.

One of the fundamental practices in an Islamic funeral is the recitation of the Qur'an before, during and after the burial. It is believed the spiritual energy generated by the recitation of the Qur'an benefits the soul of the dead person [ABU DAWUD, *FUNERALS*, 24]. It is a common practice to recite the *Fatiha,* the opening chapter of the Qur'an, and dedicate it to the soul of the dead in an unknown grave or all the dead buried in a cemetery.

In this way, the Qur'an informs, inspires and spiritually nourishes a Muslim from birth to death. Naturally, the level of connection depends on the devotion of a family and a Muslim to Islam and its principles.

How do Muslim teenagers react to Islam in Australia? Is it hard to educate your children in Islamic principles in Australia? Do Muslim children go overseas to learn about Islam?

Irrespective of what ethnic or religious background they might come from, most teenagers go through the turmoil of adolescence. So do Muslim teenagers. Fundamentally, there are three characteristics common to all teenagers – physical self-awareness, a sense of belonging and wondering about meaning in life.

In the case of physical self-awareness, the reaction of Muslim youth may not always be in line with Islam. The dominant Australian culture and modern lifestyle provide an easily accessible way to satisfy newly discovered physical pleasures and emotions. Unless they have a strong Islamic education and practice, a certain portion of Muslim youth goes through a conflict with Muslim values and what modern lifestyle has to offer resulting in going into excesses that damage the individual, the family and the immediate community.

On the other hand, professed Muslim teenagers quench their sense of belonging in Islam's call for a worldwide community of Muslims, transcending national and racial boundaries. Again, if a youth does not receive a good Islamic education, the strong sense of belonging may result in negative nationalism. In order to survive as a minority some parents may also emphasise the national ties to their country of origin with the hope that their children are not assimilated and lose their Muslim identity as a result.

Many Muslim youth throw themselves in the oasis of Islam from the vast spiritual desert that modern societies have become. The quest for finding a meaning in life and the need to find answers to questions such as "Why am I here? Where do I come from? Where am I going?" leads youth to Islam since it satisfactorily answers the spiritual questions of an inquiring mind. The alignment of Islam with human reason is one of the main reasons why Islam is attracting youth worldwide.

Although one does not have to travel overseas to learn Islam, a handful of young or older men travel overseas to study Islam in universities in Muslim countries. In Australia, there are many Islamic colleges, after-school or weekend classes that give children, youth and adults basic Islamic education. There are also some initiatives to teach Islam at the academic level.

There are about 300,000 Muslims in Australia, with 36% of this population having been born in Australia. In its forty years of history, the Australian Muslim community went through two phases of development. Now they have entered the third phase and I believe, as described below, the fourth and fifth phases will come sometime in the future decades.

Phase 1 consisted of mass migration and the establishment of the community during the sixties and the seventies. The first Muslim migrants were from a diversity of Muslim countries. They first needed employment, housing, places of worship and a need to belong somewhere. This has resulted in Muslims concentrating in Sydney and Melbourne and more particularly in a few suburbs within these capital cities.

Phase 2 was the need to have continuity and identity in their culture and this phase lasted through the eighties and nineties. This made Muslim communities introverted in order to preserve themselves. Realising that it was very difficult to educate their children, some parents opted for a permanent return to their country of origin. However, often they had become overly attached to Australia and therefore most of them came back for the second time. Realising they were to stay in Australia permanently, they started to venture into educational institutions to educate their children and to preserve their cultural identity.

Phase 3 is the period entered since the year 2000, when the Muslim community started to open up to the wider society, led by the second generation Muslims who are articulate and have the skills needed to develop relations with the wider non-Muslim society. The true integration of the Muslim community within the wider society will occur in this period.

Phase 4 is yet to come. I believe that, in time, Muslims in Australia will develop their own unique Australian identity and culture detached from the countries the original Muslim migrants came from. Australian Muslims will also be spiritually independent from the rest of the Muslim world by educating their spiritual leaders here in Australia.

There is also Phase 5, which is the interdependence of Muslims in the West and Muslims in traditionally Muslim countries positively influencing the development of one another.

Q88

How is Islam practised in Australia? What is it like to live as a Muslim in a secular culture? Is it difficult for a Muslim to practise their religion in a Christian community? Are there many Western converts to Islam?

It is estimated today that around one third of Muslims globally are minority groups in their country of habitation. In countries designated as Islamic republics, or where Muslims make up the majority, it is their duty to establish Islam in their own lives and to help establish and maintain Islamic principles such as the rule of law, freedoms and minority rights within society and an Islamic polity. As a minority group in a society having a majority of non-Muslims, Muslims are expected to survive as a community and to strive to ensure they have religious freedom to live Islam both as individuals and as a community. This is what Muslims strive to do in Australia within the secular and democratic framework of the Australian ethos.

Notwithstanding the freedom of religion inherent in secularism, many Muslims and indeed those of other religious persuasions, believe that secularism (removing religion from its inevitable social manifestations) to a great extent undermines religious values and morality. It may certainly become more difficult to adhere to prayer five times daily in a secular workplace, or to explain to children why the festivities of Christmas and Easter are not religiously relevant to them or to purchase foods that adhere to dietary rules. Although the early Muslim polity established by the Prophet Muhammad in Medina was somewhat secular since it defined the rights and responsibilities of citizenship irrespective of one's religious convictions, essentially there is no distinction for a Muslim between state and religion; the spiritual and profane. Recognising that men will govern other men, the highest level of escalation and hence true governance belongs ultimately to God [QUR'AN, 4:59]. The principles of Islam have a direct bearing on the whole of life and not just the personal domain.

Muslims in Australia respond to the challenges of a secular society differently depending on their level of faith and commitment. While some fully adapt to the society, others try to minimise some of the damaging effects on their faith and identity by strongly associating with their religion and immediate cultural community. There is also an emerging group of Australian-born Muslims or the second or third generations of the first migrant community, who have the skills to interact properly with the greater society while being able to maintain their religious identity and practice. I believe these Muslims in time will develop a unique Australian Muslim identity and culture.

Islam is not a hard religion to practise. It has great flexibility in its rights and requirements. Since Islam is lived on a daily basis, the practice of Islam sometimes unavoidably places a Muslim at odds with their workplace and social environment in a foreign or purely secular culture.

1. Praying at work. Those Muslims who want to observe the noon and afternoon prayers in particular have a challenge to find a suitable place and even the time to perform these duties unless they are close to a place of worship or the employer is tolerant to the needs of Muslims.

2. Finding *halal* meat [SEE QUESTION 73 FOR MORE ON WHAT MAKES A MEAT *HALAL*] in a society where Muslims are a minority.

3. Avoiding social gathering where alcohol [SEE QUESTION 71 FOR MORE ON ALCOHOL] is served. A practising Muslim would not consume alcohol. Because of the observed fact that the behaviour of people sitting at a table where alcohol is freely served and consumed for an extended time will usually be inappropriate, some Muslims do not attend functions where alcohol is served.

In situations like this, some Muslims elect to compromise while others stay firm in their practice. Almost in all cases practical solutions are found because of the flexibility inherent in Islamic practice. For example, a person can combine two prayers in one when travelling. Missed prayers could be made up at a more suitable time. Meat of the lawful animals slaughtered by Jews or Christians could be consumed. If unsure of how an animal was slaughtered, Prophet Muhammad recommended his followers to say *"in the name of God"* and eat it. There are many other alternatives and flexible practices found in the other obligations of Islam. The key message the Prophet Muhammad gave to his followers is summarised in the following narration: *"Facilitate things for people (concerning religious matters), and do not make it hard for them, give them good tidings and do not make them run away (from Islam)."*

Since Islam is a public religion and it is visible in daily life it will shift the normal line of demarcation between the individual and the society that exists in the West. How can one not notice Muslim women who cover their hair or how can one avoid being aware when thousands of people fast for one month in Ramadan or pray in the park and in the workplace? The secular norms in the West are not used to religion being so visible. This visibility will unavoidably result in a new point of equilibrium in the secular society we live in. This should not be seen as a negative development or a deliberate attempt to damage secularism. Rather, it is a natural consequence of the presence of Muslims in any society.

So far as adherence to religion is concerned, Muslims in countries such as Australia and the US, which are essentially Christian by nature, face far greater trials in life than their Muslim brothers and sisters in Islamic nations. Muslims in a predominantly non-Muslim country find themselves without the supportive layers of culture and social institutions. This causes a person to either be a very strong

Muslim or detach from the Islamic and Muslim community altogether. Muslims believe that those who face greater challenges in life and succeed in overcoming them will also be greeted with greater rewards in the hereafter and in this life with increased self-esteem and stronger identity.

Despite these challenges, more and more Muslims are starting to practise Islam. People are also being drawn to Islam in great numbers and Islam is attracting many converts. Growth rates currently stand at about 235% globally, the fastest growing religion in the world at present. Islam is the fastest growing religion in the USA and the third fastest in Australia (after Buddhism and Hinduism). While the greater part of the growth rate is by birth, there are a considerable number of converts in Western countries.

**How does Islam view sex before marriage?
And how does it view homosexuality?**

Although sex before marriage is not viewed as seriously as adultery, Islam only endorses sexual activity within a legitimate marriage.

One should bear in mind the commandments and prohibitions of Islam are structured to protect basic human rights – freedom in belief, the right to live, the right to reproduce, the right to own assets and to protect the human mind. Preservation of these rights is universal, that is, they do not change over time or from one culture to the other. They ensure that no-one's rights are transgressed in an interdependent society. In addition to protecting basic human rights, Islam's goal is to facilitate a wholesome and balanced spiritual development so that we find happiness in this world and the next.

We know from the experiences of the Western sexual revolution that four decades of free sexual experimentation have not resulted in overall happiness, personal satisfaction or better social structures. This is in spite of the fact that the levels of education and material comfort have increased. The ever-increasing rates of rape, exploitation of women, theft and increased cases of depression prove we are worse off. This is because of the reality that our physical desires have no limit. The more they are stimulated the less satisfied they become – especially sexual desires. People who get bored with their partners want to "experiment" with others to fulfil new fantasies.

There are serious personal and social consequences from extramarital sexual relationships. Firstly, the woman in the relationship is left in a vulnerable position. If the man leaves her, she would be deprived of her chastity, which is held in honour in many cultures around the world. Her life could be ruined as a result. Secondly, the relationship may produce a child. In this case, she (and the society) would also be left with the liability of looking after the child. This has serious consequences, especially in societies without a welfare system where abandoned children provide examples of tragic humanitarian neglect. Moreover, there is a high risk the child would not know who his or her father is and would come to the world inherently disadvantaged and be troubled during their upbringing not knowing who their biological father is. This can pave the way for the child to be more unsettled during their upbringing putting an even greater burden on the mother. In other words, the child's basic human rights would be violated even before entering the world scene.

It is for these reasons that Islam does not approve of sexual relationships outside of marriage. That is, Islam seeks to protect women's and unborn children's welfare and rights. Islam proposes marriage as the means of satisfying one's sexual and personal needs. Only through marriage can healthy families be established and maintained. Healthy family units, in turn, ensure a healthy society and happiness and safety for all members of society.

The usual argument is "what's wrong with having sex when both parties are willing and there is protection against the pregnancy?" The counter question is, do you go through the red light at night when there are no cars around? Of course you don't or you shouldn't because you might develop a habit of going through red lights. One day, out of habit, you might go through a red light at a busy intersection with devastating consequences. Similarly, promiscuous sexual relationships develop a habit, which generally results in one's inability to establish long-term relationships or cause late marriages with few children. We will see the full impact of the sexual revolution of the sixties when the next few decades will produce very lonely old people and a pension system unable to cope with the demand. Lack of a sustainable younger population means that developed countries (such as Australia) have to continue to have a yearly migrant intake to maintain their economies. Furthermore, Islam came for all times and all people. Medication to prevent pregnancy even today is not available for everyone, so the problems associated with sexual relations outside of a marriage still pose social and individual problems for most people in most countries.

Homosexuality is very similar to the case of sex outside of marriage in that Islam does not approve of homosexual relationships. Just as we believe it is not right to make people of homosexual orientation outcasts and oppress them, it may not be right for gay people to go marry or adopt children to appear as a normal family. "Test-tube" babies of the eighties are now adults and are looking for their true parents. Similarly, children born through an unknown surrogate mother will one day want to know who their real mother and father are. Knowing one's true parents is a fundamental human right.

In the Qur'an, God tells us that man and woman are designed physically and emotionally to complement one another [QUR'AN, 2:187, 30:21]. Their differences combine to produce a collective person in a family. Sexual relationship plays an important but only a partial role in the whole relationship between a man and a woman [SEE ALSO THE ANSWER TO QUESTION 76].

The Qur'an also talks about the fact that everything is created in pairs: *"Glory be to Him Who created **pairs of all things**, of what the earth grows, and of their kind and what they do not know."* [QUR'AN, 36:36] In addition to being a description of a scientific fact unknown at the time of revelation, this verse says that pairs of opposite nature are the rule in the universe. Although there are exceptions to this law, exceptions do not change the fact that the divine intent in creating humans was for them to establish families in the way of a male and a female. Whether one accepts this or not, the stark reality is that this is the norm. Only the family unit made up of a male and a female can produce an interdependent entity that produces more value than the sum of its individual components. This value is the child produced and the support structures that exist in the extended family (something that is also partly eradicated by the sexual revolution).

Islam's view on homosexuality can be summarised in three broad categories. I know this issue is political and there have been human rights abuses against gay people, which tend to prevent an open discussion. Islam treats "sinners" with compassion and views them as people in need of support rather than alienation. When a person spoke critically of a person for committing adultery, the Prophet Muhammad stopped him saying, *"but he loves God and His Prophet"*.

1. In the first category are those homosexual relationships practised by bisexual individuals and omnisexual people who do not care with whom they have a sexual intercourse as long as they satisfy their insatiable libido. This category is clearly prohibited in Islam, as it is clear that there has been a choice to engage in homosexual relations when a heterosexual relationship could equally be chosen.

2. The second category covers individuals who are sexually attracted to the same sex and have no attraction to the opposite sex. There is currently a claim that this situation is genetic. Assuming this is the case, then one could ask whether this is a sexual disorder similar to the sexual condition of "impotence" (having no sexual drive) bearing in mind parity of reasoning. Could one then propose the development of a medicine to cure homosexuality, just as there are drugs for the treatment of impotence? If homosexuality is not treatable, then would it be considered as a disability? These questions can be asked and beg answers in the current debate. Islam recommends a person in this category to be patient and promises the reward of Paradise for the inherently disadvantaged (the analogy

is drawn from words spoken by the Prophet Muhammad to an epileptic woman).

3. The third category covers those who have some physical traits of both sexes. Islam gives them the choice of selecting the sexual identity they prefer.

As there are no religious clergy in Islam, the issue of the ordination of gay people, or for that matter, women in religious posts does not arise.

Islam is not against the satisfaction of sexual desires in the form of a legitimate marriage. This is the balanced path between the two extremes of no sexual desires (impotence) and having indiscriminate sexual activity with just about anyone. Any physical desire unchecked eventually becomes self-destructive for the person and the society.

Chapter 9

Contemporary Issues Facing Islam and Muslims

September 11, 2001, war in Afghanistan and Iraq, suicide bombings – these have dominated the recent headlines and global politics. Muslims, and therefore Islam, unwittingly seem to enter into discussions in relation to these events. Yet, few of us really know about Islam, the faith of one in every five people on earth spanning the globe from Africa to Asia, from the United States to Europe. Islam and Muslims have often been viewed through a series of stereotypes as fundamentalists, extremists or radicals, which distort our understanding of the world's second largest religion.

In this chapter, I will provide a clear and concise look at some of the contemporary issues: Islam and democracy, secularism, Islam's views on terrorism, concept of jihad, Muslim response to modernity and future directions.

What is holy war? What is *jihad*?

Literally, the Arabic word *jihad* means "to struggle" or "strive" and applies to any effort exerted by anyone. In this sense, a student strives to get an education and pass their exams. A businessman strives to make money and expand his business. A mother strives to bring up her children to be good citizens. In its general definition, *jihad* means doing one's best to achieve a desired goal.

In the religious context, the broadest definition of *jihad* is *the inner and outer struggle in proactively confronting adverse circumstances* that one might find oneself in. That is, *jihad* is the endeavour to positively influence the circumstances, which are adversely affecting the well-being of the individual and society or overcoming the barriers that may exist in the way of achieving this goal. Islam expects a Muslim not to be overly submissive or aggressive, but to find the middle ground. For these reasons *jihad* is a very important concept not only in Islam but also in any civil society. The practitioner of *jihad* (*mujahid*) is one who devotes himself or herself to a struggle against adversity.

There is no concept of "holy war" in Islam. The phrase "holy war" is not used anywhere in the Qur'an, in the authentic sayings of the Prophet Muhammad or in the early Islamic literature. The Arabic term for "military war" is "*harb*" and for "fighting" is "*qital*", not *jihad*. According to Islamic teachings, it is "unholy" to instigate or start a war, while it is recognised that wars are sometimes inevitable and legally justifiable.

In the words of the Prophet Muhammad, there are greater and lesser aspects of *jihad*. The *greater jihad* is the pursuit of intellectual and spiritual enlightenment, despite the emotional barriers within. It consists of fighting superstition, wrong beliefs, never-ending desires of the flesh and the evil inclinations of the self. This is called the *greater jihad* since it is always present and comes both invisibly and in many facets. The *lesser jihad* involves encouraging others to follow this path. While it includes military defence, the *lesser (outer) jihad* is much more comprehensive. It consists of the social activism of a believer or a believing community to advance the cause of Islam through lawful channels.[20]

The Prophet Muhammad combined these two aspects of *jihad* in a balanced manner. Testimonials to his unequalled courage and resolve in defending the emerging faith and the community of Muslims are found in numerous history books. We also find many accounts of his spiritual battles during the night and while fasting. When his wife Aisha questioned whether his praying was excessive, he replied, *"Shall I not be a grateful servant to God?"* Aisha would often wake up to find him supplicating in prostration in the pitch darkness of the night.

For Muslims, the word *jihad* is used in conjunction with all forms of striving and has developed various special meanings over time. Two of the most important sources in Islam, the Qur'an and the sayings and actions of the Prophet Muhammad (*hadith*), use the term *jihad* in quite differing contexts, as listed below.

- Recognising the Creator and loving Him above anything other [QUR'AN, 9:23–24].
- Resisting the pressure of relatives, peers and the society to do wrong [QUR'AN, 25:52].
- Staying steadfastly on the straight path of faith and equilibrium [QUR'AN, 22:78] [QUR'AN, 3:142].
- Striving to do righteous deeds [QUR'AN, 29:69].
- Having the courage and steadfastness to convey the message of Islam [QUR'AN, 41:33].

---

20 Fountain, January–March 2002, p. 44.

- Defending Islam and the community [QUR'AN, 22:39–40] as well as helping allied people who may not necessarily be Muslim.
- Removing treacherous people from power [QUR'AN, 8:58].
- Gaining freedom to practise Islam as well as to educate and convey the message of Islam in an open and free environment [QUR'AN, 2:217].
- Freeing people from tyranny and oppression [QUR'AN, 4:75].

The Prophet Muhammad advised a man wishing to join a military expedition, to start his *jihad* (strive) by serving his parents [SAHIH AL-BUKHARI, 5972]. On another occasion, a man wanted to know a better form of *jihad,* and Muhammad responded, *"a word of truth in front of an oppressive ruler."* [SUNAN AL-NASA'I, 4209]

A military *jihad* becomes necessary as a last resort in self-defence against aggression. There is to be no aggression on the part of Muslims, since, *"God loves not the aggressors"* [QUR'AN, 2:190]. The Qur'an also provides detailed guidelines and regulations regarding the conduct of war: who is to fight and who is exempted [QUR'AN, 48:17, 9:91], when hostilities must cease [QUR'AN, 2:192], and how prisoners should be treated [QUR'AN, 47:4]. Most important, verses such as 2:294 emphasise that warfare and response to violence and aggression must be proportional: *"Whoever transgresses against you, respond in kind."*[21] Peaceful solutions to disputes are preferred to military ones. In the event of unavoidable war, every opportunity to end the war must be pursued. The Qur'an directs, *"But if the enemy inclines towards peace, then you must also incline towards peace…"* [QUR'AN, 8:61] Certain rules must be adhered to in military warfare. War can only be declared by nations, not by individuals. *Jihad* cannot include offensive action or war for personal ambition or over nationalistic

---

21 Esposito, John, *What everyone Needs to Know About Islam*, Oxford University Press (2002), p. 118.

disputes. Muslims cannot engage in indiscriminate killing and pillage. Women, children or the elderly cannot be deliberately killed. Trees and crops cannot be destroyed.

Today, as a solution to their problems, mainstream Muslim activists call for *jihad* to revive and restore Islam. They maintain that social problems are caused because of people moving away from the teachings of Islam. Many Muslim activists believe this *jihad* should be done with the pen, that is, through education.

Some also call for a political struggle, *jihad*, against corrupt authoritarian regimes, dictatorships and oppressive secular governments that hold back the country and repress freedom. Western powers, especially the US, are perceived to support these regimes in order to exploit the resources of Muslim countries. Some radical few take this to be violence against governments and their leaders. Unfortunately, some Muslims have reduced the concept of *jihad* to equate it with violence. People like Saddam Hussein and Osama bin Laden called for a physical *jihad* to rally support for their causes. Fortunately, the great majority of Muslims are able to judge the invalidity of these calls.

The confusion is further intensified by the way the media connects Islam with political and regional conflicts, which are only seen through the lens of religion. Muslims view this as an unfair connection that results in the false linkage: "Islam equals terrorism".

Does Islam encourage terrorism?
Will the "Islamic religion" contribute to world peace?

Islam does not permit nor tolerate terrorism. Even in the literal definition of the word "Islam" we find connotations of "peace" rather than "terror". Literally, the word "Islam" means "submission" or "surrender" and the word "Muslim" means "one who has surrendered". The word "Islam" also comes from the root word *"seleme"*, which means "peace". Thus, in the religious context, a Muslim is defined as a person who has surrendered him or herself to God in deep faith and as a result found peace within and with his or her social and natural environment.

Furthermore, by being a Muslim, a person synchronises with the perfect order seen in the universe for, according to the Qur'an, every entity within it has submitted itself to the Will of God by following Divine laws laid down in nature and the universe [QUR'AN, 3:83]. For example, the earth always follows the same route set for it by God. In a sense, it has submitted itself to God. Consider how bees always make honey and spiders always craft their webs. We could say that both the bee and the spider have also submitted themselves to God by living according to their predetermined dispositions. So it would be fair to say that the earth and the bee are in fact Muslim. In effect, anyone who has submitted himself or herself to God can be considered a Muslim. A Muslim therefore can only contribute to harmony, not disorder. Furthermore, the Qur'an clearly instructs Muslims not to harm people who bear no hostility against them: "*...if they leave you alone and do not fight you and offer you peace, then God allows you no way against them.*" [QUR'AN, 4:90]

On the other hand, a "terrorist" is someone who generates terror in people, causes disorder and triggers chaos. Hence, a true

Muslim cannot be a terrorist nor a terrorist cannot be a Muslim. The words "Muslim" and "terrorist" have completely opposite meanings, and therefore cannot be used together in the same phrase.

Like millions of other Muslims, I understand Islam to be a peaceful and compassionate religion. Muslims start any basic task by saying *bismillah-ir rahman-ir rahim* ("in the name of God Most-Compassionate Most-Merciful"). The primary source of Islam, the Qur'an, gives a message of peace in that Islam was sent as a mercy to humanity [QUR'AN, 10:57], not as a menace. The Qur'an asks people not to make mischief on earth [QUR'AN, 29:36]. *"O mankind! We created you from a single (pair) of a male and a female, and made you into nations and tribes, so that you may know each other (not that you may despise each other). Verily the most honoured of you in the sight of God is the most righteous of you…"*, says the Qur'an [49:13]. The Prophet Muhammad also said, *"the Muslim is the one whom others are sure no harm will come from his hands and words."* Clearly it is very difficult to reconcile acts of terrorism with Islam.

Then why is there such a negative image of Muslims? There are two sides to this question. On the one hand, the actions of a few Muslims hold the whole religion and the worldwide Muslim community at ransom. On the other hand, centuries old propaganda against Islam in the West deepened the misunderstanding. With the purpose of drumming up support for the Crusades, a campaign of spreading hatred was started in Europe. Count Henri de Castri, an orientalist of the 19th Century, mentions the practice of hired storytellers, who travelled Europe spreading negative and false information about Islam and Muslims. Many Muslims often view the modern media taking on the same role, especially when generalisations are made with expressions such as "Muslim terrorist" linking the actions of some individuals with Islam. When Muslims don't see the use of expressions such as "Christian terrorists" in

Ireland or "Jewish terrorists" in Palestine, they think that the media is biased and working against them. This compounds mistrust and the incorrect image people already associate with Islam and Muslims through centuries of misinformation.

Islam promotes justice and instructs its followers to adhere to absolute justice, to the degree that it equates the unjust killing of a single person to the extermination of all mankind [QUR'AN, 5:32]. Therefore, it is inconceivable to justify the killing of innocent civilians by the teachings of Islam. Because of these fundamental teachings, Muslims in general have a very good humanitarian record in history. Islam has been dominant player in the world for 1300 years, from the 7th to the 19th centuries. When Muslim nations were strong, they were a source of peace and stability in much of the world. Before the appearance of Islam, people never experienced security, peace and harmony over an extremely large portion of the then known world. Since the last Muslim State, the Ottoman Empire, lost its influence in the early 20th century, the world has seen two world wars and more than 80 million people killed in conflicts where Muslims played no part. The Balkans, the Middle East, Iraq and other places that were governed in peace for centuries on the basis of the tolerant principles of Islam, have never been the same since. Much of the world's unrest still originates from the lack of a positive Muslim presence and influence as a balancing power.

Islam has greatly contributed to human progress and world peace for centuries and certainly it has the potential to do the same in the future [SEE QUESTION 100]. This is provided that three root issues afflicting the general Muslim world are resolved first. These issues are lack of education, poverty and social fragmentation within any given Muslim society. All other problems are relatively minor and could be resolved rather more easily.

I have read in the paper that if a Muslim kills a Christian he will go to heaven. Is this true? Why are Muslims so antagonistic towards non-Muslims?

The answer, simply, is no. On the contrary, any Muslim who kills an innocent person irrespective of the religious background of the victim is punishable by God in the hereafter. The Prophet Muhammad cautioned Muslims not to harm non-Muslims in a clear warning: *"Whoever harms a dhimmi (a non-Muslim citizen), I am his foe. Whoever is my foe, I shall deal with him on the Day of Judgment."* [22]

Islam equates the life of a human being to the lives of all mankind, *"…If anyone kills a single person, not in retaliation of murder or for spreading mischief in the land, it would be as if he killed the whole mankind, and if anyone saves a life, it would be as if he saved the life of all mankind…"* [QUR'AN, 5:32] The verse gives two exceptions where the life of another human being can be taken – capital punishment for serious crimes like murder or inevitable killing in a defensive military action. In both cases, authorities with public legitimacy have to make the decisions, not individuals.

Islam gives Jews and Christians the title of "the people of the book", recognising the fact that they have received revelation in the form of a book from God. The Qur'an does not condemn Jews and Christians or in fact any group of people to Hell. Rather, it focuses on those who have the attributes of non-belief or flawed dogmas and criticises them instead. Whenever it does this, it also reminds people that there are always exceptions: *"Not all of them are alike: Of the People of the Book is a portion that stands (for the right): They rehearse the Signs of God all night long, and they prostrate themselves in adoration.*

---

22 An-Nabhani 3:144; Acluni 2:218; *New Hope Journal*, January–March Issue 2004, p. 21.

They believe in God and the Last Day; they enjoin what is right, and forbid what is wrong; and they hasten (in emulation) in (all) good works: They are in the ranks of the righteous. Of the good that they do, nothing will be rejected of them; for God knows well those that do right." [QUR'AN, 3:113–115] For this reason, Muslims have always been tolerant towards religious minorities living under their rule throughout the long history of Islam. As a result, Muslims never initiated Crusades against other religions and there were no holocausts, inquisitions or forced conversions.

Some people cite the first part of the Qur'anic verse 9:5, *"When the sacred months have passed, slay the idolaters wherever you find them and take them and confine them and lie in wait for them at every place of ambush…"* to argue that Islam is inherently violent. This is the same passage that religious extremists use to justify their violent actions in recent times. When one takes this passage out of the context of the complete verse and the other verses that come before and after it, the whole intent could be missed. The verse continues to say, *"…but if they repent and perform prescribed prayers (salat) and give charitable alms (zakat) then let them go their way, for God is Oft-Forgiving and Most Merciful."* [QUR'AN, 9:5] Chapter 9 of the Qur'an was revealed in 631 CE, a year after the peaceful capture of Mecca by Muslims that ended the aggression led by Mecca towards Muslims who thereafter legitimately held popular power in Arabia. Although the organised aggression against Muslims ended, some individuals were still attacking Muslims in a way that we classify today as terrorism. So, Muslims were subjected to acts of terrorism by a few remnant idolaters and minor tribes who refused to accept the Muslim victory and government of the Prophet. This chapter is an ultimatum to these individuals and tribes, telling them to end their aggression. Verse 4 clearly asks Muslims to fulfil their obligations towards tribes with whom they have a treaty. Verse 6 also commands Muslims to treat well any idolater refugee who seeks protection with Muslims and asks them to be escorted to a place where they can feel safe. From all of this additional information we understand that *"slaying those idolaters"* mentioned in verse 5 only applies to those individuals who are carrying acts of terrorism against a peaceful Muslim society and a legitimate government. This is quite similar to the current (2004) American policy to kill Al-Qaida members wherever they find them because they feel they are at war with them. Muslims never understood verse 9:5 as an open licence to kill non-Muslims.

We cannot come to a conclusion about a religion by only reading part of a verse out of context. Take for instance the following quotation from Jesus in the Gospel of Matthew: *"Do not suppose that I have come to bring peace to the earth. I did not come to bring peace, but a sword. For I have come to turn a man against his father, a daughter against her mother, a daughter-in-law against her mother-in-law. A man's enemies will be the members of his own household."* [MATTHEW 10:34–36] Are we to conclude that Jesus has taught violence? Of course not. A well-intended examination of these verses and the context leads to the understanding that Jesus was really talking about the inevitable consequence of a conflict that would arise between those who believed in him and those who did not accept his massage. In a similar way, the Qur'an should be read with the same intent and the reader should understand verses within the spirit of the religion which is peace and goodness.

We have to look for a cause other than a religious one to explain the current anger and violent behaviour of some Muslims towards various European countries and in particular towards the US.

One of the reasons is the complete European colonisation of the Muslim world in the 19th and the first half of the 20th centuries. Muslims remember that Britain, France, the Netherlands, Italy and Russia were the major European powers responsible for the complete collapse of their civilisation and loss of their freedom.

Muslims also observed that once Muslim countries gained their independence, dominant world powers installed leaders with whom they could work in spite of the wishes of the masses. The perception is that the rule of corrupt dictatorships, oppressive secular regimes or military elites was sustained by Western support in order to exploit the rich natural resources of the Muslim world. Muslims also see that atheism and its Western materialistic philosophy not only attacked Christianity but Islam as well. On top of this, the establishment of the State of Israel by Britain at the expense of the majority indigenous Palestinian Muslim population came as the final indignity in the heartland of the Muslim world.

Furthermore, the Western ideals of democracy, self-rule and human rights are seen as hypocritical double standards. Muslims find it hard to understand how the swift action against Saddam Hussein's occupation of Kuwait occurred in 1991 while at the same time the world had watched Serbs massacre Bosnian Muslims for three years. Muslims ask in bewilderment and suspicion why the US imposed sanctions against Pakistan for developing nuclear weapons, but did not do the same to Israel and India.

These external factors give the real impression that the very survival of Muslims and Islam is in danger. This root cause coupled with the frustration of people who endure poverty and lack of education and equal opportunity in an increasingly global world have made Muslims very angry towards the governments of the Western powers. As we have seen in recent times, this anger developed into rage which inevitably manifests itself in violence by people who have a tendency towards extremism. Unfortunately, human psychology means that people cannot be persuaded by rational or even religious arguments to end a destructive behaviour in a state of anger unless the source of anger is removed.

Endangerment can be signalled not just by an outright physical threat but also, as is more often the case, by a symbolic threat to self-esteem or dignity: being treated unjustly or rudely, being insulted or demeaned, being frustrated in pursuing an important goal... Anger builds on anger; the emotional brain heats up. By then rage, unhampered by reason, easily erupts in violence. At this point people are unforgiving and beyond being reasoned with; their thoughts revolve around revenge and reprisal, oblivious to what the consequences may be.[23]

I should stress that while the majority of Muslims are not satisfied with the status of the Muslim world, they do not see the solution in violence. There is a growing tendency within the Muslim world to examine itself and come up with feasible non-violent methods of social activism and to engage in an intellectual struggle rather than a physical one.

---

23 Goleman, Daniel, *Emotional Intelligence*, Bloomsbury, London (1996), pp. 60–62.

Q93

Those Muslims who resort to violence often justify their actions by referring to the Qur'an or the Prophet Muhammad. If Islam is against terrorism, why and how can they do what they do? I watched a program on the television depicting Muhammad as a "warrior prophet". Could it be that violence is in the nature of Islam?

In order to understand the behaviour of some violent Muslims, people reason that since these individuals look and sound very religious, there must be something about Islam that makes them violent. After all, they reason, *"didn't the Prophet Muhammad fight wars?"* Other people, who know of the moderation of the Prophet Muhammad and that Islam does not sanction violence against others, simply cannot understand the dichotomy between the behaviour they see in these Muslims and the teachings of Islam. So why do these religious Muslims resort to violence? Do Islam and the Prophet Muhammad really endorse their actions?

It is true the Prophet Muhammad led a number of battles and the Qur'an talks about warfare. However, this fact is not a disadvantage but really an advantage for Muslims and Islam. The Qur'an talks about warfare in order to regulate it, not to endorse it. It lays down clear principles to define when a state can engage in warfare, when war should be stopped, what to do with prisoners of war, the level of force to be used in response to aggression and so on. Without these guidelines Muslim history would have been very different indeed.

The Prophet Muhammad's involvement in wars also provides Muslim political leaders a solid example, an etiquette dealing with how to behave in warfare. Muhammad himself was a religious and political moderate. Struggling to stay alive after thirteen years of oppression in Mecca, a fledging Muslim community was established in a new city, Medina. Their former oppressors and many tribes wanted to exterminate the Muslims. Muhammad being the Prophet and the leader of Muslims, staunchly defended them from aggression in order to ensure the very survival of his followers and Islam. In this struggle for survival, Muhammad never initiated aggression. His time in battle only adds up to one and a half-days out of his 23 year mission. More often than not he tried to resolve conflict through diplomacy and signed many treaties with neighbouring tribes. He honored all these treaties. To ensure peace, he even signed disadvantageous treaties (such as the treaty of *Hudaybiya*) much to the surprise of his followers and dissension among them. He declared a general amnesty when Mecca eventually fell to Muslims without warfare in a diplomatic victory. This was despite the fact that these were the same people who persecuted Muhammad and his followers for 20 years. Certainly, the civility Saladin showed during the Crusades came from the positive example he finds in the Prophet Muhammad, while Richard the Lionheart killed whole cities of civilians, perhaps because he lacked guidelines and a good role model. Moreover, Muhammad guaranteed rights to minorities in the treaty of *Hudaybiyah*, which served as the first constitution in human history and defined citizenship rights regardless of the religious convictions of the citizens belonging to the new state in Medina. Jews, for example, were allowed to practise their faith freely and even have their own laws. They were exempted from the application of Islamic law and military service.

    The Prophet Muhammad called his followers to respect the rights of women. He championed a campaign of education. He continually warned Muslims that nations were destroyed when people went to extremes. He even forbade excessive praying and fasting, pointing out that life should include the family and recreation. As a testament to the tolerance he preached, Islamic history had no forced conversions, Holocausts, Inquisitions, bloody Crusades or other large scale tragedies on its record.[24]

The answer to the perceived dichotomy between Islam and the behaviour of some Muslims lies in human psychology. The psychological term "cognitive dissidence" describes a condition in which a person simultaneously holds two conflicting views about himself or herself. Since we define ourselves as rational beings, this situation is unsustainable and so we tend to *rationalise* in order to resolve the conflict. When we rationalise, we change our perception of reality to suit our actions. After all, it is easier to change our perceptions than our actions. In this way we feel good about ourselves even though our action may be wrong. How many of us keep on smoking knowing that it is really harmful?

The same thing happens for a Muslim who knows that he is not supposed to kill civilians in acts of violence but feels compelled to do so out of desperation and a feeling of revenge for the injustices done to him, his relatives or other Muslims elsewhere in the world. In this dichotomy, he unwittingly distorts his understanding of certain verses of the Qur'an in order to justify his actions. A Muslim does not come to the conclusion that he should resort to violence after reading the Qur'an or examining the life of the Prophet Muhammad, but rather he feels compelled to resort to violence due to the adverse circumstances he is in and then justifies his actions through an appeal to the Qur'an.

It is customary to rally support for the cause of any organisation. The use of Islamic rhetoric and argument lends an apparent legitimacy to a cause. This is similar to the behaviour we saw when Nazis used Christian references to justify hostility towards Jews. American

---

24 Emerick, Yahiya, 2002, *Muhammad*, Marie Butler-Knight, United States (2002), p. 130.

slave owners often justified the practice of slavery by saying they were Chritianising the black Africans. Similar rationalising is seen in India when Hindu fundamentalists justify their violence against Muslims by saying they are bringing them back to their former true religion of Hinduism.

Without doubt, the Israeli-Palestinian conflict is the prime source of Muslim frustration and anger as well as a root cause of terrorism. "Imagine if you were forced to leave at gunpoint your home and farm where you lived for centuries. The only place you can live is in hills where there is no water, no electricity and no schools. Many people in similar circumstances join you to establish a tin-roof town, which you can only leave by showing your identity card at checkpoints. The only job you can find is in the fields that were seized from your parents. While you are working, you see new shiny houses built at the same place where your house stood. You decide to fight back but you only have stones and small arms while the other side has tanks and Apache helicopters made in US. Your friends are gunned down mercilessly while you are arrested. You know that you could be tortured and held for years without trial. You have no rights. Meanwhile your baby sister died of malnutrition and your cousin's house was bulldozed to the ground. The chances for a future look grim. While in prison, you see on the side of supply boxes "made in America". Your anger at the people and the soldiers are so great that you begin to transfer some of it to those who are supporting them. You don't have an army to fight the invaders nor an organised resistance. Your only way of action is through individual actions such as bombing. Thus, a terrorist is born. But in his eyes the real terror was done against him and his people first."[25]

---

25 Emerick, Yahiya, *The Complete Idiot's Guide to Islam*, p. 173.

Two major concerns of many religious traditions are those concerning euthanasia and abortion. What is the Muslim view on these matters and what is taught about them?

Life is the most important aim in the universe and its greatest result... Life is the distilled essence and the most perfect fruit of the universe... Life is a miraculous reality, which makes the tiniest creature comparable to the whole universe... Life is the most extraordinary miracle of Divine power that connects living creatures to every other being in existence.

In addition to its intrinsic value, life attains a spiritual dimension in the human sphere. Human life is a great mystery giving rise to thanks, worship, praise and love, which are the most important Divine purposes in the universe and the most important fruits of the whole tree of creation.

Although Islam treats the life of all creatures as valuable, it gives a greater honour to human life. Humanity and therefore human life is distinguished from the rest of the creation in three distinct ways.

1. Humanity is created in the best composition [QUR'AN, 95:4].

2. Humanity has been given the capacity to learn through reflecting on universe and thus gain knowledge of God [QUR'AN, 2:31-33].

3. Humanity's acceptance of God's trust. This trust is said to be the self-awareness and freedom of choice enabling humans to develop spiritually, leading to belief in and submission to God willingly and consciously [QUR'AN, 33:72].

All the injunctions of Islam and therefore Islamic law hinge on the protection of five fundamental rights and freedoms: (1) freedom of the mind (speech & belief), (2) the right to live, (3) the right to own personal property, (4) the right to reproduce, and (5) the right to lead a healthy life, both mental and physical. The issues concerning contraception and abortion are related to the rights to life and reproduction.

Islam allows contraception before conception. There are reports from the Prophet Muhammad that affirm this. When a follower asked if he could use the popular contraception method of the time to prevent pregnancy, the Prophet allowed him to do so. Muslim scholars are in consensus that all forms of contraception that do not damage the health and the reproductive capacity of the person, male or female, are permissible. This is because sexual activity within the confines of a marriage serves both as a means to continue the family lineage as well as a means to improve and sustain love and intimacy between the partners in marriage. Since healthy family units are the foundation stones of a healthy society, the intimacy between partners lies at the core of the family. Healthy sexual activity within marriage is even considered sacred.

Once conception occurs then the principle of the "right to life" steps in. This is because of the fact that there is now a physical form with all of its characteristics determined (through DNA) by God and has the potential to be fully human.

There is consensus among Muslim scholars that to end the life of a fully developed foetus is definitely prohibited. There is also consensus that after four months of pregnancy the embryo becomes a fully functional human being, which has the right to live. This view is based on the narrative from the Prophet Muhammad that the human spirit is added to the foetus 120 days into the pregnancy. There are clear injunctions in the Qur'an [81:8, 6:151] that prohibits the inhumane pre-Islamic practice of infanticide. Muslim scholars draw an analogy to this injunction and deduce that the abortion of a foetus older than four months is definitely prohibited. Just as it is a crime to willingly kill a baby after birth, it is equally a crime to end the life of a foetus while it is in the womb of the mother. Parents do not have the right to decide whether to abort the life of the foetus because God is the Giver of Life and Owner of all that exists and only God has sole authority over life. Just as a normal person has a right to live so similarly does the foetus or the baby have the right to live. In this respect, Islam protects the life of the unborn child.

There is a difference of opinion among Muslim scholars concerning the case of abortion during the embryonic stage of the conception, that is, when the embryo is less than four months old and not a fully functional human being. The Qur'an talks about the changing of the embryo to "*...another creation*" [QUR'AN, 24:14] and the spirit being given to the embryo at this stage. Some scholars argue that the embryo becomes human at this stage. Therefore, they condone the abortion of the embryo during the first four-month period. However, the great majority of scholars are of the view that abortion must not be undertaken even at this stage because the embryo has the full potential to be a human being if allowed to develop.

The only exception is in cases where there is a serious health risk to the pregnant woman. In this case abortion can take place, based on the principle of necessity overriding the general rule as an exception [QUR'AN, 16:115]. This is also based on the key Islamic principle that when one is faced with only two bad choices, one takes the lesser of the two evils. When it is a choice between whether the mother or the child should live, the decision hesitantly favours the mother as her death would create a greater negative impact on the family than an unborn person who does not yet have any social ties. In any case, a qualified physician objectively makes the decision rather than the emotional parents.

Similarly, a person does not have the right to end his or her life, since God has entrusted life to him or her for a temporary period. Only God owns the life and therefore has the sole right to end life.

QUESTION 94

Euthanasia is considered to be suicide, which is a major sin in Islam.

Islam considers suffering in terminal sickness as an opportunity to compensate for one's past sins or to rise to higher ranks of spirituality in the Court of God. Although it might be a painful experience, there is the promise of great reward in the hereafter. The Prophet Muhammad says, *"the sins of a person fall like leaves off a tree"* if a person endures suffering in sickness. There are also reports that point to gaining the rank of martyrdom and the reward of Paradise if one is patient in the case of terminal diseases.

If the person is on life support in a vegetative state, then the majority of scholars are of the opinion that life support can be removed because the person is not aware and life as a place of trial has ended for him or her. The decision rests with qualified doctors and family members.

Q95

What are the main Islamic symbols and their significance? Some symbols used in Muslim traditions are the sword, the moon and the star. What do these mean and are there other symbols?

Islam is a religion that focuses on practical reality. It emphasises the first hand experience of spirituality in life and in the inner self. It is not a religion of symbolism. Muslims do not use any symbols for God or religious concepts. The Prophet Muhammad did not use symbols. As a flag, he used plain white or black banners with no other writing and symbol on them. Nevertheless, in time, certain entities came to be associated with Islam. These symbols emerged from the perception of people of other nations and faiths as well as their use by Muslims themselves. The following short list gives some of the main symbols of Islam generally accepted by all Muslims.

■ ***Ka'bah***: Just as the Opera House with its unique architectural design and prominence in the most populated city of Sydney came to symbolise Australia, so the *Ka'bah* came to represent Islam [SEE QUESTION 54 FOR MORE ABOUT THE *KA'BAH*]. To an outsider, the spectacular role of the *Ka'bah* during the month of Pilgrimage, and the unique function and design of the building make it a symbol. To Muslims it symbolises the legacy of humanity and monotheism.

■ **Minaret:** A domed mosque with a number of tall *minarets* came to symbolise the existence of Islam and the freedom of Muslims' religious practices in a land. Again the unique function and the design of the *minaret* makes it a distinctive symbol identifiable with Islam.

■ **Azan:** If there were ever to be a real symbol of Islam it would be the *azan*, the Muslim call to prayer. Established at the time of the Prophet, five times a day its resonance announces the creed of Islam throughout the land. To Muslims it represents the existence of Islam and freedom of religion in a land.

■ **Crescent Moon:** In response to the use of the Christian cross during the Crusades, Muslims used the crescent moon as a symbol. Even today the humanitarian organisation equivalent to the Red Cross in Muslim countries is named the Red Crescent. The crescent moon has entered Muslim consciousness as it is used in religious terminology to signify the beginning of the month of Ramadan. Its use on the flags of the Ottomans and on the flags of many Muslim nations reinforced its use as a common Muslim symbol. However, it is important to note that the crescent moon does not represent any faith-related concepts. The Byzantine Empire also used the crescent moon as its imperial symbol.

Other symbols such as swords, stars or religious phrases used on the flags of some nations are not necessarily religiously oriented symbols. The colour green is also used as a symbol, especially in funerals, following on from the tradition that when the Prophet died he was covered with a green-coloured garment.

In addition to these commonly found symbols, Muslim architects and artists out of their own initiative used natural motifs and architectural features of a mosque to represent certain concepts of religion [SEE ANSWER TO QUESTION 55].

Is there a spiritual leader of all Muslims in the world, like the Pope? What is the role of an *Ayatollah*?

Currently, there is no single political or spiritual leader for the worldwide Muslim community. The political unity of Muslims ended with the collapse of the Abbasid caliphate in 1258 as a result of the Mongol invasion. Following the collapse of the Ottoman Empire after World War I, the newly formed Turkish Republic removed the Ottoman Caliphate on the 3rd of March 1924. The Caliph had represented the spiritual unity of Muslims for many centuries.

The institution of the Caliphate (succession to the Prophet) appeared immediately after the death of Muhammad. It impacted the intellectual, administrative, social and political development of the Muslims throughout their history. The Caliphate is a system in which people manage religious and worldly affairs under the leadership of a Caliph. Initially people elected the first four Caliphs (their total period in office was 30 years). Due to the prevailing circumstances of the time and the norm around the world, the democratic process lapsed back into a leadership by dynasties. This development was predicted by the Prophet Muhammad, who said, "*the caliphate is for thirty years. After that will come dynasties.*"

Although the Caliph was the leader of the universal Muslim State, throughout Muslim history the Muslim world consisted of smaller regional powers and states whose leadership would seek legitimacy and approval from the Caliph. The institution of the Caliphate was used to its full potential to unite and defend the Muslim world by the Ottomans from the 16th century onwards.

The Caliph represented all Muslims but did not interpret religion or bring new changes to it. Religious interpretation lay with the learned scholars and the people themselves. There is no official clergy or institutional body in Islam [SEE ANSWER TO QUESTION 59]. Interpretation of religious sources and spiritual leadership are open to any Muslim who appeals to the people, who accepts and acknowledges them by a process of natural selection.

For Sunni Muslims, who form the majority of the followers of Islam, the Caliph or the *Imam* (leader of Muslims) is elected from among the Muslims on the basis of competence and qualities of leadership. Any leader is fallible. In the Shiite tradition, which makes up about 15% of the total Muslim population in the world, the *Imam* is the head of Shiite Muslims. He is a pope-like figure who is considered infallible. He should come from the descendants of the Prophet. The *Imam* leads people through a group of men with titles such as *Mullah, Ayatollah* (the sign of God) and *Hojatulislam* (the proof of Islam). Ayatollah Khomeini, who led the 1978 Iranian Revolution, attained the highest spiritual rank within the Shiite clergy and was considered infallible.

Sunni Muslims do not recognise the *Ayatollah* as their leader. Hence, the ruling (or *fatwa*) of an *Ayatollah* only has a bearing of influence on the minority (15%) Shiite population. The religious establishment of Iran appoints the *Ayatollah* without an election.

How does Islam view the environment?

Modern attention to the environment and its protection has been on the agenda for less than a century. Only after the full scale of the damage done to the planet's environment, did we become serious about the environment and its preservation. The extinction of wildlife, clearing of rainforests, the hole in the ozone layer and the greenhouse effect threatening the climate of the globe underscore the contemporary concerns not only of sensitive individuals but also of many governments. The irony is that modern concern for the environment stems more from selfish reasons than from a sincere concern. "We do not have another planet to go to" becomes the rationale for environmental activism. Environmental protection as a scientific field rests on two main disciplines.

1. Waste minimisation and control
2. Conservation of environment: air, land, water, vegetation, animal life and natural resources

Before I comment on what has been Islam's record, we need to look at Islam's theological perspective on the topic.

The Qur'an tells us that human beings are created from an earthly essence [QUR'AN, 7:11, 17:61] and more generally that every living being is created from water. *"Have not those who disbelieve known that the heavens and the earth were of one piece, then We parted them, and* **We made every living thing of water?** *Will they not then believe?"* declares the Qur'an [21:30]. We do have a common physical existence with everything else on earth. There is, however, a profound difference between the way humans along with plants and animals function in the common home we call the earth.

When we examine nature and living beings from the perspective of their contribution to the natural environment, we realise that every living being adds value to its ecological system. Consider a grapevine, for example. It sucks muddy water from the soil and turns it into sweet and nutritious grapes. Sheep consume grass from the meadows and produce milk, wool and meat. Trees inhale carbon dioxide and exhale oxygen, thus, cleansing the atmosphere for animals and humans. Every animal and plant species adds value to its natural environment, either by the end products that they produce or by the functions they perform. Human beings, on the other hand, consume the best of what nature has to offer and turns it into waste that is flushed away in a hurry. Humanity, in a physical sense, adds no value to the ecological environment. This observation has two consequences:

1. Humanity is not really part of the ecological system, as it functions independently of humans. Humans are designed to utilise the materials provided by the earth and to live within the environment but are really alien to the ecosystem.

2. For human existence, one has to look for a purpose other than its mere physical existence. The finer intellectual and spiritual faculties are given to us for a more comprehensive and willing spiritual enlightenment and worship [QUR'AN, 51:56]. The Qur'an also talks about the worship of everything that is in the heavens and the earth.

We live on earth and inevitably interact with the environment. Not being part of the ecosystem, the result of our inevitable interaction with the environment is in the form of consuming its value-added products without returning any tangible value. Human life and ecosystems are not mutually exclusive and certainly not interdependent. Humanity depends on the environment but the environment does not depend on humanity. In fact, the whole planet would rejoice if we all packed our bags and left the planet for good.

The only real value we can add to the environment is by protecting and preserving it. Islam addresses the issue at three levels.

We only take care of things if we believe they are valuable. So, the first thing Islam does is to give immense worth to the environment. Islam asserts that all life is special and valuable because it is the life and the art displayed by each creature that connects it to the Divine. To a Muslim, God has created this universe like a majestic palace. He fashioned the earth like a huge exhibition hall within the palace. He then decorated the hall with his fine works of art for those conscious beings who can appreciate the art and recognise the Artist behind it all. It is this connection, the work of art with the Artist, which makes every living entity valuable because of the Artist, God, just as the painting of a master artist gains immense value, beyond its material worth, because of the art in the painting. Therefore, in Islam, the natural environment and animal forms are sacred and valuable. On the other hand, not recognising God reduces the value of all creatures to their mere material worth.

Although Islam treats the life of all creation as valuable, it gives greatest honour to human life [QUR'AN, 95:4]. However, this honourable position is not absolute. The level of human development one attains is the measure of every person's status with respect to other beings. Just as it is possible to reach levels above creation, it is also possible to fall far below it. What might appear to be an advantage can turn out to be disadvantageous. The reality is that we have the opportunity and the freedom to determine our own destiny.

With the freedom of choice comes accountability. This is the second level in Islam's education of humans with respect to environmental protection. One of the roles given to humanity in the Qur'an is that of vicegerent (*caliph*) on earth [QUR'AN, 2:30]. This role gives the human being authority over the creation, rendering the creation on earth at human disposal. This is not an unconditional authority, as accountability is a natural consequence of authority. Therefore, Islam teaches that on the Day of Judgment humanity will be questioned about its treatment of animals and the environment: The Prophet Muhammad declared, *"Fear God in your treatment of animals"* and *"Verily, there is heavenly reward for every act of kindness done to a living animal"*.

The third level is the recognition that the vegetable and animal worlds establish ecosystems just as humans develop interdependent communities. The Qur'an clearly talks about living beings existing in ecological systems. It declares [QUR'AN, 6:38], *"There is not a moving creature on earth, nor a bird that flies with its two wings, but are communities like you. We have neglected nothing in the Book (of Our decrees). Then unto their Lord they will be gathered"*. The comparison of animal species to human communities is very significant. Since human societies are complex systems made up of numerous interdependent individuals: the comparison in this verse leads us to the modern concept of ecosystems for the vegetable and animal worlds. The plural "communities" also leads us to the conclusion that there are many concurrently existing independent ecosystems.

It is the culmination of how Islam gives value to the creation, the theological responsibility and accountability given to humankind and its recognition of ecosystems that shapes Muslims' perspective on the environment and its protection.

How is this theology put into practice? The Qur'an states [7:31], *"O Children of Adam!... Eat and drink but waste not in excess, for God does not love the wasters"*. While Islam encourages people to enjoy the blessings of life it clearly lays down as a precondition that there be no waste. Also notice the verse does not address just "Muslims" or "believers" but the whole of humanity with the proclamation "O children of Adam!"

Islam takes efforts to minimise waste to a higher level in the words of the Prophet Muhammad, who asked people not to overuse water even while having the ablution for prayer next to a flowing river. While this recommendation is aimed at waste minimisation, it is also saying that waste minimisation should not only be confined to times of shortage but, more importantly, even when there are ample resources. This is because wastage usually occurs when there are more resources than needed. There is not much to waste when there is a shortage, is there? The attitude of waste in abundance causes later shortages.

Muhammad also said that the lowest manifestation of belief in a person is that one should remove harmful objects in the path of people. Since it is good to remove waste and harmful objects, it is better not to litter in the first place.

In a well-known saying, Muhammad recommends that we *"lay in the ground the plant at hand even if it is the Last Day"* on earth. It is characteristic of the sayings of Muhammad, that there is always the hint of a very important teaching in every recommendation. In this case, while people are being encouraged to plant a tree, this is not to be done for an immediate benefit, but for the benefit of future generations. We also know that when the Prophet migrated to Medina, he initiated a tree planting campaign along with a push to improve public literacy.

The Prophet Muhammad enjoined people to show kindness not only to each other but also to all living souls. He forbade the practice of cutting the tails and manes of horses, of branding animals at any tender spot, and of keeping horses saddled unnecessarily (Sahih Muslim). If he saw any animal over-loaded or ill-fed he would pull up the owner and say, *"fear God in your treatment of animals"*. (Abu Dawud, Kitab-ul Jihad)

We see many examples of how the Prophet educated his followers in relation to the treatment of animals. Once a companion came to him with the chicks of a bird in his sheet and said the mother bird had hovered over them all along. He was directed to replace the bird's offspring in the bush where they were found (Mishkat, Abu Dawud). During a journey somebody picked up some bird's eggs from a nest. The bird's plaintive cry and fluttering attracted the attention of Muhammad, who asked the man to replace the eggs (Sahih Bukhari).

Islam is arguably the first religion that introduced animal rights along with human rights. Muhammad stated, *"Verily, there is heavenly reward for every act of kindness done to a living animal."* It is also believed in Islam that humans will be judged on their treatment of animals on the Day of Judgment.

Clear pronouncements in the Qur'an and the example of Muhammad gave Muslims the impetus to preserve the environment and to get a good record for their treatment of wild life and domestic animals. During the Ottoman reign (1299–1923), for example, comprehensive waste and environmental management regulations were stipulated as early as 1539. In 1502, local government legislation regulated the loads of animals and the number of days they could be worked in a week. There were even organisations dedicated purely to treating storks injured on their annual migration. Centuries before similar regulations were introduced in the modern world, hunting was regulated on the basis of need and no hunting was allowed during the breeding season. When mosques were built, the architects provided covered nesting areas for birds under the facades.

In its long history Islam not only produced a culture of charity but also a "green" culture centred on a world view that places humanity in harmony with nature and the environment.

Q98

Is there an Islamic state?
Is Islam compatible with democracy?

Islam primarily focuses on the immutable aspects of life and existence, while political, social, and economic ideologies concern only certain variable, social aspects of our worldly existence. When comparing religion or Islam with democracy, one must remember that democracy is a system that is being continually developed and revised. Therefore, it is important to note that only Islam's perspective on society and the physical world can be compared with existing notions of democracy.

The Prophet Muhammad said, *"All people are as equal as the teeth of a comb"*. He also declared, *"You are all from Adam, and Adam is from earth. O servants of God, be brothers (and sisters)."* According to Islam, then, those who have wealth and material power or those who belong to certain families or ethnic groups have no inherent right to rule over others.

Islam does not propose a definite form of government or attempt to shape it. Instead, Islam establishes fundamental principles that orient a government's general character, leaving it to the people to choose the type and form of government according to time and circumstances. Islam also upholds the following fundamental principles:

1. Power lies in truth, a refutation of the popular idea that truth relies upon power.
2. Justice and the rule of law are essential.
3. Freedom of belief and rights to life, personal property, reproduction, and health (both mental and physical) cannot be violated.
4. The privacy and immunity of individual life must be maintained.
5. No-one can be convicted of a crime without evidence, or accused and punished for someone else's crime.

6. An advisory system of administration is essential.

As Islam holds individuals and societies responsible for their own lives and actions, so too people must be responsible for governing themselves. The duties entrusted to modern democratic systems are also those that Islam refers to society to address. People cooperate with one another by sharing these duties and establishing the essential foundations necessary to perform them. The government is composed of all of these foundations. Thus, Islam recommends a government based on a social contract. People elect the administrators and establish a council to debate common issues. The society as a whole participates in auditing the administration. There are many sayings from the Prophet that encourage people to speak up and oppose the wrongs of leadership. The first successor to the Prophet Muhammad, Abu Bakr, in his inauguration speech welcomed justified opposition, saying, *"O people, I have been chosen to be your leader, even though I am no better than any of you. If I do right, help me. If I do wrong correct me."* [26]

Especially during the rule of the first four caliphs (632–661), the fundamental principles of government mentioned above, including free elections, were fully observed. After the fourth caliph, Ali, the political leadership was at first confined to a dynasty and then gradually changed into a monarchy, which was the global norm at the time and a system that provided greater stability than an untimely democratic system. Unlike in the caliphate, power in the monarchies was passed on through the sultan's family. Even though free elections were no longer held, government and society maintained other principles that are at the core of today's liberal democracy.

Considering the discussion so far and the status of countries where Muslims are in a majority, one could easily conclude that the

---

26 Emerick, Yahiya, *A. Complete Idiot's Guide to Understanding Islam*, p. 289.

ideal principles of government stipulated by Islam are not fully functional. Countries with an "Islamic" label in their name do not really deserve to have such an attribute as they are far from implementing the key principles of Islam pertaining to the governing of people. In fact, at no time in Muslim history has a label such as "Islamic" or "Muslim" been used in the name of a state. Therefore, at the moment there is no country on earth, which can be shown as a good example of an ideal Muslim state. Many modern Muslim countries are going through a transitional period. Hopefully they will eventually settle into stable political systems, at which time Muslim nations will be able to help propel global democracy to greater heights.

The Christian world solved the problem of the relationship between society (politics) and religion (the church) by separating the two in a secular state. Why can't Muslims do the same?

The assumption behind this question is that the social upheavals in Muslim countries are caused by a lack of secularism. In reality, however, most social problems are caused by extreme secular regimes [SEE THE ANSWER TO QUESTION 101 FOR MORE ON THIS]. Apart from this paradox, two observations cause people to ask this question. The first is the call of some Muslims for an "Islamic state" and the implementation of Islamic law in certain majority Muslim countries such as Afghanistan, Sudan and Nigeria, giving the impression that Islam has a tendency to govern a country by a theocratic regime. This is usually associated in these countries with a lack of democracy, rule of law and basic human rights. The second observation is the inevitable visibility of Islam in a society while other religions seem to be more or less invisible.

The Western experience of religious freedom has been a long and a painful one. Forced conversions, the influence of the church on the State and the resulting eras of violence led the French Revolution (1789) to separate state (politics) and religion. While this total separation has ended the domination of the whole society by one interpretation of religion, it has also removed religion and spirituality from the social scene. This has led to the spiritual deprivation of the masses and associated moral decline and perhaps to a greater level of killing (about 80 million people) in the 20th century.

"Philosopher John Gray calls secularism 'the absurd myth because it replaces one God with hordes of cults and pseudo-religions. Secularism, he says, is the unthinking creed of conformists who repress religion as a natural human impulse just as the Victorians repressed sex'. The religious desire is

hard-wired into the species like sexual desire, says Gray... George Orwell, a dedicated secularist, wrote in 1944, 'The problem of our time is to establish the absolute sense of right and wrong when the belief that it used to rest on – that is, personal immortality – has been destroyed'. This problem remains."[27] The benefits and perils of present forms of secularism call for a critical examination.

In my answer to QUESTION 98, I have shown that Islam aligns well with the principles of democracy. Further, Islam enjoins the rule of law, the protection of basic human rights, a government system that is based on a consultative decision-making and the restraining of rulers by the people. Nevertheless, some Muslims and non-Muslims argue that since the Prophet Muhammad was both a prophet and a political leader, Islam can never be secular. How did Muhammad and his early followers really govern the young polity that he established in Medina?

Since people swore allegiance to Muhammad when they converted to Islam, in effect they also chose him as their leader. He appointed governors to cities and regions under Muslim control and empowered them with extraordinary freedom in their rule. The only stipulation to governors was they adhere to the Qur'an and the Sunnah in dealing with matters relating to the people. This stipulation fostered the rule of law, in that the governor could not make arbitrary decisions and rules. People were allowed to dissent from the rulings of a governor by direct recourse to the Prophet himself. In some instances governors were replaced as a result of complaints. The Prophet appointed officials on the basis of performance and competence rather than kinship. He purposely did not appoint his kin to state office to avoid the slightest suspicion of nepotism.

---

27 Brennan P., A Wish and a Prayer for the Godless Society, *The Australian*, 15 October 2003.

A city charter for Medina was put together which became the constitution of the new polity. In return for shared responsibilities, the charter guaranteed the rights of its citizens, irrespective of their religious beliefs. The Prophet, and therefore the State, was legally impartial to all faiths. When Jews brought cases before him to judge (they did not have to do this, by the way), he judged according to Jewish law and not according to Islamic law. Having basic human rights and not being restricted by a religious law (if one is not a believer) are the cornerstones of modern day secularism that Islam fulfilled fourteen centuries ago.

It seems almost too good to be true, but no-one, including the Prophet himself, was paid for the tasks of state. All work, including the managing of state expenses, was done on a voluntary basis and by donations. There was no standing army or bureaucracy. The first caliph after the Prophet hesitated to accept the offer of a small salary, as he knew the Prophet took no salary.[28]

The Prophet always involved people in decision-making. He had an advisory council made up of tribal elders or individuals respected by the people. All decisions were discussed in the mosque (which acted like a parliament house, since there were no other suitable buildings in the city) and were transparent to the whole community. Anyone could join and take part in the discussions. Women were involved in the consultation process. By and large the Prophet always followed the consensus of the people. When discussing the defence strategy to follow in the wake of an attack on Muslims in Medina, for example, he went ahead with the majority view of defending the city out in the open even though his personal view

---

28 In fact, when Abu Bakr died he left a pouch-full of coins and a note. The note said, *"these are the leftovers of my salary after my essential expenses to be returned to the state treasury"*. This note made the second Caliph Omar shed tears.

was to defend it within the walls of the city. When in the subsequent battle of Uhud, Muslims were almost defeated, he neither blamed nor punished anyone for the misfortune.

Although the Prophet Muhammad had religious and state leadership, he made clear what was revelation and what were his own thoughts so as to empower people to challenge his views. This is the key demarcation point that separated the religious domain and the worldly domain, although the principles of Islam informed the whole. In the defensive battle mentioned above, when the Prophet positioned the army, one of his companions approached him and asked whether he positioned the army because of a revelation or by his own judgment. When the Prophet said that it was his personal judgment, the companion suggested a better positioning for the army, which the Prophet accepted. He often said, *"I am a human being too. Do as required when I ask you to do a matter pertaining to religion. However, when I give you my opinion (over worldly matters) know that I am a human being too."* [BUKHARI, *SALAT* 31; MUSLIM, *AKDIYA* 5]

In summary, the rule of the Prophet was not a theocratic regime but was a balanced rule that delivered the benefits of both religion and secularism. Therefore, a call for Western style secularism is not really relevant or necessary in the case of a Muslim society.

The second aspect of the question of secularism has to do with the visibility of religion in a society. The total removal of religion from society is not possible in a Muslim society because Islam is a public religion. The practice of Islam is so intermeshed within life that its visibility is inevitable. Muslims need to pray five times a day. When the time for prayer comes, a Muslim will look for a place to pray in the workplace, at school or in a park. How can you hide the fact that you are fasting for a whole month? When your friends ask you to go for lunch you are going to say that you can't because you are fasting. Muslim women wearing the veil are also clearly visible.

For these reasons a Muslim society cannot be like a Western society, where religion is almost totally invisible in daily life.

As with everything else, the position of Islam on this question is therefore somewhere in the middle ground. It does not allow for a theocratic regime while at the same time it does not accept the other extreme of complete removal of religion from law and society. The increased presence of Muslims in Western countries will slightly shift the secular equilibrium point that currently exists between religion and society. This should not alarm people into thinking they are losing secular ideals. It is simply that Muslims are practising their religion.

If Islam is as good as you described why are the Muslims that we see in the media so bad? Islam and Muslims are going through a hard time in the world scene at the moment (2004). Is this caused by the lack of understanding of Islam by the Western World or by the actions of some Muslims?

The present dilemma is caused by both a lack of understanding of Islam and Muslims in the Western World and an inappropriate response by some Muslims to what is perceived to be injustice inflicted on them throughout the world. The violent behaviour of some Muslims is not because of, but in spite of, Islam and ignorance of what Islam is. There are many complex historical and current reasons for the present predicament. I will explore both sides of the coin.

Firstly, centuries old propaganda against Islam in Europe etched a deep canyon of misunderstanding between Islam and the Western World. With the purpose of drumming up support for the Crusades, a campaign of misinformation was started in Europe. Count Henri de Castri, an orientalist of the 19th Century, mentions the practice of hired storytellers, who travelled Europe spreading negative and false information about Islam and Muslims. The European fascination with the private lives of Muslims led them to fantasise about the *"harem"* with erotic stories and pictures, when *"harem"* was simply the home of the Sultan where his family resided.

Many Muslims often view the modern media taking on the same role, especially when generalisations are made with expressions such as "Muslim terrorist", linking the violent actions of some individuals with Islam. Professor Terence Lovat of Newcastle University observed *"in one national daily soon after '9/11', I counted the phrase 'Islamic terrorism' or 'Islamic terrorists' twenty-six times in the first 4 pages, with the word 'terrorism' on its own not appearing once."* When Muslims don't see the use of expressions such as "Christian terrorists" in

Ireland or "Jewish terrorists" in Palestine, they get the impression that the media is biased and working against them. This compounds the mistrust and the incorrect image people already associate with Islam and Muslims through centuries of misinformation.

The second major cause is the European colonisation of the Muslim world and the devastation it has inflicted on Muslims up to the present. This was the third major catastrophe to hit the Muslim world since the Crusades (1095–1453) and the Mongol invasion of 1258. This time round the catastrophe was not only a military one but also affected the political, cultural, economic and religious domains, resulting in the complete collapse of Islamic Civilisation.

Coinciding with the European revival and the Industrial Revolution, the power and prosperity of the Muslim world took a sharp downturn. Following the fall of the Safavid Empire in 1736, the Mughal Empire was abolished in 1857, when Britain declared India a colony. The Ottoman Empire came to an abrupt end in 1923 after heavy losses in World War I. Islamic civilisation was finally conquered after more than a thousand years of Muslim world domination. Turkey was the only free Muslim nation. It was only recognised on condition that it applied a sweeping program of secularism.

There was a greater calamity that attacked the core of religion itself. The materialistic philosophy and its challenging assertions about faith, which again originated in Western Europe, was now threatening Islam after delivering a devastating blow to Christianity. In the West, all of a sudden, everything was thought to be explained by science. Charles Darwin with his Theory of Evolution explained biological life on earth. Durkheim extended the evolutionary concepts of natural selection to social life and society while Freud tied everything in human behaviour to sexual impulses. Finally, the ironic proclamation of Friedrich Nietzsche, "God is dead", was taken literally and accepted by the majority of intellectuals.

Although the damage done to Islam by materialistic philosophy was much less than that done to other religions such as say Christianity, nevertheless, a minority population, who either became atheists or distant to religion, spawned in the Muslim world. This is an important fact because Muslim societies in the 20th century are characterised by an intellectual, religious and political struggle between the religious majority and a minority elite who hold power and are alien to people and their religion. This polarisation of life deepened the problem of social and political fragmentation in Muslim societies.

After World War II, Muslims started to gain their freedom and small states with borders drawn by "Winners" emerged on the scene. Churchill said he drew the borders of Jordan in one afternoon. There was no educational, political and economic development during the almost 50 years of Western rule over almost the whole Muslim world. The new leadership in these countries turned out to be oppressive secular regimes or dictatorships or kingdoms. The power lay in the hands of elites, military generals or religious or secular extremists who did not represent the majority. In order to perpetuate their power, their rule was characterised by suppression of dissent, elimination of critics, annihilation of independent social and administrative institutions and prevention of religious education. The predicament of this political cycle continues to this day.

What circumstances gave rise to these regimes and how do they seem to persevere regardless of their obvious failure? The reasons are many. "*Suffice to say that the euphoria of Independence; the aura surrounding the 'founding fathers' of the nation; the intoxicating appeal of nationalism; the relative weakness of countervailing social and political forces at the time of Independence; certain deeply ingrained cultural attitudes about authority; and the centralising tendencies of the ideology of development and the development itself have all conspired to reinforce the power of the ruling* class. To this we should add the role of imperialism in perpetuating authoritarianism within the nation state."[29]

The British government signed the Hussain-McMahon treaty (1915) with the Shareef Hussain of Mecca "as representative of the Arab peoples", promising Arab people self-rule over the Middle East, including Palestine. However, in 1917 the same British government pledged itself to "the establishment of a national home for the Jewish people" with the famous Balfour Declaration. Arabs felt cheated when the state of Israel was finally established. For them, it symbolised the great indignity inflicted on the Muslim world and the double standards of the "West".[30] In this heated political climate, the majority of the Muslim population was not given a chance to govern themselves, resulting in dissension not only towards the ruling elite but also towards the West and giving rise to an "Islamic Resurgence".

In the religious sphere, the struggle has been no different. After a short period of shock and being caught unprepared for the new challenges, Muslims very quickly realised that Islam was in danger as it has never been before in history. Many Muslims felt a sense of responsibility to do something about it. Almost simultaneously and spontaneously, religiously sensitive Muslims all around the Muslim world embarked on the task of defending and reviving Islam within Muslim societies. Spiritual leaders such as Hassan al-Banna in Egypt, Muhammad Iqbal in Pakistan, Said Nursi in Turkey and many others in almost every Muslim country spontaneously emerged to lead this revival.

The revival movements aimed to strengthen faith and to emphasise Muslim identity through the reflection of Islamic prac-

---

29 Chandra M., "Civil Society in the Muslim World", In *Islamic Education* Vol. 7, Issue 10.

30 Lang J., *Struggling to Surrender*, 1998, Amana Publications, pp. 219–220.

tice in personal and social life. Mosque attendance and the number of fasting people grew many times over. With the aid of mass transportation, people making the Pilgrimage numbered millions every year, a development that was unprecedented in Muslim history. Islamic resources, schools and associations grew exponentially. As a result, Islam once again proliferated.

Among religious movements of the time, the impact of Said Nursi (1876–1960) on Muslim thought has been significant and it represents a good example of non-violent methodology that delivered success. For Nursi, the problem facing the Muslim world lay deep beyond current events. The root cause was the collective attack of materialistic philosophy and its atheistic assertions, which were causing people to have doubts and leave religion altogether. Lack of faith, in turn, was driving people to vices that were threatening the very fabric of society. According to Nursi, the remedy was to reconcile science and religion and therefore protect and strengthen the faith of people. Consequently, all people of religion, including Christians, should combine their efforts to repel the atheistic tides sweeping across the world. Nursi said that it was futile to have a political struggle, since it was not the root cause nor was it effective. All efforts had to be exerted in an intellectual struggle. He proposed that solving the problems of the Muslim world would have to start with education that combined religious sciences and material sciences so that wisdom could prevail rather than religious bigotry or atheism. This proposal was largely put into practice by M. Fethullah Gulen (b. 1938).

Corrupt and despotic regimes and the failure of existing governments to solve deep social, economic and political problems, despite decades of opportunity coupled with a revival in Muslim identity, led Muslim activists and the masses to take their chance at politics, being confident of popular support. People started to call

QUESTION 100

for the creation of an "Islamic state". The tendency gained momentum when the Iranian revolution (1978–79) successfully overthrew the monarchy in Iran. These were some of the circumstances that prepared the way to the rise of fundementalism[31] and terrorism.

Although we are led to believe that fundementalist aberrations are confined to Islam, this is not the case. Fundamentalism is an extreme form of religious response to secularism and it can be seen in many religious traditions. Karen Armstrong says, *"Fundamentalism is a global fact and has surfaced in every major faith in response to the problems of our modernity. There is fundamentalist Judaism, fundamentalist Christianity, fundamentalist Hinduism, fundmentalist Buddhism, fundamentalist Sikhism and even fundamentalist Confucianism. This type of faith surfaced in the Christian world in the United States at the beginning of the twentieth century."*[32] One example is the famous Scopes Trial in Tennessee in 1925, when Protestant Christians violently opposed the teaching of evolution theory in schools. According to Karen Armstrong, the fundamentalist phenomenon has two common chracteristics irrespective of where it comes from:

1. It expresses a deep disappointment with the negative outcomes of modern life. Fundamentalism becomes the "litmus test" to indicate a polarisation between those who enjoy the life brought about by secularism and those who dread its existence. Secularism here means to confine religion to the sphere of personal life and remove it from society and, as an extension, from politics.

---

31 I should point out that Muslims in general are offended when they are classified as fundamentalists. The term "fundamentalism" was coined by Western sources to define an extreme response given by a group of people to a rapidly changing world. For the lack of a better word, it is used in line with extreme form of behaviour displayed by some Muslims.

32 Armstrong, Karen, *Islam. A Short History*, 2001, p. 140.

2. There is a real fear that the secular establishment is out there to wipe out religion. In an instinct of survival, fundamentalists feel that they are cornered and there is no where to go except to fight their way out.

Certainly in the Muslim experience, the fight for survival has been real. The coercive and sometimes militaristic secular practices have left a great mark on Muslim consciousness. In almost all Muslim countries thousands of people were rounded up and killed in the name of progress and modernisation. Even a simple practising Muslim is seen as a threat by the secular elite, which makes sure they don't end up in an influential place in society. For example, Said Nursi, an advocate of non-violence, was exiled and placed under house arrest for writing theological books. Although the great majority of Muslims neither practised violence nor condoned it, it was inevitable that a certain minority would distort religious tradition and highlight defensive mechanisms existing in its teachings to justify aggressive behaviour. Certain minority Muslim groups resorted to violence out of desperation and deep disappointment. Some individuals, such as Osama bin Laden, took the response to the level of terrorism. There is also a lot of evidence that Muslims were set up and dragged into violence by the same forces that opposed them in the first place, with the hope that Muslims would be discredited. The events of Algeria in the 1990s could be given as an example.

The misunderstanding between Islam and the general non-Muslim world is deep. This is partly due to the centuries old spread of misinformation, lack of dialogue and partly due to the violent behaviour of some marginal Muslims, whose actions are unwittingly generalised to represent all Muslims by the media. Muslims had a raw deal for so long, both within their countries and by the intervention of external forces that it has inevitably caused a minority group of Muslims to take up arms.

What direction does Islam have for the future?

For the reasons mentioned earlier in QUESTION 100 as well as lack of education, extensive poverty and political and social fragmentation, the Muslim world looks like it is in a mess. Where do we go from here?

As far as the sources of Islam (the Qur'an and the example of the Prophet Muhammad) and the spirituality of Islam are concerned, Islam maintained its freshness and vitality through the philosophical challenges of the last century. Authentic Islam is here to stay and requires no change. This is the shared outlook held by the majority of Muslims throughout the world.

The reflection of Islam in society, on the other hand, requires development in the contemporary world. The consequence of the major world upheavals that I have mentioned earlier meant there is a 150-year gap in the development of Islamic law. Struggling to survive or to attain freedom, Muslims did not get a chance to adopt the social aspects of Islam to the needs of a new world. For Muslims, the transition from being European colonies to mature and developed states with strong civil institutions is still in progress.

There are three key problems the Muslim world has to overcome: lack of education, poverty, and social and political fragmentation. These are also the same internal factors that caused the decline of Islamic civilisation.

1. Social and Political Fragmentation. After losing their vision of representing and peacefully spreading Islam, no new vision was developed that could hold the Muslim world intact. The political ambitions of individuals and clans came to the foreground and caused political disintegration and loss of unity and political stability, preventing the ruling administrations from dealing with real problems. Political fragmentation brought with it nepotism in administrative appointments. There is further fragmentation within any given Muslim society between pro-secularist and religious segments.

2. Economy. With the discovery of the American continent, millennium old trade routes took a dramatic shift. The Muslim world was no longer on the direct trade routes. Muslims could not change fast enough to compete with the rising European competition and the advent of new manufacturing technology and the associated consumerism. The total GDP of the 57 Muslim countries is much less than the GDP of the United States.

3. Education. Perhaps the most serious mistake was that knowledge was split into religious knowledge and material knowledge. Scientific education was neglected while religious sciences were the only subject matters taught in madrasas (schools). Once the champions of knowledge and science, Muslims lost their original scientific advantage to European developments in science and its associated applied technology.

In short, Muslims were strong when they had a strong vision beyond the self, an emphasis on trade and economy and took knowledge as a whole. The decline started when these were reversed. The remedy is therefore a strong visionary leadership that unites people, a bias for competitive economic success and a fervent struggle against ignorance.

There are hopeful signs the decline has been reversed and there are important developments on all three fronts. For the first time in 80 years, religious Muslims have finally achieved political success in Turkey. In time, if the final remnants of the secular-religious rift ends, Turkey seems to provide a good political model for the rest of the Muslim world. The economic success of Malaysia, Dubai, Turkey and other Muslim states can be replicated in other Muslim countries. There are many religious movements that focus on contemporary and religious education in a unique blend. Schools built on contemporary models are spreading fast around the Muslim world.

Concurrently with these developments, Muslims are engaging in interfaith activities in Western countries. These engagements are removing centuries old misunderstandings, while people in the West are getting a chance to explore Islam as a spiritual religion and Muslims as devout humans just like them. Building bridges between religions and cultures will be key to world peace in the 21st century.

When Muslim nations were strong they were the source of peace and stability in much of the known world. Until the arrival of Islam, people never lived in security, peace and harmony over an extremely large portion of the then known world. Islam has been responsible for the prosperity and peace for almost half of the world for more than a thousand years. Since the last great Muslim State, the Ottoman Empire, has lost its influence, the world has seen two world wars while the Balkans, Middle East and other places where it governed in peace for centuries, based on the tolerant principles of Islam, has never been the same again. Still much of the world's unrest originates from a lack of true Muslim presence and influence in these regions.

I believe the Muslim world is coming out of its period of adolescence and will complete its transition in the first half of the 21st century. It will then start to contribute positively to human civilisation in the second half of the 21st century and beyond.